Examining Trust in Healthcare

Examining Trust in Healthcare

A Multidisciplinary Perspective

David Pilgrim
Floris Tomasini
and
Ivaylo Vassilev

First published 2011 by
PALGRAVE MACMILLAN

Palgrave Macmillan in the UK is an imprint of Macmillan Publishers Limited, registered in England, company number 785998, of Houndmills, Basingstoke, Hampshire RG21 6XS.

Palgrave Macmillan in the US is a division of St Martin's Press LLC, 175 Fifth Avenue, New York, NY 10010.

Palgrave Macmillan is the global academic imprint of the above companies and has companies and representatives throughout the world.

Palgrave® and Macmillan® are registered trademarks in the United States, the United Kingdom, Europe and other countries

ISBN 978–0–230–53791–0

This book is printed on paper suitable for recycling and made from fully managed and sustained forest sources. Logging, pulping and manufacturing processes are expected to conform to the environmental regulations of the country of origin.

A catalogue record for this book is available from the British Library.

10   9   8   7   6   5   4   3   2   1
20   19   18   17   16   15   14   13   12   11

Printed in China

Contents

List of Figures and Boxes

Figures

Boxes

Foreword

One of the great paradoxes in public services is that those organisations, which are created to protect vulnerable people sometimes do them harm. This book explores the possibility that one factor in this failure to care is a breakdown in trust. This can occur at the personal level, at the organisational level or both. The authors provide original perspectives on an enduring problem. They show how trust has become a fundamental property of healthcare systems, particularly in the relationship between healthcare professionals and patients. However, this can be abused not only in malign environments, which show no respect for the primacy of patients' rights, but also in benign systems where there is no intention to harm. Medical paternalism, which is common in developed healthcare systems, can generate trust and confidence that 'doctor knows' best but can ultimately undermine crucial interpersonal relationships because of the values which it embodies and the differentials in power which it sustains.

The book draws upon insights from different disciplines to cast light on the nature of trust and the problems, which are created when trust is corrupted or absent. It demonstrates the enormous complexity of the concept and shows that definitions (and the expectations which they reflect) are not always shared. They change and adapt according to their social context and over time. The essential qualities of trust in the healthcare setting are said to be 'competence, honesty and integrity'.

In a National Health Service, which has been largely free at the point of use for 60 years, trust in the institution itself has been a striking feature of its popularity. It acquired an iconic status almost unheard of in market-based, diversified healthcare systems. As this book shows, this confidence has sometimes been misplaced. Some of the tragedies described here persisted for so long because no one could conceive that individuals who were drawn to work in a system, founded upon the principles of care and concern for the sick, could possibly do them harm. The authors explain that this 'blind faith' can be understood not just in terms of a sentimental attachment to a much loved social institution but also through psychological factors which account for attachment and dependence when people become ill. They show that 'followship' in a wide range of organisations derives from power relationships, which may make people inappropriately trusting and uncritical.

The relationships between trust, attitudes to risk and models of regulation are complex, but central to all modern health systems. The book charts the shift from a two-dimensional approach in which patients trusted doctors and doctors regulated themselves to one in which formalised, external, structures are created to manage and monitor professionals. The implication is that, once trust in health professionals (as a group or as individuals) is lost, it is lost forever. New governance arrangements, or even legislation, may be introduced which afford a degree of protection for patients but the personal bond between patient and professional is weakened. The 'high trust' model of the past may have been naïve and unjustifiable but it had qualities which cannot be replicated in artificially created mechanisms imposed from outside.

We cannot measure how much trust we had in people, organisations and healthcare systems or how much we have lost. What we do know, from this book, is that trust cannot be assumed and that it must be earned. That is a valuable insight.

PROFESSOR DAME JOAN HIGGINS

Introduction

The question of trust or, more often, its lack in healthcare has been raised often in recent times. Healthcare has been beset by medical scandals and controversies that have put a lack of trust centre stage in various arenas of debate and reflection. In Britain, scandals and controversies such as the GP Harold Shipman, and the children's hospitals of Alder Hey in Liverpool and Bristol Royal Infirmary are now notorious. These have been discussed widely in the media and have been a background for the development and justification of new government policies aimed at improving public confidence.

As we deliver the manuscript for this book (the end of February 2010) news has broken about what the BBC describes as 'one of the worst scandals of NHS history'. In 2009 the Healthcare Commission investigation (Commission for Healthcare Audit and Inspection, 2009) into poor care at Stafford Hospital calculated that between 2005 and 2008, 400 more patients than expected died. A group of relatives of deceased patients are still campaigning for a public inquiry about the scandal. By the end of this book we hope the reader will understand how events like these might be understood and why, despite nearly two decades emphasising consumerism in the NHS, a myriad of checking mechanisms introduced by government and an extensive list of official watchdogs, healthcare can still let any of us down badly.

Yet, despite this background of national scandals, health professionals and the National Health Services (NHS) are consistently ranked by the UK public as highly trustworthy. For example, in a recent study conducted by Ipsos-MORI (2009) 92 per cent of people trusted doctors to tell the truth as opposed to 16 per cent trusting government ministers and 13 per cent trusting politicians. The irony here, of course, is that it is the least trusted professionals, the politicians, who are trying to act as guarantors for health professionals who are already most trusted by the public.

However, arguments highlighting the continuing trust of the public in healthcare do little to address the high-profile health scandals or the more mundane stories from patient websites on everyday neglect and poor patient care. Furthermore, there is the concern about the ready availability of particular treatments and post-code lotteries, where some receive better healthcare than others. Fears about the availability of services and equity of treatment, which on the founding principle of the NHS, free healthcare for all at the point of access, are often highlighted by the mass media. With a limited budget and rising demand for both types and amounts of service, there is an apparent 'disconnect' at times, between the ideals of the NHS on the one hand and economic constraints and consistent management of healthcare on the other, which can lead to anger, frustration and distrust.

There is also the matter of the continuing politicisation of healthcare services, which attracts revolutionary zeal and continual reform from either side of the political spectrum. In the UK this has led to increased levels of bureaucracy and the distrustful surveillance of professionals, amongst a number of other general trends. In respect to the political discourse about healthcare quality, this is often reduced, crudely, to matters of access. Just recently, for example, defenders of the NHS have been offended by hostile opponents of President Obama's planned healthcare reforms in the USA who used the NHS as a dire warning about the risks of socialized medicine.

This kind of debate singularly focuses on access and overlooks the wider and more complex matter about the inherent trustworthiness of healthcare. It also highlights that healthcare is an emotive topic prone to rhetorical claims which arouse anxious fantasies. For example, in the USA conservatives in the debate warned that socialized medicine would lead to impersonal committees deciding who would live and who would die (Brendan, 2010). In the UK fear of compromising a service paid for from central taxation and available at the point of need (even though rationing is actually inevitable and so availability is not unending) has led conservatives to be wary of unpicking a social democratic reform established over 60 years ago.

When we come to think about trust in healthcare, questions arise that take us beyond access for all and equity of treatment. Are 'health' services (which by and large deal with morbidity so are mainly illness services) an unequivocal and trustworthy force for health and well-being? Will our deepening reliance on healthcare genuinely improve the health and well-being of the population? Will our rights and autonomy be safeguarded? Will we be treated with respect and consideration? Satisfactory answers to such questions precede ones about fair access and equal treatment. Without that confidence in the quality and trustworthiness of healthcare we end up in the paradoxical position of defending equitable access to healthcare free at the point of need, whilst at the same time being wary of what might happen to us as patients.

Despite the focus in our case study material on the breakdown of trust, we want to avoid giving the impression of a false dualism. That is, it is not a matter on the one hand of healthcare being a disaster area to be distrusted with good cause by all of us all of the time. On the other hand, in the light of the case studies we offer, it is naïve for any of us to simply accept what healthcare does, and what it offers, in blind faith. We wish to critically examine how trust has already been achieved, as well as how it fails and how such failures point to aspirations or formulae to re-build trust in healthcare. This said, we offer no apologies about the complexity of our analysis. Questions like 'should we trust healthcare?' or 'how do we trust those caring for us?' do not have simple answers because context is all important – a point we return to recurrently.

This book involves two enormous and complex topics (trust and healthcare). By applying one to the other, our task is limited and focused to some extent but we still have much to do. The problem of trust is now all around us. Sometimes the very authoritative social institutions we expect to safeguard our interests let us down badly. Governments and banks are common contemporary examples and during the writing of this book both have incited angry distrust from the general population. Considerations about a crisis in confidence in those institutions are similar to those about our trust in healthcare. They beg questions about the sources and reasonableness of our expectations and the criteria we might apply to the trustworthiness we invest in those allegedly acting in our interests.

In developed societies healthcare is a taken for granted part of our daily landscape, with our nearby primary care health centres and the range of hospitals we regularly pass or enter in our locality or far away. The readership of this book predominantly will work in or research those settings but we are all also patients from cradle to grave (with costly and emotive attention being particularly evident at each end of the life span). As a consequence, we all in different ways have known healthcare intimately. Like schooling it is one of those social institutions that we all in our particular ways are experts about by experience. As sick children, parents to be and in practice or relatives of those dying, we develop a strong sense of what healthcare is about (even if we are never in its employ). If we do work in healthcare, then our perspectives are particularly rich, as we see it in operation from both sides of the relationship.

By the end of the book we will have taken the general context we all inhabit and just described and examined it in some depth, especially in relation to those who provide, receive and manage healthcare. But in the first part of book in order to clear the way for this, we will examine some general but important aspects of trust in our lives. This will involve us considering trust as a useful way of thinking about ordinary human processes, especially about how we relate to ourselves and one another. Because trust is *both* a personal *and* a social matter, it is not sufficient to consider it as one or the other.

It is a notion that is contradictory in many different ways. Thus, on the one hand trusting others is risky, could make us vulnerable, and could reduce our autonomy, while on the other hand it is an important aspect of growing up and becoming autonomous individuals, as well as for building and sustaining relations of intimacy and solidarity. Trust could be based on rational calculation, but it is also an emotional and emotive topic and experience. When we invest trust in others and it is rewarded with reliability this imbues security, warmth and confidence. If trust is broken we can be left distressed, desolate and angry (depending on the importance of the matter and the people involved).

Applying these opening comments to healthcare, then trust is a matter of importance to us in the particular biographical contexts in which we are most vulnerable and dependent on others. Although we are now used to healthcare, like all aspects of the health and welfare systems being framed for us as 'services' we utilize as 'customers' or 'consumers', there is something inherently inadequate about this way of describing our role as patients or as relatives of the sick and dying. If we go to the cinema and the film breaks down or our holiday flight is cancelled, this is frustrating and annoying. However, the range of personal implications these events create pale into insignificance compared to the scenario, in which the 'service' of healthcare lets us down as 'customers'. For this reason, we have refused in this book to accept that healthcare is a service like any other to be evaluated using the simplistic principles of consumerism.

Simplistic descriptions are proved inadequate from the outset when we come to explore trust in healthcare for another reason. The role of healthcare in developed societies remains perennially problematic and contradictory. Everyone wants access to good quality healthcare but *even when this is achieved* it does not prevent us from being sick or from dying – these happen to us all eventually. And yet, like children, constantly looking for and expecting to be looked after by omnipotent parents, we all, to some extent (and some much more than others), expect healthcare to cure us and ward off death. Healthcare does often do these things but often it does not. One way or another we all die and many of us remain chronically sick before then. And when death occurs, an institution, preoccupied with cure and the restoration of health, has been less than impressive at attending to us sensitively. The technological fix of curative healthcare is not only often overrated and overstated, it has few answers for us when we go the way of all flesh. In this context, we need to look at some deeper questions about trust in ourselves to deal with sickness and death on one side and to protect our own health on the other. Healthcare cannot do everything for us about health, sickness and death and it never will, no matter how much of it is available and whatever technical progress is made.

CHAPTER 1

Connotations of Trust

This book examines the role of trust in healthcare. In this short opening chapter, we start by offering an overview of the structure of the book. We then move on to our approach – one that takes both a multi- and an interdisciplinary view of trust in healthcare. The discussion then moves on to how we use the word 'trust' in different constituencies of debate; in other words, what the word connotes or denotes according to different people in different settings.

Overview of the structure and rationale of the book

This book builds in complexity. In this chapter, we start with less technical meanings of the word 'trust' then move from ordinary language connotations of the word to those that are more technical and academic. Then, in Chapter 2, we examine interpersonal trust (in healthcare) in a fairly non-technical way. Chapters 3, 4, 5 and 7 are disciplinary and give more technical perspectives on the notion of trust in healthcare, starting from the sub-personal (Chapter 3, psycho-social and psycho-ethical aspects of trust), moving on to the ethical (Chapter 4) and social aspects of trust (Chapter 5) and ending with systemic or trust in systems (Chapter 7). These chapters build a case for examining different levels and disciplinary perspectives of trust in healthcare. Chapter 6 is an exception to the rule, reversing the emphasis from disciplinary perspectives, to an examination of case studies where trust in health has become an issue. This chapter examines trust from a more empirical perspective – investigating how trust has been broken, brought into question and rebuilt, all through a series of case studies. Chapter 8 concludes the book by examining the risks and challenges to trust in healthcare that we need to question today.

Overview of our approach to analysis

To deal with the complexity of our analysis of trust in healthcare, we introduce the idea of triangulation – *three intersecting modes of analysis, which gives us a richer, deeper and more pluralistic account of trust in a healthcare setting*. It is these intersecting modes of analysis that interleave throughout the book and can be so described in the chapters that follow:

Perspectives on trust. By perspectives we mean how we embed and contextualize talk about trust: that is, whether it is an ordinary language examination of trust in healthcare or whether it a more technical, academic and disciplinary one. Each chapter represents different perspectives that involve either ordinary language discussions or disciplinary and sub-disciplinary discussions of an academic nature.

Levels of trust. By levels of trust we mean sub-personal, interpersonal and systemic aspects of trust, each of which represent particular levels of analysis at which particular disciplinary discourses can be brought into play. In other words, trust operates at different levels in people and in society. It works at psychological level (trust in oneself), at interpersonal and social level (trust in others) and at the levels of systems and institutions.

Depth and relational proximity of trust. By depth and proximity of trust we mean how it reflects our relationship with ourselves and others. This is significant because trust cannot always be considered an entirely rational affair. In other words trust may also have a more emotional and intuitive aspect in closer more proximal relationships and may therefore be of a different character to the trust built up, for example, between relative or even complete strangers.

To do justice to a complex analysis, this book attempts a triangulation of analysis using these three basic modes of enquiry throughout.

Having provided a brief outline of the structure and the approach, we now turn to some of the connotations of the word trust.

How we use and understand the word 'trust'

We use the word 'trust' in relation to healthcare in different ways throughout. *To understand the meaning of the word, one needs to be sensitive to its use.* In other words, we are less interested in what the word denotes and more interested in what it connotes in different constituencies of argument and debate. Broadly speaking we can consider trust as it is used in everyday language and how it has been theorised in more technical and academic language. This latter constituency of debate can be further divided and sub-divided into academic disciplines and particular kinds of debate within those disciplines. Also we can look at the concepts that are *implicitly related* to the understanding of trust. In particular, trust needs to be linked to power, risk and ethics. In other words in both practical and academic debates, 'trust' does not stand alone but is part of a wider discussion about uncertainty in our lives. To do justice to this, our analysis is unashamedly complex and multidisciplinary, although throughout we attempt to use our more technical understandings to illuminate examples in healthcare. In short we consider:

- Ordinary language descriptions of trust in *everyday use.*
- Technical descriptions of trust *explicit* in academic literature.

First connotation of trust – ordinary language and everyday scenarios

The risk in adhering too closely to ordinary language definitions is that they often understate the complexity of an academic topic. However, in this case we are dealing with one that is ubiquitous: arguably trust is a human universal and so has already grown in complexity. Some version of it, like 'suffering' or 'happiness', seems to have existed in all times and places and so it is likely that any ordinary language definition might be quite elaborate. To confirm this point, let us (rather unimaginatively) begin with a look at the dictionary, as might an anxious student writing an essay on our topic. In the case of the word 'trust', a very lengthy entry can be found, which hints immediately at the complexity of our topic. In the Concise Oxford Dictionary we find no less than 14 versions, which are *actually abridged* here to save space namely:

1 (noun) firm belief in reliability, honesty, veracity, justice etc of a person or thing ... confidence in expectations that ...
2 person or thing confided in ...
3 reliance on truth of statement etc. without examination

4   commercial credit ... .
5   responsibility arising from confidence reposed in one ...
6   (Law) confidence reposed in person by making him nominal owner of property to be used for others benefit; right of the latter to benefit from such property ...
7   thing or person committed to one's care; resulting obligation ... .
8   (organization managed by) body of trustees; organized association of several companies for purposes of reducing or defeating competition etc ...
9   BRAIN (s) trust ... trust deed, deed by debtor conveying property to trustee for payment of creditor ...
10   (verb) place trust in, believe in, rely on the character or behaviour of ... trust person with, allow him to use thing because one is confident he will not misuse it ... .
11   consign ... place or leave without misgivings ...
12   allow credit (to customers for goods)
13   entertain an earnest or confident hope ...
14   place reliance in ... .

Some initial reflections on this list might be that before we get at all interested academically in trust, its everyday use as a noun or verb is quite wide ranging and complicated. There is a specific reference to care and confidence in being treated well (items 7, 10 and 11). Another is that so much of the concept refers to economic transactions, as well as interpersonal investments (items 4, 6, 8, 9 and 12). Also other words soon flow from trust – especially hope, confidence, honesty, reliance and reliability. Thus trust seems to refer to interactions, which can be described as outer (especially interpersonal) events but also an inner orientation or subjective stance is also strongly implied.

Other words not mentioned but maybe implied in the definitions are power, security, risk and predictability. In the latter regard, at its simplest level, trust implies predictions about both the impersonal and personal worlds we inhabit. In the first of these we trust that when we turn a tap on then water will flow from it. In the second, we trust that the shopkeeper will provide the correct change when we buy an item and offer a large banknote for payment.

If these predictions about the inanimate world or people break down then we become in some small way distrustful and encounter life as risky. In these everyday contexts, trust connotes reliance or confidence in the routines of the world that are taken for granted in a very deep and fundamental sense – it reflects our daily expectations or anticipations based upon our past experience and knowledge of people and events. The clock will strike on the hour, the sun will rise in the east in the morning and people will drive on the left hand side of the road in Britain but on the right in France, etc.

The legal aspects of trust in the list (item 8) also reminds us of a particular term used currently in the Britain – that of an 'NHS Trust', with the emerging 'Foundation NHS Trusts' being given powers of autonomy to compete with others. Across the list we then find the word of interest to us in ways that describe trust in financial and legal arrangements, trust in things and trust in people. If societies always require trust to work (which they do) then the particular political and economic arrangements of particular societies will be always coloured by trust. The study of trust is thus one pathway into studying society.

Another implication of trust is that it might be framed as the other side of the same coin as risk. Risk is also about making predictions (latterly it has come to mean negative outcomes but originally it referred to the prediction of success, as well as failure). Certainly trust is at times like placing a bet on the outcome of an event; if I trust the train timetable and go to the station just before a train is due to arrive then I will soon catch the one I need. But sometimes the train is late or cancelled; while this maybe not a wholly predictable event, it is unreliable enough for me learn that relying on a train to get to an important appointment is a form of risk taking.

On the other hand, trust as a positive experience is not risky – in its anxious, negative sense – but comforting. When we place our regular trust in friends and relatives in ongoing predictable relationships, we are rewarded with a sense of well-being and belonging. Thus the *positive* risk we take by trusting others is to enjoy being alive in the presence of others, rather than being lonely and disconnected from people.

Turning to the personal aspects of trust we encounter on a daily basis, it begins as an inner relationship. For example, can we trust ourselves to tell the truth, not swear, eat properly or abstain from alcohol this week? Given that we are people, the relationship of trust can be thought of as turning inwards not just outwards to others. These aspects of trust in ourselves point it up as an expression of resolve or intention, where an 'I' feels that they are in the driving seat about their lives and conscious about the factors required in choices, decision making and moral obligations.

And yet trust in an everyday sense is not *only* about our good intentions and commitments and promises to ourselves; others are typically implicated. Trust can also entail decision making in uncertainty, where we are reliant on information from the world in general or particular individuals to know what to do. We have to trust in others at times and rely on *their* knowledge and decisions not our own. The latter is particularly the case with experts and, for the purposes of this book, this means healthcare systems and healthcare professionals. We can only know so much from the world to make trusting decisions and we are not likely to fully understand what experts know about us, even if they do their best to be 'patient-centred' and keep us informed. Trust in these circumstances is partially blind. It approximates less to choice and more to faith.

In the items noted above (1, 2, 7, 8 and 9) there is an allusion to trust being in things or organisations not just in particular people. Moreover trust as a fully conscious intention or choice, whether it is about things or people, may be suspect for two reasons. First, our intentions stated to ourselves and others are not reliably expressed in action. What we intend to do and what we actually do are sometimes different (hence the expression 'the road to hell is paved with good intentions'). To complicate matters further some intentions are never tested in action to check their outcome.

Second, psychoanalysis and cognitive science inform us that our inner life, by and large, is not accessible to us – our capacity to know why we are thinking or doing what we are thinking or doing is very limited. We give accounts of our past conduct and future intentions but they are always partial in form and often biased by a positive glow to flatter ourselves.

For example, when asked, most people believe that their driving is far better than average. But actually *most* people's driving is *necessarily* average. Freud called this aspect of mental life 'the unconscious' and 'defence mechanisms', Sartre talks of 'bad faith' (a state of self-deception we fall into to avoid anxiety of authentic encounters with the world) and cognitive psychologists talk of 'cognitive errors and biases'. In other words trust might start as an inner relationship, but because we are often self-deceiving, this may be a shaky start.

Before leaving the dictionary we can look further down to find 'trustful' to mean 'full of trust, unsuspicious, confiding ...' and 'trustworthy' meaning 'worthy of trust, reliable ...'. The second of these meanings is highly represented in the academic literature but before moving to that realm of inquiry, note that we are already getting a sense of the complexity of our topic and the futility of conceptualising trust in simple unambiguous ways. It is already emerging as a *polyvalent concept* – it means different things in different circumstances, at different times to different people. However, within this brief exploration stimulated by dictionary definitions, we find that three main sorts of trust are being considered: trust in oneself; trust in others and trust in organizations or systems.

Second connotation of trust – technical and academic

There are a number of ways trust is understood, within academic discussions. The latter often focus on one specific aspect or context of trust, while also making assumptions about other aspects of the notion that tend to remain invisible to the reader. While this is a necessary process in academic writing, we feel that outlining these different uses is important in order to understand assumptions in specific arguments. Also, given that specific notions, such as, for example, person, personal, systemic, risk, are used in relation to different aspects of trust debates, such an awareness makes it easier to identify connections between apparently unrelated arguments. Therefore, it is useful to outline and unpack these in this introductory chapter in order to be able to differentiate the focus and assumptions of the debates addressed later in the book. We highlight the different ways this is done throughout, to introduce the reader to some of the key ways we talk about trust in later chapters.

Rational and affective accounts of trust

A good starting point for a rational account of trust is Hardin (2006), who argues that we can think of trust primarily as 'encapsulated interests'. He suggests that trust can be explored first by thinking of being *trusting* (as a moral orientation or commitment to others) and second about trust being expressed as *trustworthiness* (an attribution of character or disposition about a person or system). Hardin favours more of a focus on the second aspect of trust (because it is outward, behavioural and thus measurable). He acknowledges the first notion, of a personal moral orientation, but is less keen to use it as the focus of academic exploration. His basic argument is this:

> As a rule, we trust only those with whom we have a rich enough relationship to judge them trustworthy, and even then we trust only over certain ranges of actions. Hence, trust is a three part relation: A trusts B to do or with respect to X. (Hardin, 2006: 12)

Hardin goes on then to argue that it is in the interest of those deemed trustworthy to be that way and part of acting in self-interest is to take the interests of others into consideration. Your interests become encapsulated in mine. As social animals, in a moral order, it suits us all to consider one another's interests; self-interest and the interests of others coalesce as shared interests. Common expressions of encapsulated interests are that we: are mutually respectful; cooperative; loyal; love one another; recognise each others' right to be autonomous, etc. For Hardin, trust is *calculative* and so altruism or acts of kindness certainly exist but for him they are indirect forms of enlightened self-interest.

Whilst we see Hardin's logic, and it has much to commend it, we consider it to be a partial and thus unsatisfactory account of trust. This is because for human beings, trust is about *feelings* not just the rational calculations that, for example, could be made by a computer but the decisions of the latter would only correspond partially to human decisions. There is a natural bias in trusting relationships; we trust those, most deeply, whom we are closest to, our family, friends and closest colleagues. Depth of trust seems to be associated with proximity of care. One way we examine this is through the struggle for recognition – which has an emotional as well as rational dimension. Both of these have different connotations for the kinds of trusting relationship we enter into.

For example, whilst we might want unconditional *justice* for our fellow humans on the basis of the fact that we recognize them, as fully human, we reserve unconditional *love* and regard for those closest to us, where trust entails more than securing fair justice or fair play. To understand trust, we argue, we need to understand its 'affective' (emotional) as well as rational dimension, which exists on societal and cultural levels as well as personal ones. In this way we can talk about trust in terms of malign and benign cultures, with a range of contexts that encourage or discourage trust between people.

Inner and outer trust

Trust is more often than not theorized in relation to external events and behaviours. For example, other people are deemed to be trustworthy if they are reliable, competent, honest and so on. However, we often miss the fact that trust depends on whether we are trustworthy ourselves. At a simple level, trustworthiness points to the consistency of our own behaviour. But whether we are trustworthy or not is more than just whether we are consistent in our external behaviour towards others who may rely on us, it also points to our inner lives: how secure we feel about others, the life decisions we make, the values that we hold, etc.

To understand trust, we argue, we need to delve deeper than its current interpersonal dimension; it is also bound up with our personal histories. Trust, we believe, starts from a *basic trust* in the self (or *self-trust*) and manifests in human values that we associate with trust between people: honesty, competence, integrity. Our capacity (and sometimes our naïvety) about trusting others now is bound up with whether, in younger days, we discovered personal consistency in others (such as parents and teachers) and, via them, *confidence within ourselves* was established.

Thus the interpersonal field in which trust is both judged and risked now is coloured by the extent we have an inner confidence to trust ourselves and others. That confidence itself was bound up with an interpersonal field in childhood. This is taking us a good way from Hardin's 'encapsulated interest' focus. It suggests that to understand trust we must be sensitive to *both* the emotional *and* rational aspects of relationships. Our current confidence, that our future welfare will be protected or enhanced by trusting others, is affective not just rational and it is built on the historical foundations of our lived experience.

Levels of trust

Another key theme in this book is the idea of theorizing different levels of trust. As we have just noted, trust can be understood intrapersonally (trust in oneself/self-trust or 'basic trust'), interpersonally (trust in others or interpersonal trust) and systemically (trust in systems). All these different levels of trust matter in examining trust in healthcare. The easiest to grasp is probably, interpersonal trust, where the relationship is between people in their different social roles: health professionals and patients, and so on. However, trust also operates sub-personally in that malign professionals, or overly suspicious patients, may have fallen victim to a breakdown in inner trust. That is, patients may lack confidence (and so be 'counter-dependent' when asked to comply with health advice or the patient role) and some professionals may exploit the vulnerability of patients to gratify their own needs in some way.

Furthermore, we also examine trust in respect to systems, where trust is more about accountability, for example, checks and balances in systems that maintain fairness, prevent incompetence or malign intent. Systems are both aspirational and preventative in relation to trust. They aspire to best clinical practice and in the reliable governance of healthcare. They are also preventative in that they develop ways of holding professionals to account for errant behaviours (making practitioners anxiously concerned about ensuring good practice), as well as developing ways of learning from mistakes.

Risk, power, trust and ethics

The final theme that runs through our more technical treatment of trust in healthcare is that it is linked recurrently to risk and power. We cannot understand trust in its various expressions unless we also consider these related matters. For example, to avoid risk we must be constantly on our guard about things going wrong or people getting it wrong (or seeking to blame others if the latter occurs). This is inherently a *distrusting* personal stance. Similarly, by accepting the power that is held over us by professionals, when we are in the patient role, we trust that that power is exercised wisely in our interests. This is inherently a *trusting* stance. In other words trust and distrust are bound up with immediate contexts of risk or power or both.

Also at a more personal level, trust is connected to ethics because it signals the striving for moral certitude. The ideas of 'good will', 'virtuous character', 'principled autonomy', or 'the greatest benefit for the greatest number' are technical terms from philosophical ethics that attempt to delineate ethically trustworthy actions. These are reflected in more applied forms (professional ethics) in the idea of 'the virtuous doctor', 'duty of care', 'patient rights' and 'ethical accountability' (at a more systemic level). At an intrapersonal level, basic trust relates to security of our moral convictions. That is, trust is also connected to the authenticity of the ethical decisions we make. At an interpersonal level, trust is an important feature of ethical practice, which is expressed positively as beneficence and negatively as avoiding maleficence.

Disciplinary emphases

We approach this book with a shared interest in the topic of trust applied to healthcare settings but from different academic perspectives of political sociology (IV), moral philosophy and the philosophy of psychiatry/psychology (FT), clinical psychology, medical sociology and health policy (DP). Between us we know enough to recognize that trust is examined differently by political scientists, psychoanalysts, social psychologists, sociologists and philosophers. All of these cannot be represented in equal measure or with consistent confidence by us.

However, we hope that as authors we are informed enough collectively about the topic of the book to provide the reader with a wide ranging, informative and stimulating exploration. Having discussed the connotations of trust, we now briefly discuss what we think trust is.

What is trust?

It is already evident from our discussion above that trust is both positive and negative, calculative and non-calculative, rational and emotional. Moreover, trusting could lead to risk and vulnerability as well as to intimacy, solidarity and empowerment. But if all those opposing poles can be equally relevant in defining trust how can we answer 'what is trust'? Here we will argue that if we have to describe the 'core nature' of trust this can only be done with reference to its internal contradictions: for us trust is contradictory and socially situated. This does not mean that the question 'what is trust' cannot be answered beyond that point, but it means that such an answer will always be situated, and not valid across all contexts.

Following that we can argue that the only way in which we can define trust as, for example, being primarily about risk, or calculation (a dominant trend in the literature on trust) is by situating our definition of trust. This could be done within disciplinary (psychology, sociology, philosophy) and empirical frames of analysis, as well as within specific political projects, cultural (individualistic or communitarian) and social fields (health or economics). While there is nothing wrong with embedding the meaning of trust in such a way (it is actually important for understanding concrete contexts, such as healthcare and the NHS) it is problematic if we try to generalize about the meaning of trust on the basis of, what are essentially *specific*, cultural or academic frames of reference. Therefore, we argue that in our discussion of healthcare we need to keep this distinction in mind, between generalized discussions and specific context, in order to be able to understand practical dilemmas and debates about trust in and within healthcare.

This is not an easy task. It requires drawing on concepts that are used in different academic disciplines and some of which are immediately trust-related, such as 'confidence', 'belief', 'faith', 'familiarity', 'competence', 'honesty', 'integrity', while others are not so closely associated with trust but are nevertheless trust-relevant, such as 'power', 'risk', 'attachment', 'autonomy', 'authenticity' and 'recognition'. Offering an analysis of trust that is both grounded and relevant to everyday dilemmas and policy decisions, but which also offers a critical distance from those, as well as providing relevant questions and possible explanations, is another challenge that we had to address when writing this book.

Summary

- The book reflects on two constituencies of debate: practitioner and academic
- Trust is examined throughout from both an ordinary language and a technical academic perspective
- In the more technical examination of trust we are interested in rational *and* affective accounts of trust; outer *and* inner accounts of trust; different levels of trust and finally; how trust relates to values in society
- To understand what trust is we need to look at how it is used and embedded in different debates
- To understand trust we need to have an understanding of trust-related concepts.

CHAPTER 2

Interpersonal Aspects of Trust

Introduction

This chapter begins with an examination of successful clinical encounters before moving on to those characteristics of professionals, which, we tend to assume, will increase their trustworthiness for patients. These professional features of competency, honesty and integrity are expressed within relationships and so the role of patients is also important to consider. Moreover, the interpersonal dynamics which accrue between professionals and patient always exist in social contexts and so the latter also has to be taken into consideration.

The context of clinical encounters is shaped by factors such as supply and demand, the impact of social inequalities and the rise in consumerism in health policy. In subsequent chapters we examine how trust as an intra-psychic and interpersonal phenomenon has to be placed in the context of these supra-personal features. By the end of this chapter we begin to outline an overture to these chapters.

Assumptions about successful clinical encounters

A successful interaction between professional and patient entails an implied contract in order to maximize the efficiency of diagnosis and treatment. The first is that patients should present themselves voluntarily in a way that the professional considers appropriate in order that the latter can use their expertise to its maximum value. The second is that once the patient puts themselves into this amenable position, then the professional should ensure that they respond competently and respectfully at all times.

In health services, these relational aspects of trust often run

13

smoothly leaving both patients and professionals reasonably happy with the process and outcome of care. The type and success of clinical encounters are shaped from the beginning by help-seeking (an exception to this is when services are imposed on patients, for example under mental health law).

Rogers *et al.* (1998) note that help-seeking has several dimensions:

- Patients vary in their understanding of illness when they make decisions about consulting professionals.
- Their approach to healthcare access is shaped by past experience – it has a 'recursive' character.
- Most symptoms are contained in the community without professional intervention (the 'clinical iceberg'). Thus self-care is ambiguous – is it a success at limiting demand on services or is it a failure to consult professionals when required?
- Help-seeking is shaped by networks of influence in families and neighbourhoods.
- Healthcare systems both encourage and discourage demand in their public information profile. Patients are told not to waste professional time and use services cautiously but also they are also warned not to leave presentations of illness too late.

This list is a strong reminder that from the patient side, we have to interpret the stance they take within a relationship with a professional, in the context of their social and cultural background, which contains both current and historical influences. For this reason moral judgements and psychological descriptions of conduct of those in the patient role cannot be limited to understanding them as individual agents. Their context can and should also be illuminated if we are to develop a full understanding of their success or failure in that role.

When we discuss parents resisting mass childhood immunization later in Chapter 6 we find that lay people demonstrate 'situated rationalities' about what healthcare offers or expects. These situated realities may or may not chime with professional expectations. When there are clear discrepancies between the positions of each party then trust will be missing or depleted. People enter the patient role during their help-seeking and then come up against professionals who they assume to be trustworthy. This assumption is tested out and confirmed in degrees by the characteristics of the professionals being consulted by patients. We now turn to those personal features.

Trusting the professional: competence, honesty and integrity

In developed countries we are raised in a context where professional life is all around us. Generally we assume that professionals are trustworthy. Indeed the term 'professional' brings with it three main positive connotations of trust for most of us. The first is that professionals can be trusted for their *competence*. The second dimension is that professionals can be trusted for their *honesty*. The third is that they can be trusted to take care of our interests – that is, we assume that they always act with *integrity*. These three aspects of trust will now be explored further with specific reference to healthcare professionals.

Competence

Superficially this is the most easily assured aspect of professional action. Professionals are trained to act with appropriate skill to carry out their role. A nurse understands how to put up a drip and take a patient's blood pressure. A physiotherapist knows how to exercise a recovering limb. A doctor knows how much of a drug to prescribe for a particular condition. Patients put their trust in professionals in this apparently clear domain of technical competence, where roles and responsibilities are well recognised by patients and the law. The latter generally makes it clear who can use an anaesthetic or advertise a particular clinical role.

Credentials gained in higher education are the formal record of competence and fitness to practice. However, patients' general trust in technical competence can break down on a number fronts, despite these demonstrable credentials. The reason is that competence may be found lacking in practice in some contexts.

- Because professionals are human, they make *mistakes*. That is, a professional may be genuinely competent and well practised in a routine clinical act but may omit it or perform it wrongly occasionally. To fail once may have dire consequences and an experienced practitioner may be exposed as incompetent. Of course, as in any part of life, mistakes can often go unnoticed, especially when there are no adverse consequences.
- Their competence may be *undermined on a temporary basis* because of distractions or illness. Routine and guaranteed competence in any task requires that the professional is focused on their work and is fit and well.

- A practitioner may become *deskilled*. To take a simple and obvious analogy, many people who have been driving for many years would fail their driving test. All tasks involving particular skills begin to incorporate bad habits. Another aspect of this truism is that as we get older we find it more and more difficult to incorporate new knowledge. Thus a particular practitioner may fail to learn new and better skills.
- Practitioners may lose competence because their *work context* does not enable them to keep up to date with best practice.

It is usual and legitimate to hold individuals responsible for their own actions. Consequently it is easy to make the matter of technical competence a narrow judgement about individual professionals. What is contentious is the extent to which they are wholly blameworthy when they manifestly act incompetently. Health services appear to contain two contradictory approaches to technical malpractice. On the one hand, blameworthy individuals are subject to disciplinary action, overseen by their professional bodies and their employers. On the other hand a 'no blame' or 'low blame' ethos has been encouraged to understand the root causes of 'critical incidents'. More will be said about this contradiction in the next chapter.

Honesty

In January 2007 a serving police officer who had been suffering from the early symptoms of multiple sclerosis sued his health authority. His complaint was that his diagnosis was known to medical practitioners for many months but neither his GP, nor the neurologist he was referred to, disclosed their dialogue about his condition. At the centre of this complaint was not medical negligence about treatment (at the stage of the development of the illness, a 'wait and see' policy would be normal). The claimed negligence was in relation to transparency; the patient considered that he had a right to know his diagnosis.

Whilst it may seem self-evident that patients have a right to truthfulness from professionals they consult, there have been well rehearsed professional arguments favouring deception. Indeed, until recently, withholding information from patients was sufficiently common that it was not a matter of either self-doubt or disciplinary action.

Gillon (1986) rehearses three main traditional arguments for sometimes keeping patients in the dark. The first is that to communicate bad news is psychologically harmful to patients. This is an interpretation of the Hippocratic stricture of 'first do no harm'. The second argument for deception is that diagnosis and prognosis are often inherently uncertain.

They are often probability statements rather than fixed and clear statements of fact. The third argument is one of paternalistic presupposition. That is, professionals might consider that the patient would rather not know the truth. They shield the patient from grim reality, much as a parent might do with a small child.

These grounds for deception of course are invoked at the very point of connection between a patient and a professional when honesty might result in dire news being communicated. It is easy for a professional to be frank about a self-limiting and non-life threatening condition because it is a trivial existential matter for the patient. Indeed, to be honest in these circumstances actually constitutes a positive assurance to expedite recovery – it reinforces the placebo effect. By contrast, the three arguments noted by Gillon are most likely to be invoked about serious matters – when a life changing opinion is offered (as in the case of a chronic degenerative condition) or when a life-threatening condition is the focus. The commonest example in the latter regard is a diagnosis of malignancy.

Do these three arguments constitute an ethical defence of professional dishonesty? The answer is in the negative. The arguments are understandable and even at times well intentioned but they are not defensible ethically. The main reason is that they fail to respect the patient's autonomy. Patients might find bad news upsetting, but as autonomous and self-determining beings they have the right to deal with the news as they see fit (just as much as enjoying good news or coping with everyday tedium). Morally, dishonesty is in effect a form of stealing; stealing someone's possibility to live their lives as they see fit. Psychologically, lying is often about protecting ourselves. So, lying to a patient may involve darker motives (than paternalism) and may have to do with professionals protecting themselves from having to deal with the fall out of giving a patient bad news. Even if ones motives are essentially paternalistic and good, the desire to protect the patient from bad news is a dangerous presupposition that is impossible to validate. How does a professional know that this particular patient would rather not know this particular fact or opinion? The answer is that they cannot. This is not to say that that they may not be correct in their speculation some of the time. However, as they cannot know *when* they are correct or incorrect, a blanket policy of paternalistic deception is not defensible.

As for the uncertainties of diagnosis and prognosis, why should they be a reason for dishonesty? The logical and empirical problems that healthcare professionals have for themselves about certainty are real enough but why should that lead to deception? The flawed rationalization, that professionals should always be certain to patients even though they harbour personal doubts and can share the latter with colleagues, makes no sense, except as part of maintaining a professional persona of competence (see earlier section).

The case example given of the man with multiple sclerosis is useful here. Uncertainty often attends the early diagnosis of the disease. Moreover, its prognosis is very uncertain. It remits episodically and its course varies from patient to patient. However, that confusing and uncertain picture is one that the public have a right to understand, just as much as professionals. Whatever the legal outcome of the man's action, he had a strong ethical case to make a complaint. The professionals should have shared their own problem solving and uncertainty about his symptoms from the outset, instead of keeping him in the dark.

Finally in this section on honesty, there is a particular nuance that can affect trust which can be summarized as *considerate diplomacy*. Given that the difficult topics typically evaded by professionals are serious in nature, when they are discussed frankly it can be anticipated that many patients and their significant others will be distressed. Out of humane consideration, tact and empathy are implicated. To be brutally honest or curt when delivering bad news can be cruel and harmful. Thus honesty may be one interpersonal building block of trust but it is more solid if expressed with due consideration for the feelings of the recipient.

Integrity

This final aspect of interpersonal trust in professionals has been the focus of two forms of discussion. The first is part of a principled objection to professional ethics. Gillon (ibid.) cites Watt (1980) along the lines that inconclusive debates about ethics are best replaced by ensuring that practitioners are people of integrity. Here the assumption is that people of good conscience will do their best in particular clinical circumstances and should be supported in this regard. They should be left to exercise their clinical judgement, knowing that they will be trying to do their best for their patients.

But this wholesale dismissal of ethics in favour of good character and conscience is not persuasive to ensure probity in all aspects of healthcare. For example, it is clear that some of the major arguments within medical ethics (in relation to say voluntary euthanasia, abortion or cloning) have opposing protagonists, who all may be of good character and conscience. This suggests that the latter personal qualities may be generally desirable in daily clinical care but they cannot provide ethical answers in themselves. This is because two practitioners, both of impeccable character, may take completely opposing positions about good practice or the role of healthcare in society.

Nor does personal integrity necessarily engender trust in practice for patients. A woman wanting an abortion is hardly likely to feel confidence in staff who she knows object to the procedure. It is of little comfort to her that practitioners are of good conscience in that circumstance. Integrity is thus a necessary, but not a sufficient, condition for trust between patient and practitioner.

The second way in which integrity has been discussed is in relation to impropriety. This goes beyond the mistakes, negligence and rationalisations discussed in the sections on competence and honesty. It takes us to the deeper question of professionals knowingly behaving badly – an arena of conduct in which selfishness, fecklessness and malevolence intermingle. In particular, it refers to the practitioner putting his or her own needs before those of the patient. Examples that can be given here are of sexual or financial exploitation of patients. The most malign exploitation of whimsical homicides (considered in Chapter 6, when discussing the Shipman case) is very rare but it is an obvious example of the breakdown of integrity. Another example of exploitation is in relation to medical researchers indulging their intellectual curiosity and advancing their academic careers at the expense of others (the Alder Hey case also to be discussed in Chapter 6).

Power, risk and context

The notion of exploitation raises a related matter – the relationship between trust and power, which we discuss in subsequent chapters. Here it is worth noting that exploitation (or lesser expressions of disrespect such as rudeness or even simple indifference) is largely possible *because* there is a power discrepancy between the patient and the professional. However, this is not only one-way traffic. The patient may fail to comply in a variety of ways with reasonable expectations from their carers. They may act in a disrespectful or unreasonably demanding way. They may even be abusive – hence the policy in the NHS to take legal action against violent patients, which is advertised widely in A&E and outpatient clinics.

Nonetheless, the sociology of the profession's literature largely emphasises the dangers for patients rather than health workers in relation to power. People with health problems are inherently vulnerable because their illness creates some degree of regression to childhood – a time when parents would care for their maladies – and more will be said about this in the next chapter. Even without this regressive side to the relationship, the sick person is reliant on the technical expertise of experts to mend their health, just as much as they are reliant on a mechanic to mend their car.

In other words, the discrepancy in knowledge between the two parties puts the patient in a relatively powerless position. There is little surprise therefore that those of us who are resentful about professional expertise because of the power it contains are often counter-dependent (by evading consultations and coping alone). Objections to the power discrepancy have even led to the collective opposition evident in health movements (such as women's health groups and the mental health service users' movement). These tend to be anti-professional in ethos.

When we look across the three sections above it is clear that power over patients can be expressed in three separate or interweaving ways. First, the professional is typically more competent than the patient in understanding and correcting their health problem (though at times this is not the case). Second, the professional has the discretion to deceive the patient in large or small ways. The patient has to rely on the honesty of clinicians. Third, the professional may take advantage of the patient's vulnerability by putting their own needs first in the relationship. A mundane example would be professional aloofness and indifference and a less common example would be of murder.

Permutations on these interactions are interesting. For example, a GP may not be technically very competent but they may be liked by patients because they are treated well at a personal level. Other patients may resent a poor bedside manner but they might also appreciate obvious competence in the same physician. In another example, although, as was argued earlier, deception is not ethically defensible, some patients may prefer to be kept in the dark sometimes, so they may respect their doctor for it.

Moving from these general points about power discrepancies to particular situated actions it needs to be noted that the role of patient is highly varied. It can be thought of on a continuum, with the following scenarios marking its points:

- The first point is the counter-dependent or self-caring sick person who does not approach professionals for help. Trust cannot be betrayed in these circumstances because there is no relationship and so no power discrepancy.
- The least dependent role in service contact is that of an otherwise healthy patient consulting for advice and treatment for a minor ailment.

- More dependency is expressed by the patient who consults frequently for a range of maladies in primary care.
- If a sick person has to attend for a hospital appointment as an outpatient or day patient for diagnosis or treatment, then they enter less familiar territory than their local health centre.
- Next in dependency comes a period in hospital for days or weeks. The patient's routine autonomy in their home surroundings is disrupted.
- Long-term hospitalization extends this disruption to routine autonomy.
- The most extreme point on the continuum is where the patient has treatment imposed upon them. One example would be the comatose patient in an intensive care unit. The other is the psychiatric patient detained and treated under the mental health act.

The above is an indicative not exhaustive list of nuanced points on the continuum. It highlights that the notion of trust in a health setting is highly variable and that the risk of it being betrayed increases with the decreasing power of the patient to resist unwelcome intervention or to express their autonomy. This is not to argue that at the least autonomous end of the continuum trust *will* be betrayed, merely that the risk of this outcome increases. Also, at the other end of the continuum, professionals may still be incompetent, dishonest, disrespectful or exploitative. However, the risk of these interpersonal eventualities is much lower because the patient's autonomy is manifestly present. In other words the context of care determines the chances of trust being gained or lost as much as the personal qualities of the professional.

Trust and confidentiality

One specific aspect of integrity of particular relevance to healthcare is that of confidentiality. Patients expect details of their ill health and personal circumstances over time recorded by practitioners to be kept confidential. This has two aspects to it. One is dealt with in the next chapter because it refers to health records in a system of care. The other, relevant here, relates to the personal responsibility of practitioners not to divulge information about patients to third parties. The expectation of absolute confidentiality has its roots in both medicine (Hippocrates demanded it) and some religious rituals (for example in the priest–penitent relationship in the confessional).

However, in practice most complex healthcare systems do not permit practitioners to abide by it as a strict principle. Shared notes and frequent communications between different disciplines involved with a patient mean that absolute confidentiality is regularly compromised. What the patient can still reasonably expect though is that their personal records are only shared on a genuine 'need to know' basis. That is they are not shared carelessly or whimsically with others who do not need to know. This expectation thus still places a responsibility upon practitioners to carefully respect patient confidentiality. Indeed now that in practice the latter is no longer absolute, the practitioner has to be more vigilant, moment to moment in their practice, that any reason to share information is justified.

Apart from the modern norms of multidisciplinary team work, professional bodies do make exceptions explicit even in relation to the (outmoded and unworkable) notion of absolute confidentiality. For example the General Medical Council in Britain allows professionals to disclose aspects of health records in order to prevent harm to third parties. Exceptions are also permitted in relation to *bona fide* clinical research and at times for paternalistic reasons. Gillon (1986) notes that the first exception is readily justified on moral grounds but there is a much less clear defence in relation to the others.

For our purposes here the personal question is not whether professionals can defend the violation of absolute confidentiality but what expectations patients have about those rules. For example, if a patient believes that absolute confidentiality exists but then discovers that it does not (because of routine information sharing in multidisciplinary teams) then this may cause offence and distress and reduce trust. Or in, another example, the relatives of deceased patients may consider that researchers have no right to access the records of their loved ones. Again if post-mortem research is conducted using health records then trust may be diminished.

These examples suggest two types of tension around the norms of confidentiality, which might jeopardize interpersonal trust. The first is that health professionals may aspire to absolute confidentiality but in practice, at best, they deliver limited confidentiality. Second, patients' trust in professionals can be undermined when their expectations about confidentiality are not met in practice. The latter can happen if the professional acts in a negligent way but it might also occur because professionals find reasons to excuse their transgressions about confidentiality (reasons which are explicitly supported by their peers).

Mechanisms for maximizing personal trustworthiness

Returning to the three main dimensions of trustworthiness of professionals (competence, honesty and integrity) what mechanisms have emerged to boost their personal presence in the encounters between professionals and patients? Essentially there are two. The first covers the question of competence alone and the second all three dimensions. It is important to note that these mechanisms do not guarantee trustworthiness: they merely claim to increase the chances of fitness to practice for most practitioners most of the time. A number of empirical questions are then raised about the success in practice of these mechanisms. Given that the credibility of professionals, individually and collectively, is bound up with the presence of these mechanisms, there may be a tendency to over-state their success. We will return to this point later.

Turning to the first 'safety mechanism' to increase the probability of personal trustworthiness via competence, this was noted at the outset – credentials. Indeed 'credentialism' is for many still the touchstone of personal reliability in professional life; is the practitioner demonstrably qualified to carry out their role? Vocational courses in health and social care are largely sited now in higher education. This siting signals the sophistication of the knowledge base of care practice. Healthcare practitioners are *both* trained *and* educated in higher education – not one or the other.

The phrase 'trained and educated' indicates a distinction and sometimes tension when higher education hosts vocational socialization. For example, although healthcare professionals can become graduates, their qualifications are not purely academic in nature. Instead they are underpinned by a range of pure disciplines (in the biological and social sciences) that inform healthcare training. In the case of nursing, there is a particular question raised about whether care (an ordinary human process) can or should be framed as a form of academically informed activity. Can care be theorized and codified as transferable skills or is it simply intrinsic to life? Can it be taught as a set of skills or is it simply present or absent as a personal quality in relationships?

Take another example – clinical psychology. Whilst psychology is an academic discipline, applied psychology (with its clinical, educational, occupational, counselling and forensic branches) is a form of postgraduate vocation. Strictly these branches are professions not disciplines, even if the latter term is often used in care agencies and organizations to stand for the former. When clinical psychology first emerged in Britain, its leaders argued that it should only be involved in the disinterested understanding of patients (diagnosis or assessment) – it acted initially like a discipline not a vocation. Treatment was seen as value-laden and so at odds with the scientific ethos of the *academic discipline* of psychology (Eysenck, 1949). This position soon broke down as clinical psychology increasingly colonized therapeutic activity. However, the initial tension about disinterestedness and helping intent highlights the difference between an academic discipline and a caring profession.

This question about the relationship between vocations and academic knowledge focuses our mind on the confidence we might have in taking technical knowledge as the necessary and sufficient basis for personal trustworthiness. The doubts about nursing care being framed in academic terms and the query just described about whether clinical psychologists should be therapists highlights this point. Credentials are probably not a good reason alone to trust professionals (though most of the time they are a necessary starting point for that trust).

In the light of this discussion, there is a tension between the certainties demanded in daily clinical routines and the tolerance of uncertainty, which is often encouraged in the academy. In the latter, competing theories are rehearsed and there is a frequent plea for the necessity of more research. By contrast, the daily life of professionals requires practical decisions to be made with some certainty. Most of these decisions are routine and rapid. The average practitioner is not expected to dwell on knowledge on the margins of his or her practice (cf. the ground-breaking realm of new research), nor are they often permitted the luxury of uncertainty and inaction.

Thus some have argued that too much higher education might paradoxically undermine our confidence in the *practical* aspects of professionalism. They lament that practitioners are 'over-trained' and that their academic knowledge and its tendency towards theorization, speculation and disputation may be inappropriate for practice (Freidson, 1970). This is mentioned because it is at odds with another typical cultural assumption that more education leads to more trustworthy practice.

Trusting the patient

In the everyday discourse of health professionals, frustrations with patients are common. In broad terms, these tend to coalesce around the following set of complaints and assumptions, expressed with varying amounts of neutrality, humour, resignation or contempt:

1   Many patients do not look after themselves well (e.g. they drink and smoke too much, eat fatty foods, have unprotected sex and do not take sufficient exercise).
2   Many patients are ignorant about their bodies and the link between action and health (e.g. they are not aware of the risks of the bad habits just mentioned and they lack a basic understanding of human anatomy and physiology and how it might go wrong and for what reasons).
3   Many patients do not present themselves at the right time for help (e.g. men avoid their GPs and so miss the opportunities of early diagnosis and treatment).
4   Some patients present themselves too often and unnecessarily for help (e.g. frequent attenders who waste the professional's time – so called 'heart-sink patients'). In its most extreme form people may abuse health services by presenting with fictitious illnesses directly or vicariously (via their children) by faking symptoms or creating deliberate harm to produce bodily signs. They also might malinger for some sort of financial or other gain.
5   Some patients tell the professional about what is wrong and what to do about it (e.g. the patient, who having consulted the internet, has self-diagnosed and simply wants a particular treatment from the professional, independent of the view of the latter). These patients do not know their place and threaten to de-role the professional.
6   Some patients do not comply with advice and treatment (e.g. those who do not complete a course of antibiotics when the symptoms abate).

This list can be thought of in terms of two phases. In the first, the person avoids timely help-seeking and does not promote their health. In the second, the patient acts inappropriately in their role. Taken together, from a professional perspective, in various ways lay people *cannot be trusted* to act in their own interests about their health. However, that lack of trust can be placed in context.

First there is the role of information in making choices. Poor decision making for all of us about anything can be a function of ignorance and so this is the reason that *informed choices about health* have to be understood in relation to trust. Professionals may make poor decisions because of their ignorance (see earlier discussion), though generally we assume that the risk of ignorance is far greater for lay people – after all *ipso facto* they are not experts about health. Thus health professionals might distrust patients because the latter are assumed to be in a state of partial or total ignorance about how to maintain their own health via preventative measures and optimal help-seeking. The problems generated by lay ignorance have been codified by health service planners now as 'health literacy' (Council on Scientific Affairs for the American Medical Association, 1999). This term is explained on the website of the Department of Health in London in 2007 as follows:

> Health literacy is defined as the cognitive and social skills that determine the motivation and ability of individuals to gain access to understand and use information in ways that promote and maintain good health. This means much more than transmitting information and developing skills to undertake basic tasks. By improving people's access to and understanding of health information and their capacity to use it effectively, improved health literacy is critical to empowerment.

Thus knowledge is offered as a form of power to patients. The website continues by justifying the need for this empowerment by citing research on health literacy, which demonstrates amongst other things: that over 60 per cent of patients did not understand standard instructions about informed consent; 40 per cent of patients could not understand instructions about taking medication on an empty stomach; and over a quarter of patients did not understand information on an appointment slip. A two-year follow up of this sample found that those with low levels of literacy were twice as likely to be hospitalised (Baker *et al.* 1998). Thus ignorance is seen as an impediment to health improvement and for our purposes evidence about that ignorance would seem to warrant weak professional confidence in lay people's decision making about their health.

The second reason that professionals do not trust lay people relates not to knowledge but to intent. The lay person who does not care for their health (evidenced by their unhealthy habits and inappropriate healthcare utilization) may do so for a range of reasons not related to ignorance. They may not care about suffering and dying prematurely. For example, the irascible British writer, John Mortimer, who died recently, proudly told the world that he was happy to indulge himself habitually with rich food and alcohol because he saw no point in living an extra three years on a geriatric ward. There is also the matter of poverty – people may be poor and oppressed and look to unhealthy habits as sources of comfort. Also some people may gain in a range of ways from being ill (the malingerer gaining access to extra welfare benefits and the 'Munchausen' patient).

Thus in this second domain of reasons for patients being untrustworthy (beyond reasons of simple ignorance) is that at best they tend towards being unhealthy because of their passivity, nihilism, fatalism and fecklessness and at worst because they use help-seeking and illness presentation for manipulative reasons (Rogers, 2008; Halligan *et al.*, 2003).

Paternalism and the prospects of mutuality

The above sections have summarized the various reasons why patients might not trust professionals and vice versa. If mutual trust is to be consistently present then both aspects of the relationship have to be considered. The scenario of 'fully engaged' and 'empowered' patients who look after their own health and that of their significant others and then present at the right time for the right reasons to optimally utilise healthcare seems to be one prospect. From the other side there is a scenario of professionals acting in a competent, sensitive and respectful way at all times towards all patients. Stewart *et al.* (1995) suggest that this sort of 'win–win' outcome can be achieved by adhering to six principles in order to achieve patient-centred practice:

1 Professionals need to be psychologically sensitive to patient's communications. They need to be aware of the patient's knowledge, understanding and the unconscious as well as conscious motives for help-seeking.
2 Professionals need to think holistically and try to understand in a sensitive way the cultural and social context of a patient's account.
3 Professionals need to identify a common ground with the patient in order to develop a working collaboration in which expressed needs are respected and shared goals identified.
4 Professionals incorporate health promotion and preventative screening in their work.
5 The professional discloses uncertainties and is willing to act as advocate for the patient rather than simply having authority over them.

6   Professionals are realistic and admit the limits of their knowledge and competence – they are willing to seek help themselves.

This list includes an onus on professionals to listen credulously to the accounts patients provide during consultations. In the light of our earlier discussion, this is a substantial requirement, which is undermined potentially from both sides. The list requires that a collaborative and mutually respectful relationship develops by the shared investment of both parties. Neither must abuse their contribution, otherwise patients are readily seen as 'the enemy' by professionals and vice versa. The patient must be judicious, courteous and cooperative when using professional expertise. The professional must approach every patient consistently with respect and with an absence of cynicism. It is clear from our earlier discussion that this takes recurrent effort, if distrust is to be truly overcome in both directions. A break in that recurrent effort can risk a sudden collapse of trust.

Moreover, there is more to this matter than the recurrent exercise in good faith and good intentions from both sides. This expectation does not have a very long tradition in healthcare. The model of mutuality being rehearsed here is an optimal version emerging in the healthcare literature relatively recently and is becoming an unchecked working assumption; a taken for granted 'good thing' expected by all-comers. This points to the 'empowered and informed' patient preferred by user critics and health planners. From user critics it has arisen in new social movements (the women's health movement, the disability movement, the mental health service users' movement). Those involved in these consider themselves to be 'experts by experience'.

For their part, health planners have recognised that the scale of ill-health in society and the prevalence of long-term conditions mean that it is futile to expect professionals to be unilaterally responsible for the health of the general population. Thus there is a political and fiscal pressure to turn to lay people to both prevent ill health and care for themselves when they become ill.

Despite this pincer movement of service planners and the collective opposition to professional paternalism, some social groups remain resistant to this ideological shift. This is not just a matter of professional conservatism – it implicates patients as well. For example, poorer people with less education tend to retain a blind faith in medical expertise and do not expect to make much of a contribution to decision-making. This is a generational matter as well. Older people tend to manifest that dependency more than younger people. Also there are many cultural pressures to turn to professional expertise. For example, nearly every type of over-the-counter medication purchased by lay people will have a variant of the instruction – 'if symptoms persist consult your doctor immediately'.

Moreover, some types of health problem are more compatible, for patients and professionals alike, with simple mechanical rule-following, rather than elaborate joint decision making. For example, patients who develop acute symptoms or injury, where it is very clear what must be done technically (a prescribed drug, a bandage or plaster cast), are generally quite content to put themselves obediently in the hands of a professional over a short period of diagnosis and treatment. By contrast, a person who has a range of health problems and needs to cope with these over months and years is more likely to value a series of reflective and collaborative conversations with professionals. He or she also may reasonably expect to be the main person responsible for self-management or recovery.

Thus factors, such as social class, educational background, age and type of symptom presentation can shape the degree of mutuality expected during interactions between patients and professionals. We now examine this supra-personal context that situates the prospects of an ideal interaction, which is rational, efficient and mutually respectful between professionals and patients.

The social context of relationships in healthcare

In this final section of the chapter we place clinical encounters in their social context. In particular we note supply and demand, the impact of social inequality and the rise of consumerism (with more being said about these in Chapters 5 and 7).

Supply and demand

The supply of healthcare for all remains a global social policy goal. The success of this aim is shaped by the availability of a trained workforce and the fiscal capacity of nation states to build and maintain healthcare systems (compare, for example, the UK and Zimbabwe). Pencheon (1998) points out that in recent times, in developed societies, the demand for interventions has increased *and* there is an expectation that demand will be met in a way that is experienced positively by patients. Demand tends to outstrip supply in a variety of ways.

- There are the cross-national differences about fiscal capacity just noted. Often it is in those countries with the greatest demand for healthcare that there is the least capacity to supply services.
- There are tensions between fiscal priorities within countries (for example between primary and secondary care, between medical specialities and between spending on curative medicine for acute conditions and the long-term care of chronic conditions).
- Technological changes are costly and raise new patient expectations (occasionally technological innovations promise cost reductions). Innovations such as the internet have also impacted upon health-care utilisation.
- Pharmaceutical research, development and marketing expand the range and volume of medicinal products. It is the overall goal of the drug companies to maintain and improve their profits, which continuously drives this process. New products create new demands from prescribers and their patients, which have to be managed within budgetary constraints. Despite the latter, industrial competition and the search for new markets extend the range of deviations from health targeted by medicinal treatments.

The impact of social inequalities

An aspect of supply and demand is the extent to which countries provide cost-sharing schemes to ensure equitable access to healthcare. In some countries the only system is one of a fee for service. In others the latter is mixed with state safety nets, leading to a two tier form of healthcare, as in the USA, critiqued in Michael Moore's popular film *Sicko* (2007). But even in the UK with its globally recognized model of socialised healthcare (the NHS) the impact of social inequality remains. This is mainly in relation to the determinants of health (Wilkinson, 1996; Higgs and Scambler, 1998; Shaw *et al.*, 2005) but to an extent it also impacts upon healthcare utilization and healthcare delivery (poorer localities have fewer practitioners per head than richer areas).

Although there has been a cross-party consensus since 1948 that access to the NHS should always be based on clinical need, not the ability to pay, that simple vision has been clouded and undermined from the outset. Private practice has always been tolerated alongside NHS practice. Primary care – arguably the most important aspect of the NHS for most people most of the time – has been disadvantaged financially in relation to hospital-based medicine and has, by and large, been run as a series of small businesses by profit-driven general practitioners. This has encouraged the latter to have individualistic, parochial, financial preoccupations about healthcare. It has not encouraged the development of their consciousness or conscientiousness as community physicians championing health promotion in their local population.

Since the 1980s the NHS has been increasingly marketised with its encouragement of consumerism (see below). As the NHS developed, its early critical supporters began to note the 'inverse care law' (Hart, 1971); those with the least need for healthcare (the rich in society) are assured the greatest access. The 'sharp elbows' of the richer parts of the population mean that the poor have less access to systems like the British NHS, which is ostensibly 'free at the point of need'. Education and money ensure the rich access to what healthcare they demand and when they demand it; the opposite of poor uneducated people living in impoverished localities (Jarman, 1983).

The rise of consumerism

Consumerism and the marketization of the NHS fit hand in glove. Consumers make choices and suppliers of goods work hard to offer more options. As public money is spent on the latter, this has required that the NHS has become more *bureaucratized* in order to support increased marketization (an apparent contradiction). The cost-effectiveness of healthcare products and processes now must be audited or measured. Individual and collective consumer needs and their satisfaction have to be recorded, assessed and reflected on by healthcare bureaucrats recurrently. Their performance in this regard itself becomes a pre-occupation of their managers and in turn their political masters. Audit can go on and on (and in the minds of many this is already happening). System performance, fiscal probity and efficiency and clinical quality have all become a bottomless pit of audit interest and obligation (see Chapter 7).

In other words, with marketization and consumerism has come a growth in monitoring of need, cost-effectiveness and consumer satisfaction – the 'audit explosion'. The latter is now a constant backdrop to clinical encounters, which are shaped by two versions of consumerism. The first is individual, with the expectation that patient-centred choices and treatment options will be facilitated by clinical professionals. The second is that part of the NHS (for now the commissioning wing situated in Primary Care Trusts) which is charged with ensuring best value for whole local populations in relation to both health promotion and healthcare utilisation.

Whether this has led to improved standards of care is a moot point, given that healthcare systems are now characterized by a culture of elaborate accountability to a point of *explicit distrust* in relation to professional action (Sheaff and Pilgrim, 2006; Brown, 2008a). The gap in trust between managers and commissioners on the one side and practising clinicians on the other has led to a dysfunctional outcome for the NHS. We return to this difficulty in Chapters 7 and 8.

Thus the meaning of consumerism at present is ambiguous. There may have been a shift from paternalism to consumerism since the 1980s (Klein, 1989). However, an important caveat is that paternalism has also taken on a new form, with the growth of 'healthcare commissioning'; professionals with or without clinical qualifications, making wide-ranging decisions about resource allocation.

Consumerism has thus taken on a parochial form by proxy, in the hands of bureaucrats. Those working in Primary Care Trusts (PCTs) have become the earnest, audit-obsessed, performance-managing guardians of collective lay interest in every locality about healthcare. However, they are also disconnected, by and large, from the populations they serve. A handful of lay people typically turn up to the Annual General Meetings of PCTs to trouble the aims and routines of those working in them.

These small parochial organizations have provoked distrust from those expecting them to deliver 'world class commissioning' of healthcare. As the book goes to print, the new British coalition government has announced (July 2010) the imminent abolition of PCTs. In recent years parliamentarians from all parties have cast doubt on their worth. For example, the Health Select Committee of the House of Commons (13 January 2009) made the point about a review into improving the NHS that:

> There is much to commend in the Review, in particular the emphasis on quality and leadership. However, we are concerned about its implementation. This will largely be done by PCTs, but we doubt that most PCTs are currently capable of doing this task successfully. We have noted on numerous occasions, and the Government has accepted, that PCT commissioning is poor. In particular, PCTs lack

analytical and planning skills and the quality of their management is very variable. This reflects on the whole of the NHS ... We consider this to be striking and depressing.

In this new context of consumerism, patients are testing out their trust implicitly but rarely knowingly, in their local commissioners of health-care. Public engagement with the latter, who are appointed by the State (non-executive Directors) or NHS employees (Chief Executives, Directors and their staff) not locally elected, remains weak. Thus whilst patients are in a position to test out, on a regular basis, their capacity to trust the practitioners they encounter, this is not the case in relation to healthcare commissioners, who, with variable competence in the back-ground, regulate that clinical activity. Most of the population remain disengaged and often simply unaware of their powers and activity. How can trust be expressed by the population about its local NHS given this picture?

A final point to note about the ethos of marketisation and consumerism is that it is inevitably creating a confusing organizational ethos for ordinary people to witness and respond to. The pursuit of this neo-liberal solution to healthcare utilization, by Conservative and New Labour governments in Britain in the past twenty years, has been constrained ultimately by demand always outstripping supply (see earlier). This encourages a countervailing strategy of 'de-marketization' and 'demand control' (that is, rationing). In turn, this generates messages about self-responsibility for health rather than an encourage-ment of dependency on professional provision of treatment services (Sheaff, 2002). What exactly is being asked of ordinary citizens – should they avoid being patients or embrace that role as active consumers? In the light of this ambiguity, what sort of trusting orientation should be taken in relation to health? Should lay people trust themselves or trust others?

All of the above suggests that by the time the dyad emerges of a patient and professional, both parties have been affected in their approach to the other by a range of influences, current and historical. Professionals are more knowledgeable than patients and in a system in which demand outstrips supply they are looking to limit access and 'speed throughput'. At the same time, managed healthcare systems no longer rely on arbitrary professional paternalism, or professional discre-tion, to ensure effective and respectful outcomes in encounters with patients.

Consumerism and the 'audit explosion' (see Chapter 7) now put limits on that paternalism and discretion. Professionals can now spend as much time recording and accounting for what they do and managing risk, as they do carrying out the core tasks of caring. Professionals are no longer trusted simply to be motivated by good intentions towards patients; they are now expected to account for their actions, both prospectively and retrospectively, to their managers and paymasters. Legitimate complainants and litigious patients are also a constant reminder that professionals are certainly no longer a law unto themselves. They now must keep a wary eye on prospective client vengefulness and rancour in the wake of errors and misjudgements.

As for patients, the possibility of them being trusted on a routine basis to play the optimal role of patient, in line with the expectations of professionals, is limited by a number of factors. Above, the many social influences, beyond the individual, on healthy action and help-seeking were noted. Caught between messages about 'inappropriate' healthcare utilization and a failure to present for help at the right time, they walk a tight rope, which is easy to fall off for many reasons. Moreover, the patient population is not a monolith; it contains poor and prosperous, old and young, male and female, native and foreigner. All of these aspects of social group membership influence how needs are identified and expressed, once the patient role is being considered and when it is entered.

Moreover, some patients give others a bad name and encourage a pervasive distrust from professionals. Note was made earlier of the malingerers who abuse service contact for psychological or financial gain. The work-shy patient recurrently 'throwing a sicky', the welfare or insurance fraudster and the Munchausen's patient (with or without proxy) may constitute only a minority. However, their cumulative impact on professional distrust may be ever-present.

Summary

- We exist in a cultural context which has a shared view of optimal clinical encounters. We expect professionals to be competent, honest and have confidence in their personal integrity. We expect that patients should adopt the role in a timely manner and to approach the encounter responsibly.
- Clinicians have *a priori* grounds for being wary of appropriate lay action about self-care and help-seeking. If clinicians hold patients in distrust then this will affect their style of engagement in each case.

- These interpersonal considerations create a risk of de-contextualised accounts of trust in healthcare. They need then to be situated in particular daily contexts. Those contexts are affected by dynamics created by the imbalance between supply and demand, social inequalities and the growth of consumerism
- Consumerism, which is linked to the marketisation of healthcare has triggered the seemingly paradoxical outcome of increased bureaucratization – the audit explosion and reconstructed forms of paternalism (local healthcare commissioning). If trusting clinical professionals is a complex matter, the trusting of healthcare commissioners is uncharted territory because of poor local democratic engagement to date.
- There is now confusion over expectations which might impact on trust. Patients may not be clear what is expected of them. Should they use services or limit their demands upon them? How will they know when their help-seeking is appropriate? In their turn, professionals may not be clear whether they are being expected to respond to patients as needy customers to be satisfied or as threats to their authority and sources of unreasonable demand.

CHAPTER 3

Psycho-social and Psycho-ethical Aspects of Trust

Introduction

Now that we have introduced everyday and technical aspects of trust and begun to look at its interpersonal aspects specifically in healthcare, this chapter will place the establishment of trust in human beings in a wider context. This is a *psycho-social* matter because it involves *both* experiential aspects *within* and *between* intimates *and* it involves social, ethical and even political aspects of trust in our encounters with others. The psycho-social is a 'deep' notion of trust, because, first and foremost it involves a trusting relationship with ourselves (the idea of 'self-trust' or 'basic trust').

That psycho-social context begins with our very earliest experiences in the world. If we establish a secure start in life then our capacity to trust others and deal with the challenges of an imperfect world are increased. If we have an insecure start then we are made vulnerable in a number of ways in how we deal with those challenges. We may be overly trusting at one extreme or, at the other, incapable of trusting anyone. This complexity will now be dealt with in relation to the following:

- First, the newborn's experience of trust will be examined. The experience of trust is intertwined with the infant's innate disposition to seek the care of others and the capacity of caregivers to reciprocate this need. It is the platform for later trusting relationships.
- Second, the mental health implications of this early experience of trust failing are summarized.
- Third, the social, ethical and political implications of trust in malign authority are explored.

At the end of each of these sections, connections will be made for the reader about their implications for trust in healthcare.

Trust, attachment, dependency and ontological security

To become a patient is to become to some degree (and sometimes extremely) dependent on others around us. This is not new to us – it starts in infancy and so the experiences we had then are likely to orientate us in the patient role. This topic has been explored most extensively in variants of a form of psychology (psychoanalysis) which is inherently interested, because of its developmental focus, in the type and quality of relationships in early childhood. In particular, those psychoanalysts who modified Freud's original emphasis upon the Oedipus complex (the child desiring the parent of the opposite sex and learning to rescind these desires) emphasized pre-Oedipal and even pre-verbal experiences.

This group of 'object–relations' theorists, including Balint, Winnicott, Fairbairn and Guntrip argued that the developmental challenge for the infant is to find a suitable balance between fusion and separation with their caregiver (depicted at that time as the mother–child bond) in order to grow confidently as a separate individual. This basic point from object–relations theory resonates with the one we make about the importance of ontological security later on in this chapter. For example, here Winnicott talks of the early joining and separating of

> the baby and the mother when the mother's love, displayed as human reliability, does in fact give the baby a sense of trust, or of confidence in the environmental factor. (Winnicott, 1967: 372)

For Winnicott, this primary or primitive form of relating leads to the baby internalising a sense of trust when the care is good. His preferred phrase was 'good-enough' because imperfect trust also creates a space for the baby to struggle and separate from the mother to individuate. His use of the term 'environmental factor' suggests that from a psychoanalytical perspective our general trust in our environment relies on early maternal trustworthiness. Before birth the baby (usually) is held in a safe and trustworthy environment of the womb and even Freud, though less interested in the nature of pre-verbal experience, remarked on the environmental similarity between the womb and the safe comfort of the mother's arms (Freud, 1926). Some psychoanalysts suggested that the brief interlude between being safely in the womb and being held safely outside it offered the first major risk of threat to trust in the infant – hence the notion of 'birth trauma' (Rank, 1929). Moreover, even the womb is not necessarily safe as toxins can affect the placenta, a point returned to later.

For Winnicott, and other object–relations theorists, the emphasis is on mutual empathy. The baby innately trusts the mother and the mother provides a safe physical and emotional environment for the infant to grow. By implication, neglect or abuse during infancy can impair the person's capacity to trust the world generally. This would create intense anxiety which could be experienced as paranoia or chaotic madness.

The importance of the primary relationship of trust

Freud's classical theory emphasized that erotic energy was channelled through and experienced by different parts of the body as it developed through the oral, anal and genital phases. However, Balint (1952) argued that the primary relationship of trusting connection between the mother and baby actually preceded the oral stage of sucking and biting. He supported Winnicott's position that the basic need for food, which shapes the infant's experience when sucking and then, when weaned, biting, is not the whole picture in very early life. It suggests that, even before food, the infant has other needs for closeness, warmth and of feeling secure. In accordance with this emphasis on primary affection Balint used the term 'primary love' and Winnicott coined the term 'primary maternal preoccupation'. The first key process to ensure (or betray) trust is the interpersonal field between mother and child, with both parties being primed to form the bond.

Likewise Fairbairn (1952) argued that the baby was not 'pleasure seeking' (the classic Freudian assumption) but 'object seeking'. The term 'object' here may appear odd, as it actually refers to 'person', but it is based on the assumption that the pre-verbal and, by definition, egocentric, baby, at this stage of development seeks to relate to its caregivers but does not recognize their existence as whole separate human beings (yet). Support for this idea comes from the study of feral children who have been raised by animals. They seek the care of these other species and adopt their habits. The children survive, albeit in a pre-verbal state.

In other words, the infant seeks connection and attachment but does not recognize, or have a reflective sense of, the full nature of his or her carer.

Psychoanalysis and ethology: the importance of attachment for trust

These psychoanalytical ideas were joined in the 1950s by evidence from a different direction – ethology (the study of animal behaviour and its adaptive value for the preservation of a species). Bowlby (1969) was a psychoanalyst who drew heavily on the work of ethology to support his theories about attachment. The most famous and oft quoted to, and by, students of psychology is the work of Harlow. The latter studied the attachment and feeding behaviour of baby rhesus monkeys. In one version of his experiment (Harlow and Zimmerman, 1959) the monkeys were fed on demand from one of two models – one was simply a wire structure with a feeding bottle the other was cloth covered. The babies preferred the latter and spent most of their time with it whether or not they were being fed. Moreover, this preference extended to wanting the cloth model even when its milk had run out and milk was still available from the wire model.

The conclusion drawn here is that the infant's basic need to attach and relate to others precedes and is even more basic than food seeking. A further implication of this primary desire for attachment in humans (and other primates) is that our tendency towards healthy and unhealthy forms of relationship may be determined very early in life (Bowlby, 1953). Indeed it is so early in life (from an instinctive predis-position) that our later moral entitlement to receive, and obligation to give, trust as rule-following behaviour, which is codified in and learned via language, may be an elaboration of this basic tendency. This is not to argue that these later language-codified rules are irrelevant to human affairs (laws and ethical frames of reference are very important aspects of any civilisation), merely that they are an elaboration of a tendency which is much more primitive or instinctive.

Psychoanalytical and ethological interest in attachment and trust is bound up with their developmental focus. Other approaches to psycho-logical understanding also focus on trust. A good example is the phenomenological approach of Carl Rogers, the founder of person-centred therapy. Summarizing his work, Thorne (1996) makes the following points:

Person-centred therapy is essentially an approach to the human condition based on trust. There is trust in the innate resourcefulness of human beings, given the right conditions to find their own way through life. There is trust that the direction thus found will be positive and creative. There is trust too, that the process of relating between counsellor and client will in itself provide the primary context of safety and nurture in which the client can face the pain of alienation from his or her true self and move towards an integrated way of being. (Thorne, 1996: 55)

Thorne proceeds to argue that a block in therapeutic progress often arises from either the client failing to trust the therapist or because the therapist cannot trust their own commitment to progress with the client. What distinguishes this approach from psychoanalysis is that it emphasizes trust as an interpersonal field in the here and now rather than as an historical determinant of psychological functioning.

For their part, some psychoanalytical psychotherapists have emphasized the positive impact of therapy in the present, when safe and trustworthy relating is assured between patient and therapist (Guntrip, 1977; Suttie, 1935). Both analysts and Rogerians would agree that trust is a supportive condition for, and mutually reinforces, empathy in human relationships. This point would be applicable to the original conditions of trust in infancy and the current role of trust in helping people to change.

Psychoanalysis, existentialism, basic trust and ontological security

The above psychoanalytical assumptions were extended by some analysts into discussions about the existential vulnerability of some adults, who in infancy had failed to encounter good enough care in order to enjoy a sense of basic trust in the world and themselves. The strength of our existential commitments and certainties can be called 'ontological security' (see Laing, 1990) and is one useful starting point of understanding basic trust in the world.

Self directed trust or 'self-trust' is generally related to how secure we are within ourselves. This has profound implications for how secure we are in the 'ownership' of our thoughts, actions, values and beliefs that mark out our existence in the world. Self-trust can be related to how it is we belong and identify with self, place, other and situation. This then is 'ontological security' or can be discussed negatively as 'ontological insecurity'. Laing notes that:

> a basically ontological secure person will encounter all the hazards of life, social, ethical, spiritual, biological, from a centrally firm sense of his own and other people's reality and identity. It is often difficult for a person with such a sense of his integral selfhood and personal identity, of the *permanency* of things, of the *reliability* of natural processes, of the *sustainability* of others, to transpose himself into an individual lacking in any unquestionable self-validating certainties. (Laing, 1961:39 – our emphasis)

Ontological security and insecurity rely on the presence and absence of particular self-validating certainties. These vary in kind and degree. The first and most basic kind involves *belonging* to ourselves and being in one's 'authority' and 'authorship.' The ontologically secure are aware of their thoughts being their own and are willing to take responsibility for them. The ontologically insecure more usually fall into self-deception about taking responsibility of thoughts and actions that they generate in their relationship with others. In the most extreme cases 'ontological insecurity', according to Laing, leads to a divided self that invests external reality (and sometimes authority) to voices that are actually internally generated within the mind – for example, in the case of those with a diagnosis of 'schizophrenia'.

Other forms of ontological security/insecurity may have to do with *belonging* to place and/or situation, where we may or may not feel we belong: to the place we live; to the relationships we establish with others; to the situational role we find our selves in and so on. Establishing a secure and trustworthy sense of self is an existential quest for certainty: a quest for inner certainty that involves self understanding and integration.

The quest for ontological security is an existential project of belonging, where we anchor our 'being-in-the-world' with others through a sense of place and all that entails: that is, a sense of personal and shared purpose that connects us to our 'projects' with family, friends, neighbours and colleagues. It is partly, through our sense of belonging and purpose in life that we achieve well-being and self-worth, both of which are needed if we are ever to attain a sense of self-trust which radiates out to others.

Whilst excessive ontological insecurity leads to varying degrees of separation and alienation, excessive ontological security can manifest as an over-confidence in one's sense of self that may develop into inflexibility, uncritical thinking and even prejudice. For this reason ontological insecurity, *to a certain degree*, is not necessarily a bad thing; as it opens us up the ability to explore 'difference' in ourselves and others.

Because trust has an internal dimension that has to do with personal identity as well as an external one that may be more calculative in trusting others (in terms of their reliability or competence perhaps) trust is also bound up with a quest for recognition in oneself *as* another. In other words, self-trust is entangled in our relationships with others – how we recognize ourselves in another and others recognize themselves in us. This may be extended in the depth of trust we place in certain of our more significant relationships with others. For example, a significant other that 'completes' our identity in some way, is extended a surety of implicit trustworthiness that a stranger would never command. This surety we place in a significant other may have positive or negative normative implications: it is positive when a significant other is psychologically interdependent and bring out the best in us and is negative when they are co-dependent with us, colluding with our faults and failings.

Having very briefly examined the relationship between trust and recognition – see Chapter 5 for a longer discussion – we can also explore the relationship between trust, betrayal and deceit. When trust breaks down, those that we have placed our trust in, are perceived as *purposely having deceived* us, in some way. This undoubtedly happens in a lot of cases where trusting fails; that is, the trusted being straightforwardly dishonest about encapsulating the truster's interests as their own. However, this explanation does not exhaust how trust is defeated. In other words,, being untrustworthy is not simply about being self-consciously and purposely dishonest. The perception that another has straightforwardly deceived or betrayed one's trust is sometimes misplaced, because the truster might have *deceived themselves* – what Sartre might call 'bad faith' (Sartre, 2006).

However, 'bad faith' is not a conscious form of self-deception; a person in 'bad faith' does not ask themselves to believe in a falsehood. Bad faith is not *just* self-deception; it also has an element of *faith*. That is to say, when the trusted takes another's interests as their own, they do so in *false consciousness* believing that they are holding another's interest *as if* they were their own. Bad faith involves a form of wishful thinking that someone else's interest aligns with one's own. Those in bad faith believe that someone's interests are aligned to their own, only to find sometime later, that their interests are quite different or have now changed. This can lead to a circle of deceit, where either the truster or the entrusted is unaware of any betrayal; the problem being that in being able to deceive oneself about what one's interests really are, one is able to deceive others too.

Put more strongly, in the words, of Duke de La Rochefoucauld, the seventeenth-century French philosopher: 'we deceive ourselves in order to deceive others better' (La Rochefoucauld, 2003). This connects the Sartrean notion of 'bad faith' to the Freudian understanding of 'rationalization' as a defence mechanism to protect the ego and justify one's actions post hoc. At this stage, the reader may now appreciate why, in Chapter 1, we were keen to reject Hardin's 'encapsulated interest' view of trust and his emphasis in rationality as being too simplistic and partial as a model of trust. 'Rationalization' and 'bad faith' are forms of *seeming rationality* to persuade ourselves and others of forms of logic that make us feel good but are highly distorted by deeper emotional processes.

Untrustworthiness then, is not always deliberate and straightforward dishonesty, but an action born out of ontological insecurity about what one's *authentic* interests are, leading to self-deception, false consciousness and rationalization. To be trustworthy however, one needs to be in relatively 'good faith' about one's interests, either by *authentically* knowing what our true interests are and/or by encapsulating someone else's interests *as if* they *truly* are one's own. Note also, to be in 'good faith', according to Sartre, is not dialectically opposite of being in 'bad faith'; 'good faith' is simply a conscious resistance to the ever-present possibility of being in 'bad faith.' Furthermore, 'good faith' is akin to the capacity for basic trust and the ontological security on which it relies.

Implications for trust in healthcare

If we are 'object seeking' or we thrive in conditions of 'unconditional positive regard', then we are basically interdependent beings, so we inevitably construct forms of moral order to live by and within. As we will see in later chapters, that basic trust is an aspect of our interdependence as human beings and that our orientation towards experts when we need help is perfectly understandable. Moreover, when it works well interdependence in healthcare relationships celebrates a 'win–win' scenario.

During times of acute sickness dependency can be evident in both an objective and subjective sense. On the first count we really might need others to tend to our basic needs of feeding and toileting in the manner of an infant. On the second count feeling ill brings with it regressive feelings of anxiety, pain and the need for comfort. Depending on our character though, these objective and subjective features of dependence may be angrily resented (the reluctant and resentful patient) or at the other extreme actively sought out (malingerers and those described as 'Munchausen' patients). The latter are patients who invent symptoms or inflict harm on themselves to secure medical treatment. Most of us experience healthcare somewhere between these extreme points: we might tend to ignore illness most of the time; we might tend towards hypochondria; and all points between.

The developmental challenge to balance interdependency and personal autonomy is thus thrown into relief during times of illness and healthcare utilization. Moreover, the scenario just noted of acute sickness involves benign ministrations, which are anxiously sought and gratefully received. This is why the dramatic rescuing role of Accident and Emergency Departments is so readily idealised in the mass media. The further we get into the healthcare business in which chronicity is being managed and interventions are imposed, rather than desired, the more complicated the matter of dependency becomes. Healthcare systems are now responsible for many more types of sick, disabled and dysfunctional recipients than the idealised images offered and enjoyed in TV programmes such as *ER* or *Casualty*. Healthcare systems are also in the business of social regulation, which is characterized by contested ethical and political matters (see Chapters 4 and 6). In these cases, the direct symmetry of benign care in infancy and benign care in adult illness breaks down and we have to review the implications for the balance between interdependence and personal autonomy in a new light. Moreover, as the next section will indicate when we enter the role of patient or practitioner, we come with our particular history. We bring our biography of trust to bear on both the roles and our expectations of others.

The earlier points made, about ontological insecurity and bad faith, are also pertinent for our discussions about trust in healthcare. For example, we noted that ontological security is partially a function of familiarity and so it reminds us that for patients to enter unfamiliar surroundings with unfamiliar people around them will have a predictable emotional impact on many of them, especially where their self-trust is relatively weak. This would account for why patients outwardly with similar conditions might react in very different ways to entering the patient role, going into hospital, being bed-bound, and so on. Another example of this point is the range of ways in which people react and adjust to the losses encountered with a sudden acquired impairment – they are not all the same. This range of reactions reflects degrees of ontological security/insecurity.

As for 'bad faith', this means that we have deceived ourselves about the fact that we do not know what we really believe to be true. We might then become too attached to an external authority of truth to cover up our insecurity and ignorance. Being in relatively 'good faith' as patients, would allow us to resist the risks of medical paternalism, even when the latter is well intentioned and benign. As for professionals themselves, they too are at risk of entering 'bad faith', if and when they become too attached to their role as 'experts' and the sole arbiters of patient needs. This might cover over a basic insecurity about what they really think or may reduce the authentic anxiety that might be experienced about their own fallibility and the limits of their profession and its competence to restore health and ward off death. Bad faith then can ward off psychological pain for both patients and staff.

Fortunately, there are number of decision-making practices in contemporary healthcare practices that bind patient and professionals in relationships that are characteristic of being in relatively 'good faith,' where the freedom to choose and take responsibility for decisions of both parties is protected and valued. The following are characteristic of relationships based on relatively 'good faith' and can be illustrated in respect to securing patient consent:

- *Contextualizing the use of informed consent and simple/presumed consent.* Part of being in 'good faith' is recognizing the importance of context and what is and is not appropriate for consent. That is, trusting when it is appropriate to assume clinical authority in certain low risk procedures (presumed consent) and when clinical authority needs to be authorized by a patient who needs to make a decision themselves about certain treatment options (informed consent).
- *Ownership and freedom to take responsibility in ethical decision-making.* The principle of fully informed consent protects the patient's right to freely choose or refuse treatment. This aligns to being in 'good faith', where decisions about values and how they are determined are one's own.
- *Dialogic communication.* Part of being in 'good faith' involves the open space for communication, comprehension and empowerment. Informed consent is easily abused. In other words, informed consent is not about informing someone *until* they consent (a monologic

form of communication that is subtly coercive). Rather, informed consent involves empowering the patient so that they truly comprehend what the best choices for them are. This involves a dialogic form of communication where authority is used to empower free and rational choices.

- *Openness, honesty and mutuality in decision-making.* 'Good faith' is about framing limits of decision-making that requires openness, honesty and mutuality. Medical experts need to be honest, setting limits to their predictive capacity, framing 'choices' as a probabilistic gamble that makes sense to the patient and their ability to act on what only they can take responsibility for.

The failure of trust in childhood

Psychologists from a variety of theoretical perspectives agree that neglect and abuse in childhood is not good for a person's mental health (Pilgrim, Rogers and Bentall, 2009). This conclusion arises from both the psychotherapeutic traditions of psychoanalysis and person-centred therapy noted above and more recent studies by cognitive therapists about symptoms of a range of mental health problems.

Few claim that there is a consistent one-to-one relationship between neglect and abuse in early childhood and specific mental health problems. Causality is always multiple and it can also include genetic vulnerability and social stress within and around a family of origin. What is clear though is that privation (withholding care), deprivation (taking care away or providing inadequate care) and abuse (whether it is emotional, physical or sexual) significantly increase the probability of many mental health problems in childhood and later in adulthood (Browne, Davies and Stratton, 1988).

In other words, the broad claims made by Bowlby about the risks of failed benign attachment in infancy appear to be borne out empirically (Cichetti, Toch and Lynch, 1995). For example, abuse in early infancy predicts psychotic symptoms such as hallucinations, delusions and thought disorder (Read *et al.*, 2003; Whitfield *et al.*, 2005). Abuse in childhood also predicts outpatient attendance at psychiatric facilities and is significantly linked to specific symptoms such as attempted suicide, re-victimization in adulthood, substance misuse, sleep disturbances, panic attacks, depression, sexual problems and fear of others (Briere and Runtz, 1987). Parents who are over-critical and perfectionistic increase the risk of their children presenting later with social phobia or obsessive compulsive problems (Stakettee and Frost, 1998). Children who grow up feeling the need to look after their parents (role reversal) are more likely to develop chronic generalized anxiety (Borkovec and Newman, 1998).

Early deprivation and abuse also predicts a proclivity for abusing substances in adulthood and, in the case of physical abuse, it increases the probability of violent acting out (stranger assaults and domestic violence). Indeed it is difficult to find a form of mental health problem which is unaffected by negative childhood experiences, though debates still rage about the proportion of influence it has (compared to biological predisposition and one-off severe traumas or cumulative social stress). Moreover, the biological, psychological and social systems interact and influence one another in multiple and circular ways. It is worth noting that the term 'biological' here may not always mean 'genetic' because the biological environment affects the growing brain post-partum. In turn, the child's behaviour starts to affect their social opportunities at a very early age.

For example, a child in a poor family with poorly educated substance-misusing parents may start life *in utero* at a disadvantage. The mother's substance misuse affects the quality of the placenta *and* her willingness to attend to her new baby's needs. Later the child may be malnourished or hit about the head by the drunken father in a rage causing neurodevelopmental delay. The child itself becomes distractible and aggressive, as a function of learned behaviour, poor emotional nurturance and brain damage. This leads to anti-social conduct in the family and at school. School performance is affected by neurological deficits and dysfunctional conduct, early measures of IQ are low and the child suffers social rejection and constant criticism from those in authority. He becomes 'conduct disordered' and later maybe, as an adult, acquires the label of 'psychopath' or 'sociopath', when his self-seeking aggression reaches violent and criminal proportions.

The long term impact of childhood problems on personality

The early environment affects the developing personality of the child – its stable psychological characteristics in later life. When these stable features are dysfunctional the person can acquire the label of 'personality disorder'. The two commonest diagnoses given to prisoners who are deemed to be personality disordered are 'borderline' and 'anti-social personality disorder'. In the first of these diagnoses (given more to women than men) there is a consistent pattern of histories of sustained verbal, physical or sexual abuse in childhood (Widiger and Trull, 1994). Physical abuse is a recurring pattern of those with a diagnosis of anti-social personality disorder. Retrospective accounts identify a pattern of oppositional behaviour and violence from a young age.

What these offenders have in common is a marked egocentricity. With this comes a lack of empathy for others or at least an indifference to their rights and feelings. Other people only represent an opportunity for their needs being met – they are not recognized as having needs of their own, with an equal entitlement to have these needs met. At the centre of those with a personality disorder is egocentricity and a lack of mutuality, respect and trust in relation to other human beings. Others are used as sources of gratification and their needs and rights are not respected (or they are manipulated in a callous or instrumental manner for selfish ends). As a consequence of this amoral position, actions are inevitably judged by others to be offensive and incorrigible. Sustained egocentricity (rather than the transitory selfish moments and specific weaknesses of all humans) is inherently a-social and a-moral. It grows in moral, social and political significance though when it acquires the extraordinary powers enjoyed by leaders in society. This point cues our next section but first we will consider the implications of this section for trust in healthcare.

Implications for trust in healthcare

Given the above points, the failure of trust in childhood has several implications for the roles of patients and professionals. On the first count, a wide range of mental health problems dealt with by healthcare systems are traceable in large part to childhood adversity. Given that it is estimated that around a third of consultations in primary care involve mental health problems then this in not a marginal consideration about healthcare utilization. Also our experience of trust in childhood is likely to nuance the manner in which we conduct ourselves as patients (from being counter-dependent to being ultra-dependent). Put differently the *emotional* dimension to being a patient and trusting or distrusting those caring for us is relevant to consider. As we noted earlier, trust is an emotional, not just a rational, matter.

Also, if early trust can lead to pathological expressions of the personality then it will have implications for the roles of patients and practitioners. Around 10 per cent of the population warrant a description of personality disorder, which in various ways alludes to forms of egocentricity and a tendency to engage with others in a dysfunctional way. This in itself makes them both patients (in a mental health system which has few answers) and will colour the way they enter the patient role and engage with practitioners.

Turning to the latter, we will see in Chapter 6, in the cases of Harold Shipman and Alder Hey, where arrogant and narcissistic individuals found themselves in positions of power over patients and produced a gross abuse of trust invested in them. Their egocentricity led to their morbid needs being expressed at the expense of those who looked to them to be caring. Shipman cultivated misplaced trust from many of his elderly patients. Even when he was accused of his misdeeds, several of those patients retained a loyalty to him and expressed disbelief about his wrongdoing and malignant character. Shipman was a doctor who sadistically enjoyed his power over life and death. This point links to our next section.

Malign leadership and mass conformity

Trust and trustworthiness are at the centre of malign leadership. Psycho-biographical accounts of authoritarian leaders describe histories of childhood cruelty, which the dictator-to-be replays in their treatment of others. For example, although cautious about the reliability of data about Hitler's early life, Kershaw (1998) confirms that the young Adolf received daily thrashings from his father, who displayed both systematic regularity in his beatings and outbursts of temper in his family life generally. Though Hitler could trust his mother to provide benign care he could only rely on his authoritarian, pompous and pedantic father to thrash him.

Moreover, although he idealized his mother (she was possibly the only person he genuinely loved in his whole life) this supposedly perfect mother ultimately failed to protect him from her husband's cruelty. It may be significant then that his later treatment of women would oscillate between being angry and sadistic (in his abuse of his niece Geli Raubal and his long-term partner and bunker wife Eva Braun) and idealizing or masochistic (in deference towards women he considered his superior). Fromm (1973) provides an elaborate description of Hitler's oscillation between sadism and masochism in relation to these different categories of women. Both groups were prone to suicide, for

Fromm indicating the destructive impact of Hitler on those he became close to.

This oscillation between types of women may indicate a repressed anger at his mother, which had to be split off from his need to idealize her. As for his father, Hitler survived his attacks not by rejecting him but by respecting him and re-enacting his cruelty – he internalized his malevolent image. Thus Hitler's sado-masochism and obsession with domination were over-determined by a mother whose protection ultimately failed him and by a father whose cruelty was trustworthy.

To be clear this is not being offered as an explanation for the rise of fascism (a socio-political movement arising in certain economic conditions with mass support). What is noted however is that when regimes such as fascism do arise, with their focus on the role of the leader, we should take an interest in both the psychology of authoritarian leaders and the mass psychology of those who turn to them, as part of a rich accounts of political movements.

What about the followers?

These psycho-historical features of cruel dictators may well be bound up with failures of trust in their own childhood but a more curious question is not about them but their followers. This question is a psycho-social or social-psychological one. It is not about people who are cruel and enjoy dominating others *per se* but why those others embrace the role demanded of them. In some ways this question appears to be more puzzling. Intuitively we all know that cruelly treated children may well become cruel adults. But what leads others to admire or accept rather than condemn their actions? The answer to this seems to reside in malign dependency and so reveals that the seemingly adaptive desire for attachment discussed above is not always functional and beneficial for human welfare.

What needs explaining here is not malign leadership but what could be called malign 'followship'. A proportion of power-obsessed, self-aggrandizing narcissists and sadists will exist in any society but how do they acquire positions of power? Why do masses of people place their trust in these flawed personalities with predictable regularity in national politics and even within the organizational structures of democratic societies (such as in private companies or state-funded bureaucracies)?

Psychoanalytical commentators point out that the followers of Hitler, Mao and Stalin submitted themselves to omnipotent father figures. The mass adoration of Eva Peron or Margaret Thatcher suggests that this process can also be about domineering mother figures. This indicates that a dysfunctional aspect of childhood attachment is that it can lead to an uncritical stance in life and an emotionally convenient form of magical thinking. The latter involves adults relying on authority to think about and solve complex dilemmas. If we move from thinking about reliance on political leaders, to reliance on clinical professionals, the role of uncritical dependency becomes evident. This leads us on to trust and magical thinking in adults.

Trust and magical thinking in adults

An indication of the immature process involved here is when people look to politicians and experts to offer simple solutions. Complexity brings uncertainty and anxiety. Simple parental-style dictates provide certainty and reassurance. The tendency of most societies to construct oligarchies based on ideologies of race (apartheid and Nazism), tribes (tribalism), future equality (socialism and communism), present wealth production (capitalism) or timeless religious belief (theocracies) suggests that there is a recurring popular need for forms of elite leadership offering simple answers to complex questions. The latter are replaced by binary oppositions about good and bad, pre-empting the less bearable ambivalence of mature and balanced relating to others.

In developed societies, these political oligarchies have now been joined by professional elites. They all invite faith in a symbolic parent, who provides loyal and obedient adult–children with reassurance in exchange for their freedom. In the case of healthcare, the binary opposition is between sickness and health, with professional elites asserting authority over the defeat of the former and promotion of the latter. Lay people are then faced with a choice to accept or reject that authority.

A relevant experiment, which is as well known to psychology undergraduates as Harlow's studies noted earlier, is the work of Milgram. This highlights that trust can be extended to become blind obedience. In humans the benign expression of trust is one of empathy towards others, tolerance about them and a respect for their human rights. But in some circumstances trust can become dysfunctional (when people are gullible and become duped by others) or even malign (when they are complicit in human rights violations or even genocide). The classic experiment by Milgram (1963) on obedience and its critique by Fromm (1973) illustrate how we might understand this ambiguity.

The experiment at Yale University involved forty volunteers who were told that they were to be part of an experiment on memory and learning. The naïve subjects were told that they were to help understand the relationship between punishment and learning. Each subject was paired with a hoax confederate of the experimenter who was allegedly being tested on their ability to recall material taught to them. The duped subject was designated as a 'teacher' and the confederate given the role of the 'learner' by a further hoax when the (white-coated) experimenter pretended to draw random allocations of the two roles in each pair out of a hat. The experimenter lied about the random allocation – the pairs were rigged in advance. When the 'learner' in the pair gave a wrong answer, the 'experimenter' told the 'teacher' to administer a small electric shock. With each new mistake the 'teacher' was told by the 'experimenter' to increase the intensity of the shock until it became not just painful but dangerous.

A mock shock machine sat by the 'teacher', with a dial supposedly indicating this increase, and they were told by the 'experimenter' to announce the new voltage to the 'learner' with each shock administered. (There was no shock but the 'learner' acted as if they were shocked moments after the announcement.) With each 'shock' the hoax 'learner' manifested increasing distress. If the 'teacher' was worried or resistant about continuing, the 'experimenter' gave a range of prompts and reassurances for them to continue. These prompts became increasingly authoritarian, culminating in 'you have no other choice you *must* go on'. The experiment then established how many of the 40 duped 'teachers' were prepared to administer the shocks and to what level of intensity.

The outcome was that although most of the subjects complied with the instruction to give shocks, the great majority also became very distressed themselves about their compliance. Despite this distress, all of them complied with the command to give shocks up to a 'level' of 300 volts, with the hoax 'learners' by this stage screaming and kicking the wall. However, 14 (35 per cent) refused after this level and they walked away from the experiment.

Trust, obedience and the importance of context

What do we make of these findings from Milgram's experiment? One conclusion is that adults are easily duped by authority *and* they are readily persuaded to carry out cruel acts. However, Fromm questions whether this extrapolation to all real-life situations is justified. He points out that the context of the experiment was that the tricked subjects were in a prestigious seat of learning (Yale) and they were reassured and prompted by scientists. Science now has achieved the level of moral authority once limited to God and scientists now have the same right to obedience as priests. Analogously had God told Abraham to kill his only son – instead of stopping him – Abraham would have followed through. Child sacrifices in religious rituals in the past demonstrate this eventuality.

Moreover, most of the subjects did not comply ruthlessly – they were very upset about their actions. This suggests that empathy and guilt were elicited by the experiment, not malevolence or callousness. It is instructive to contrast these random volunteers with the non-random selection of torturers employed by the state or by violent gangs. The latter are atypical in their lack of distress (or even pleasure) when being cruel. The inhibiting role of conscience is shown in the distress in Milgram's duped subjects and in the fact that over a third actually defied authority once the hoax 'learners' manifested a certain level of distress.

At the centre of Fromm's argument with Milgram is not that the former denied the empirical findings of the latter but that he questioned their interpretation. Crudely the findings might indicate that ordinary human beings are overly trusting of authority and so they can be commanded to commit atrocious acts in any context. Fromm would argue that humans indeed do act atrociously, but only in specifiable contexts. In other contexts people may act selflessly and courageously.

Moreover, to complicate matters further, selfish acts might be judged differently in different contexts. Glover (2002) makes the point that the self-interested bank robber if caught is vilified and imprisoned but the self-interested politician taking his or her country to war may become a national hero. Glover goes on to describe innumerable contextual reasons why, for example, atrocities are common in the psychologically distorted setting of warfare. This distortion means that the humanity of the enemy is so thoroughly denied that combatants act in ways which are at odds with their character in civilian life. Under these conditions, in which the enemy is both depersonalized and hated, there is always the risk that 'anything goes'.

The 'real life' implication of this double significance is that human beings may in some contexts directly trust authority when being complicit in malevolent ends *and* they may be tricked into such ends indirectly by authority figures. As Fromm points out as an example, state-sanctioned cruelty was disguised by the Nazi government by an elaborate set of rationalizations and emotionally neutral descriptions offered to the German public. The latter all too readily accepted these assurances. Fromm's emphasis on persuasion and propaganda to encourage mass collusion is arguably more important than Milgram's contrived willingness to inflict pain. However, as with the minority of Milgram's subjects who obeyed without compunction or distress, there were doctors and their assistants who acted in outrageously cruel ways in the daily routines of concentration camp life (see Chapter 6). These were not fleeting moments of madness but atrocities planned, executed, recorded and justified.

The social and political downside of trust

Notwithstanding Fromm's critique of Milgram's conclusions and the subsequent ethical doubts about the nature of the research, both are ambivalent about the consequences of human trust. Both emphasize that obedience to authority has its downside. What starts as a positive construction on trust by humanistic psychologists and psychoanalysts, as an inherent life affirming human quality, which is the harbinger of mutuality, care and affection, contains within it the prospect of several dark scenarios. At a micro (one to one) level the risk is of citizens having blind faith in science and its applications (such as medicine). At a meso level there is the risk of 'group think', mob rule, gang fights, tribalism and the stereotyping of out-group members. At a macro (political) level there is the risk of the mass support for dictatorships and genocide.

Historical examples from the left and right indicate that although dictatorships usually maintain their power by terrorizing the population, using methods of extensive surveillance and ruthless policing, the *origin* of that power is populism. Marxist-Leninism and Nazism were mass movements. Hitler was elected. There were moments when Marxist-Leninism, with its single vanguard party, could have been rejected by the Soviet people in favour of a form of political pluralism before Stalin captured the state apparatus and an oligarchy ossified around him.

Earlier we noted the point made by Winnicott that a 'good enough' (that is, not totally perfect) form of care is useful because it creates the conditions for the child to discover separateness and self sufficiency. Those who admire and follow authoritarian leaders with simplistic political programmes and ways of depicting the world are unable or unwilling to risk this developmental struggle towards maturity and prefer instead the comfort of trusting others with more power. This is captured in the phrase 'the fear of freedom' (Fromm, 1941) and comes through strongly in the writings of those who have treated leadership with suspicion.

So much of the writing in the middle of the twentieth century about authoritarianism emerged in response to Stalin and Hitler; analytical reactions to regimes which, with *mass support*, exterminated millions of unarmed citizens (for example, Adorno *et al.*, 1950; Fromm, 1955). This largely psychoanalytical perspective was complemented later with accounts from political journalists and political scientists. For example, Hope (2003) traces the dynamics that linked the regimes of Mugabe in Zimbabwe, Mohammed Mahathir of Malaysia, Milosevic in Serbia and Verwoerd, the champion of South African apartheid. His focus is on their personal narcissism, their intolerance of those with opposing views, the advocacy of simplistic ideologies, which reduced complex problems to specific scapegoats and their willingness to sanction violence against their own people.

Implications for trust in healthcare

The routine clinical encounters in healthcare settings may seem to be far removed from these wider political scenarios about malign political leadership and 'followship'. However, in Chapter 6 as our benchmark for discussing trust in healthcare, we will highlight the 'othering' of human beings in Nazi Germany and democratic North America and its outcome as medical atrocities. Thus the discourse about healthcare is appropriately politicized to expose the risks we take when trusting experts.

Some, such as Thomas McKeown in his *Role of Medicine* (1976), René Dubos in his *Mirage of Health* (1987) and Ivan Illich in his *Medical Nemesis* (1976), whom we discuss more below, argue that we would be wise to *distrust* healthcare experts. They argue that instead we should orientate our attention to the social causes and consequences, of morbidity and, by implication, the false promises of healthcare. This counter-dependent and maybe counter-intuitive style of critique implies that we should face our own problems about health as active citizens and mutual carers.

At this stage, the arguments rehearsed above about mass psychology could lead to a de-contextualized or reductionist account of trust. Just as we argued in Chapter 1 that the focus on encapsulated interests to understand trust was partial rather than wrong, we would argue the same here about any psychological understanding of trust. The psychodynamic processes rehearsed are valid and can be seen all around us. Trust does not require words; it is evident in animals and in pre-verbal infants. Consequently, it seems to have a ubiquitous emotional (or affective) not just cognitive character (the limited emphasis of rationalistic approaches to trust).

However, what we *understand and know* shapes our decisions to trust others. In other words, overlaying our emotional orientation to trust our elders or betters, we also make decisions based upon what we know and our estimation of our relative ignorance. This creates the conditions for *situated rationalities* created by our particular social position and degree of education and confidence.

If lay people in general are consistently disadvantaged in relation to healthcare experts by their relative lack of knowledge and understanding, then a power discrepancy accrues. Faced with this information gap, it is understandable that trust as 'blind faith' is used as a bridge to confidence for the less powerful party. This point is at its most obvious in relation to the lesser willingness of better educated patients to comply blindly as patients. Those who are poorly educated do not have the option of resistance or challenge; their best bet is to ask few questions and simply look to experts for direction.

Thus we would argue that as with citizens and governments, patients will have a *generic* emotional or pre-verbal tendency to invest trust in those more powerful but that tendency is nuanced or inflected by the *particular* material conditions, which patients inhabit. The rich in pocket and knowledge will be able to secure a negotiated position with experts more often than the poor in society.

The same point can be made about those who are acutely ill but reflective and assertive compared with those who are chronically disabled and have a diminished mental capacity. This is why the political use of the individualistic strategy of consumerism to mitigate problems created by the knowledge–power discrepancy between healthcare experts and patients will tend to favour the better off in society (see Chapter 7). However, it offers few answers to those who are vulnerable. Instead the discrepancy of knowledge in relation to vulnerable patients can only be attenuated by advocacy and collective action by patients and relatives.

And of course the gap in power created by discrepancies in knowledge is only one, albeit important, aspect of what we might call the 'mass psychology of trust in healthcare'. It is our starting point about a trusting orientation towards people and systems. Its focus is about considering and reducing the risk of an *exploitation* of the gap in power between experts and lay people, with the many adverse or iatrogenic consequences that can accrue for the latter. These include malign action (discussed in Chapter 6) and technical failures because of poor training (discussed in Chapter 2), which lead to patients suffering or even dying as a result of contact with the healthcare system.

However, other risks still exist, which simply arise from well-intentioned human frailty and from the inevitable constraints of financial and other resources and technological capability. Here we enter the arena of honest mistakes, individual errors embedded in otherwise efficient and consistent clinical practice and the lack of resources and technology available to ensure best healthcare practice for all. As we will note in Chapter 7, even socialized forms of healthcare like the British NHS still provide uneven care standards between localities and the 'sharp elbows' of the better off in pocket and knowledge mean that they make best use of what is available anywhere.

Thus although trust is a reflection of power relationships between experts and lay people who look to them for help in their lives, trust in healthcare does require us to consider the imperfect confidence which logically flows from imperfect practitioners and systems. In modern cultures, which are both risk averse and litigious, there may be a tendency towards assuming that at some point healthcare will become perfect; that it will be populated by caring and technically competent staff at all times and that is will show no signs of systemic failure. The recurrent political promise of better healthcare for all can all too easily elide into the expectation that risk eventually will be eliminated.

This is unrealistic and creates and encourages magical thinking about healthcare. One of the most celebrated (and resented) critiques of healthcare from Illich (1976) argued that health does not come from healthcare but from social, economic and political conditions and relationships. As he notes pithily:

The relationship between the interest of the patient and the success of each specialist who manipulates one of his 'conditions' can thus no longer be assumed; it must now be proved, and the net contribution of medicine to society's burden of disease must be assessed from without the profession. But any charge against medicine for the clinical damage it causes constitutes only the first step in the indictment of pathogenic medicine. The trail beaten in the harvest is only a reminder of the greater damage done by the baron to the village that his hunt overruns. (Illich, 1976: 41)

Illich goes on to complain of three types of iatrogenesis or 'doctor-created illness'. Clinical iatrogenesis (for example, hospital-acquired MRSA) was elaborated by Illich as 'social iatrogenesis' and 'cultural iatrogenesis'. Social iatrogenesis is a description of the impact of the medicalisation of life. Everything that deviates from a physical, psychological or social norm is designated as a medical problem. This renders us all dependent on healthcare, infantilizes us and makes us anxiously concerned about our health on unending fronts. That anxiety can only then be reduced by dependence on healthcare. Birth, death and sickness are removed from our homes and placed in clinical settings instead. Our tolerance for discomfort and suffering is altered and expectations of technical fixes thus multiply. Self-care is rendered dubious.

When Illich turns to cultural iatrogenesis he describes a situation in which:

> the medical enterprise saps the will of people to suffer their reality ... Professionally organized medicine has come to function as a domineering moral enterprise that advertises industrial expansion as a war against all suffering. It has thereby undermined the ability of individuals to face their reality, to express their own values, and to accept inevitable and often irremediable pain and impairment, decline and death. (Illich, 1976: 12)

Illich may well have over-stated his attack upon the capacity of healthcare systems to improve health; an empirical-balance-sheet-type question, which can be considered in its own right. Indeed, since his critique, a defence of the population-level benefits of healthcare can now be made on health economic grounds, even though the strong impact of social context on health status for most of us also remains evident (Nolte and McKee, 2004; Bunker, 2001).

Notwithstanding this caution about Illich's nihilism, for the purposes of this book, he reminds us that clinical, social and cultural iatrogenesis are all grounds for distrusting healthcare (and our dependence upon it). Birth, sickness and dying are indeed ultimately existential matters that cannot be fixed by clinical expertise alone. The more we invest our trust in healthcare, the more we are avoiding our own authentic experience about life, suffering and death. The risk is that healthcare becomes a parent that protects us magically from our tough responsibilities and the need to be honest about our inevitable finitude and vulnerability. Bad faith, to some degree, then flows to us all from this infantilization.

Illich reminds us legitimately that healthcare systems create as well as ameliorate problems and, as a consequence, it is irrational for people to be over-reliant upon its activities. Healthcare is at its best in heroic mode with its life-saving and wound-tending responses to medical emergencies. And even here note the social and behavioural determinants of accidents and emergencies, which invite reflection on their prevention outside of the orbit of medicine. But the more that healthcare extends its remit into promoting health and dealing with chronicity, which necessarily has to be endured, because it cannot be cured, its mandate and credibility become weaker and weaker. Consequently, it is irrational to assume or hope that healthcare systems will ever become completely trustworthy as a solution to all of our health problems. Moreover, risk will not be eliminated; indeed it may increase as systems become larger and impersonal and as each new technical solution breeds new problems.

Over 20 years after Illich, McKeown, Dubos and others warned us of the inability of modern healthcare to do justice to human suffering, we now find government advisers making recommendations about how to install compassion into a system that has become depleted of it and its ordinary human context (Goodrich and Cornwell, 2008). The fact that in 2008 the British government has had to invest in a campaign of *Dignity in Care* to humanely support an ageing population is further testimony to a continuing lack of confidence in health and social care to treat vulnerable people well. It also demonstrates that the ever-increasing appeal to checking mechanisms and the 'audit culture' to be examined in Chapter 7 has not created compassionate norms within healthcare routines.

For these reasons healthcare is in a contradictory position. We are all acculturated to rely on its activities and, at an individual level, enjoy some ratio of their benefits and failings. At the same time, recurring evidence of multifaceted iatrogenesis reminds us that there are always reasonable grounds for distrusting the people and systems that constitute healthcare in modern societies. From here on, as in the past, our trust in healthcare is inevitably going to be variable and precarious. At its best, healthcare will be a testimony to our capacity to be interdependent. At its worst, it will mistreat, maim and kill us.

Summary

- The primary relationship of trust is psychologically significant in the formation of a person's ability to trust and be trusted. It has implications for an individual's basic trust.
- Basic trust has implications in healthcare, especially in how patients express their dependence when ill – dependency has both positive and negative aspects in healthcare.
- The failure of trust in childhood has implications for a person's mental health (more generally) and has specific implications for the development of the personality.
- The failure to trust has implications for malign leadership and mass conformity
- Obedience and authority in relation to trust has both positive and negative aspects and can be analysed at different levels.
- Some commentators have argued that we should distrust medical experts and orientate our attention to the false promises of healthcare.

CHAPTER 4

Ethics, Trust and Healthcare

This chapter examines the relationship between trust, ethics and healthcare. We examine three models of trust in healthcare, the first based on virtue, a second based on duty and a third based on an integrated approach to ethics. In doing so, we examine the strengths and weaknesses of these models in building and eroding trust in healthcare.

First model for ethical healthcare: virtue ethics

Before we can specifically talk about trust and healthcare under this heading, we need to have a background understanding of virtue ethics. What Aristotle means by 'ethics' may be understood by the ancient Greek root of the term *ethos*, meaning customs of a society. To speak of ethics in this sense is to speak about the customary behaviour of a people and the standards of human excellence aspired to within these customs, through which character is shaped. In this sense it includes but is more than what we might now understand as 'norms' and 'mores' in modern sociology and social psychology because it incorporates an *aspirational* quality, not just a description of customs.

A virtue is a good quality or excellence of character, predisposing the virtuous agent to *want* to do what morality requires. So, for example, truth-telling, is not an obligation or duty, but an act that is motivated by one's love and respect for truth for its own sake. A virtuous person tells the truth for the sake of the truth. It is her love or respect for the truth itself, that moves her to tell the truth, rather than her desire to be honest and duty bound not to tell a lie. In general terms being virtuous is internally driven by the question 'what should I be' rather than 'what should I do' (Van Hooft, 2006).

Psychologically speaking virtue ethics has a sophisticated and holistic picture of what motivates us to be ethical. That is to say, ethics works at the level of desire, emotion, feeling and inclination as well as at the level of reason through deliberation and contemplation. Virtues of character are rooted in what Aristotle calls the appetitive part of the 'soul' – where the soul is the forerunner of the modern notion of 'psyche' (in ancient Greek, *psuche*).

The appetitive part of the soul is based on the fact that human beings desire things and strive to attain them. Desire is an internal motivator towards action and reaction in our engagement with the world and gives rise to positive feelings such as curiosity, longing and enjoyment and negative feelings when our desires are frustrated, such as pain and anguish. When such feelings are integrated with cognition we experience emotions. Desire, in this picture, is the internal motivator and combines with cognition to lead to emotions that are purposeful and goal seeking – or teleological to use the technical term (Aristotle, 1999; Bostock, 2000).

For example, the virtue of courage may be understood in terms of how we deal with fear; do we react and flee out of fear or do we face it down? (Aristotle, 1999; Bostock, 2000) This depends on comprehending the situation we are in and responding in the most appropriate way. There is not some impartial and objective judgement that we can make on how to be courageous regardless of the situation that we are in. Neither is there some value-free point of view from which we can make that judgement. A virtuous display of courage in the Aristotelian sense is a situated event reflecting the person's orientation to themselves and the world. It is based on interplay between desires, emotions and reasons in the development of one's character, rather than an impartial judgement based on the universal power of one's reasoning ability alone. Aristotle's view of virtue draws on two deeper explanations:

1   A holistic picture of virtue and its psychological motivation.
2   A hermeneutic understanding of how we acquire virtuous knowledge.

A holistic picture of virtue and its psychological motivation

Virtue is directly related to the state of one's soul in the formation of character. Before making any sense of such a statement, we need a brief understanding of Aristotle's integrated account of the soul. Aristotelian ethics are grounded in his view of the soul and how different parts of the soul interact. Briefly speaking, Aristotle's picture divides the soul into two major parts – which are further subdivided into four. The two major divisions are called the 'non-rational' and 'rational' parts of the soul of which Aristotle further divides each into two subdivisions; vegetative and appetitive (lower part of the soul) and deliberative and contemplative (higher part of the soul). The vegetative part of the soul entails the biological functioning of the body, whilst the appetitive part concerns our basic drives, instincts and desires. The deliberative part of the soul is able to judge and reason what the external and internal goals of our actions should be. If the deliberative part of the soul engages with worldly reason and truth that we can change, then the contemplative part involves a form of reason that is directed towards eternal truths that we cannot change (Aristotle, 1999; Bostock, 2000).

There are two features of the Aristotelian picture of the soul that are important to understand in relation to ethics:

- integration of reason and emotion in a holistic and naturalistic view of a human being
- its holistic effect on moral motivation.

This Aristotelian view of ethics can be distinguished from later models, that privilege reason at the expense of emotion and inclination – duty ethics, for example, where inclinations and sentiments are *arguably* suppressed and divorced from universal reason in ethical judgement. Virtue ethics, on the other hand, integrates desire and emotion with reason and deliberation. From an Aristotelian perspective this involves the integration of at least two different subdivisions of the soul; for example, the deliberative part of the soul apprehends, comprehends more primordial desires and instincts in the appetitive part, regulating and shaping certain behaviours that have a bearing on our ethical disposition (Aristotle, 1999; Bostock, 2000)

Take the example of courage again. On a more general level of interpretation courage is a virtuous golden mean between the extremes of passionate recklessness and the cowardly paralysis of over-rationality. On a finer level of interpretation deficiency and excesses of passion and reason have underlying causes in human motivation that are rather more involved and have to do with conscious awareness and self understanding.

For example, the apparent deficiency in passion to face down fear, where appropriate, may be down to lack of insight into the nature of inchoate feelings that remain emotionally underdetermined and unexamined. This lack of emotional intelligence, so to speak, is complicated by reasons that justify inappropriate non-action, leading to self-deception where reason is not *in the service* of our feelings. So, for the soul to be balanced and virtue to be possible, deliberative and contemplative reason needs to be in the service of the feeling part of the soul, where our biological instincts and our appetitive desires come from according to Aristotle.

Aristotle's integrated picture of the soul is psycho-cultural, one that takes into account goal-orientated desires that have both an external and internal dimension. The integration of our character is co-determined by successfully attaining culturally mediated desires *and* developing an internal comportment (or desire) to them. In addition to the commonsense notion of desire, which is gratified by attaining an externally orientated goal, an ice cream perhaps, Aristotle is suggesting that we have an internal relationship or comportment to such desires, for example, whether eating such foods may be good for us. In other words, the appetitive part of the soul does not only try and fulfil desire that is external to it, but has an internal relationship to that desire, whose goal is self-fulfilment (van Hooft, 2006). Aristotle's notion of desire is thus, two headed – a fulfilment of external and culturally mediated desires *and* an internal comportment to them that, ultimately, has the goal of perfecting our being.

Aristotle's emphasis on self-fulfilment resonates with similar thoughts about two important concerns for us in this book about self-trust and virtue. If the goal of trust comes out of the experience of what is true, and the recognition of truth depends on our capacity to recognise and deliberate about the truth, then the truth – at a fundamental level – relies on our ability to trust ourselves and our experience (Block, 2002). In other words, self-trust is at the core of trusting others and being trustworthy.

A similar logic may be applied to virtue. If the goal of virtue comes out of our experience of what is excellent in cultural pursuits, and the recognition of that relies on our self-fulfilling desire to perfect our selves, then – at some equally fundamental level – virtuous perfection of our being is at the heart of being publicly virtuous.

A hermeneutic understanding of how we acquire virtuous knowledge

Providing a holistic and integrated account of virtue along with its psychological motivations still begs questions about how virtue may be acquired and learned. How can we have the right desires for the right things? On the surface, the answer is a disappointing and seemingly circular; to make an appropriate judgement about virtue requires one to be virtuous. However, on closer inspection the answer may not be as completely circular as it first appears. That close inspection requires us to attempt an interpretive understanding: it is a hermeneutic challenge for us all about understanding why we and others do good (and bad) things.

Let us return to the running example: courage. A foundational view of courage would hold that there is some defining and universal aspect of what courage is, which can be applied regardless of the situation we find ourselves in. A virtue ethicist perspective, on the other hand, has no God's eye view on what courage is; that is, courage is not simply defined and then deduced from reason but understood through particular and situated life experiences. Courage arises from a 'hermeneutic circle' of understanding (van Hooft, 2006). That is, every time we experience an act of courage in all its uniqueness and particularity, it contributes to what we already know courage to be.

This involves a benevolent circle of understanding; I *already* have *some* appreciative understanding of what courage might be like, even if it is a very vague one, in order to learn more about it. Whilst one might not have a *direct* understanding of courage, one at least has the capacity to recognise what such an act may be like. We may be told, when we are young, that this or that is courageous, to which we accrue further instances as well as expand the scope and context of our understanding, through life experience, books, films, and so on. This can be likened to not knowing the meaning of a word and looking it up in the dictionary. Even if one doesn't understand the definition immediately, one can always look a word associated with it until understanding does dawn. Learning proceeds laterally until direct experience of the word deepens familiarity through use. The hermeneutic circle of experience is benevolent, often tacit, where experience and commitment to virtue accrues through new contexts of learning.

Take healthcare work: it cannot be taught successfully in a direct way in 'one shot' of basic training. Professional competence is accrued through a hermeneutic circle of understanding acquired by problem-based learning, clinical practice, learning from 'role' models and having mentors that develop one's professional competence and trustworthiness over time.

The acquisition of intellectual virtues and virtues of character – like benevolence, non-malificence, and so on – are accrued through a hermeneutic circle of knowing. Problem-based learning in medical schools recognizes this and involves equipping students with intellectual skills as well as facts to accrue knowledge in new contexts, standing them in good stead for problem-solving in clinical practice. As far as acquiring virtues of character is concerned, nothing replaces the tacit knowledge that good role models provide through their everyday clinical practice.

Virtue ethics, trust and healthcare

Our immediate point of contact with healthcare institutions is with individuals who have professional identities of which, we as patients, expect certain standards of care. Such standards of care are, in part, shaped by what we expect the role of the professional to be. Trusting in a good nurse, a good doctor or, a good physiotherapist, for example, is related to their purposive professional role, which is partly expressed in the efficacy of carrying out that role as skilfully as possible and the character traits associated with such an achievement. In the professional role of nursing, for example, caring is not just about doing the job of looking after the sick effectively it is also about having warm, compassionate and benevolent nature.

Professional virtues can be divided into 'intellectual' virtues that consist in exercising professional judgement and reason and virtues of 'character'. Again, take another example, of a good doctor; we do not only expect her to exercise her medical knowledge to greatest practical effect (intellectual virtues), we also expect her to be truthful and compassionate (virtues of character) in exercising such intellectual judgements.

The most important intellectual virtue for health professionals is 'prudence' or 'practical wisdom' (*phronēsis*) – which involves an ability to do something which turns out well for others as well as yourself. Interestingly though, for Aristotle the motivation for prudence is self-fulfilment or self-betterment by which he means fulfilling our own efforts at doing something that requires skill. Whenever we do something that takes some concentration, skill or commitment on our part, our doing it well will be the source of accomplishment and fulfilment for us (van Hooft, 2006). In other words, the motivation is not the external achievement, in the honours bestowed on us from others, for example, but in how it fulfils and betters us when doing the task well for its own sake. Self-fulfilment is intimately related to self-trust in our worthiness and esteem to do the task well. Trust and trustworthiness (in the eyes of others) follows on from the acquisition of self-trust in one's worthiness or self-esteem.

While virtue in Aristotelian sense might be motivated by trust in self-betterment, it is also a trustworthy benefit to others. This is by no means straightforward, since context-specific professional virtues may conflict with general virtues and sentiments that arise from other identity roles of a more personal nature. So a caring husband might want to help his wife who is dying of cancer, achieve a more speedy and peaceful death. Were he asked to do a similar thing, if he were also a doctor for a patient dying of cancer, he would likely be much more hesitant, as doing so would compromise his integrity and trustworthiness as a professional where he had taken an oath to do no harm (van Hooft, 2006).

If professions have specific goals and values, then there will be virtues that are specific both to and within them. In relation to medicine the bio-ethicist Edmund Pellegrino (cited in van Hooft, 2006) has listed the following virtues as being particularly important:

fidelity to trust;
benevolence;
effacement of self-interest;
compassion and caring;
intellectual honesty;
justice and prudence.

Oakley and Cockling (cited in van Hooft, 2006) provide another list giving special importance to: beneficence; compassion; truthfulness; trustworthiness; courage, medical humility (for example the humility to recognise the limitations of medical interventions); and justice.

Virtues are reinforced by professional codes of conduct issued by professional bodies. What is and is not virtuous is therefore maintained by professionals themselves that set the standards of excellence from within and disseminate this to those who aspire to join the profession. In some ways, the Aristotelian emphasis on virtue being maintained by the virtuous is, at least aspired to, through clinical training and the desire to conform to codes of excellence that underwrite association and membership to professional organizations of all kinds within healthcare.

Having looked at the relationship between trust, virtue and healthcare, we now turn to the advantages and disadvantages of the virtue model in healthcare.

The advantages and disadvantages of the virtue model in healthcare

The major advantage of thinking about virtue as a model for healthcare is that it explains a number of naturally occurring forms of trust at the intra-personal level (self-trust or trust in oneself), and at an interpersonal level (trust between individuals):

1 At the intra-personal level, the motivation is self-fulfilment and betterment of the particular healthcare profession. In other words, to be a 'good' doctor or nurse, one has to achieve excellence in the activity of doctoring and nursing for its own sake. Trust in a good doctor, for example, stems from their own self-trust in carrying out the task of their profession excellently. Such self-trust in the virtues of character and those of the intellect, lead to a form of professional integrity. Professional integrity speaks of the unity, integration and/or wholeness of a person's virtues and ethical commitments. Persons of integrity are admired and praised by others because of their reliability, trustworthiness and capacity to act honourably. The action that the virtue of integrity calls for is to honour the trust that has been placed in you (van Hooft, 2006).

2 At the interpersonal level the main advantage of virtue ethics is that it provides naturalistic explanation for being ethical, one that conforms to our sympathies and natural inclinations towards those we love and care for in a widening circle of concern; we love our partners, children and family, we care for our neighbours, colleagues and patients. Moreover each of these relationships is characterized by particular virtues appropriate to the relationship and our desires and emotional attachments that arise from them. By having the 'right' desires we form admirable and excellent human relationships with others we care for: as lovers, as parents with children, as brothers with sisters, as doctors with patients and so on. Partiality in the respect of motivating care is an advantage, specifying the kind of love and care that is appropriate to each kind of relationship and the virtuous middle way that appears between feelings and actions of excess and deficiency.

   My concern for others emanates from a self that holds the privileged position of one who cares. We want our friends to prosper, our children to succeed, our patients to be cured and so on. Traditionally, the doctor–patient relationship is based on *philia*, a form of interpersonal care, which is akin to the relationship between a parent (father) and child. While this has come under much criticism of late, it is worth highlighting its strengths from a virtue ethics perspective. The classic doctor–patient relationship is asymmetrical in a similar way to that of the parent–child relationship: the doctor knows best what is good for his patient, just as the parent knows what is best for their child. The relationship does not need to be equitable, so long as the doctor displays a number of intellectual virtues and virtues of character in healing the sick and injured. Indeed, most of the virtues listed are not out of place in a traditional (paternal) doctor–patient relationship, that is:

- *Fidelity to trust in a doctor's integrity* as an expert whose intellectual knowledge and practical wisdom is trustworthy.
- *Benevolence of doctor's intentions and behaviour* towards their patients.
- *Effacement of self-interest of doctors helping their patients* through the recovery process.
- *Compassion and caring of doctors towards their patients.*
- *Intellectual honesty of doctors towards their patients.*
- *Medical humility on behalf of doctors* in wisely judging that the cure is no worse (long-term) than the disease.

Interpersonal trust between professionals and patients is so central because professionals have exclusive power and knowledge that others rely on. For example, if we go and see a consultant then we go not knowing enough about medicine and placing our trust in our consultant's ability to diagnose and cure us of a specific health problem that only she and others with that particular specialist knowledge, can tell us about. In other words, there is a level of some dependency that means we have *few options* but to trust both their intellectual virtues – for example, judgement required in diagnostic skills for example – and virtues of character – such as their capacity to tell the truth while at the same time being compassionate.

3 On the level of community we privilege those who are close to us because our interests our bound up with theirs; we privilege our family, friends and professional colleagues – 'our' fellow doctors, nurses or radiologists perhaps. This has certain advantages where trust is concerned, since trust expands outward into professional organisations and bodies who understand each others' concerns and self-regulate to maintain levels of professional excellence and

integrity. Virtue is thus expressed benignly through partiality where mutual understanding allows professional organizations and bodies to pass both honour and judgment on its peers.

The major disadvantage of thinking about virtue ethics as a model for healthcare is that it is open to corruption, inequity and injustice. This can be illustrated at three levels: the intrapersonal; the interpersonal; and the cultural/institutional:

1 On an intrapersonal, psychological level virtue isn't guaranteed. There is a problem with relying on the virtue of doctors and nurses, especially when so much trust is invested in individual professionals. There are some professionals that lack self-trust in virtuous motivation.

2 If professionals lack the integrity and self-trust to be consistently virtuous professionals, they are likely to display interpersonal behaviour that is at times vicious and wicked. Take the examples of the GP Harold Shipman and the children's nurse Beverley Allitt. The GP Harold Shipman was the UK's worst serial killer, murdering 215 patients under his care. The nurse Beverley Allitt murdered four children (see Chapter 6). Part of the reason for the public outrage around these scandals arises from what we the public take for granted; that medical professionals, like doctors and nurses, are beyond reproach, upholding virtues such as the sanctity and reverence for life. So, we, the public, trust certain professions more than others; medical professionals being high on the list of those we trust most. Ironically, this makes the so-called virtuous professional the most dangerous when trust breaks down, because our faith in their virtue is blind. Whilst there are statistically few that display such extreme behaviours, most virtuous practice in the medical practice is undermined by poor standards of care and neglect. Indeed, far removed from virtuous healthcare practices, there are a statistically significant number of anecdotal examples from patient feedback sites where complaints within the NHS point towards, at least the possibility, of poor medical care (see Chapter 6). For example, the website of Patient Opinion, which is open to anyone to post their experiences of healthcare in the UK, receives an approximate three-way split between stories of excellent care, those of very poor care and those which, though complaining, mention good aspects of care. In short, the classical virtue ethics model within medical paternalism in no way guarantees virtuous medical practitioners. In practice a whole range of experiences are reported by patients.

Perhaps one of the biggest difficulties with a more classical account of the traditional doctor–patient relationship – that is paternalistic in nature – is that it does not bestow any power in the patient at all. That is to say, the fruit of virtuous medical practice is bestowed on a grateful, compliant and receptive patient. The doctor–patient relationship, much like the father–child relationship, is one where the weaker party is 'infantilized' by the virtuous doctor – that is treated as 'a child', which denies their maturity and ability to make their own choices for good health and well-being. The patient is thus regarded as 'an object of information rather than a subject of communication' (Foucault, 1973). One of the implications of this is that the patient is denied autonomy and decision-making capability. This can lead to unjust treatment when there may be other treatment options available that the patient would have chosen otherwise. An extreme example of this is the Tuskegee study.

The Tuskegee Study in the USA spanned forty years and conducted an experiment on 399 illiterate black men in the late stages of syphilis, without ever being told about the nature and seriousness of the disease they were suffering from. Treated like children, they were informed that they were being treated for 'bad blood' (see Chapter 6). Whilst this is an extreme example of an abuse of the principle of patient autonomy and does not necessarily follow an asymmetrical doctor–patient relationship, classical medical paternalism is becoming increasingly irrelevant in modern healthcare where autonomous patients need to make choices in particular clinical situations.

Patient autonomy and choice is especially significant in cases of high risk to health and low certainty of outcome (as regards treatment option). In the case of certain early stage breast cancer, for example, the risks are high (if left untreated), but the treatment options present a low certainty of what might be best for the patient. In these cases there is a vital and authentic choice to be made by the patient between a lumpectomy and a mastectomy. In such cases, patient autonomy needs to be respected and no presumption of treatment should be taken. In such cases, autonomy should provide the basis for fully informed consent procedures (McCollough and McGuire *et al.*, 2007)

Once patient autonomy is increased then the practical wisdom of patients becomes increasingly relevant as generations are more informed of rival healthcare treatments through such resources as the internet. In this way the doctor–patient relationship has changed over time; the patient becoming more like a 'client' or 'customer' in which the healthcare professional becomes more of a trusted advisor to empower the patient to select between options. Such a culture is very different, from old-fashioned doctor–patient relationship where it was accepted that the virtuous doctor always knew best.

3   At the level beyond practical face work in healthcare, there are cultural and institutional considerations. Examples of institutional failure, where cultures became untrustworthy are legion. The improper retention and use of organs at Alder Hey in the late 1990s for example, highlighted cultural and institutional excesses that eroded any semblance of virtuous post-mortem practices. Importantly, such national scandals could not be dealt with through any internal regulation because the implications were national and involved other institutions as well as Alder Hey. For this reason a public inquiry into improper removal, retention and disposal of organs was justified in the public interest (see Chapter 6). Again there are other examples that are less obvious and more mundane, where cultures of neglect and poor practice do not make national headlines, are not subject to public inquiries and are internally investigated within healthcare trusts.

To recap, while virtue ethics, classically understood at least, can be non-maleficent and beneficent to the patient, it does rely wholly on virtuous character and intellectual virtues of the doctor and pays little heed to patient autonomy and patient rights. To understand this and its relationship to trust, we must look to a different model of healthcare altogether.

Second model for ethical healthcare: duty ethics

One immediate advantage an ethics of duty has over an ethics of virtue is that it does not rely on excellence of character. An ethics of duty uses 'deontic' terms – from the ancient Greek term meaning 'necessity' – such as 'right', 'wrong', 'obligatory' or 'forbidden' (van Hooft, 2006). Moreover an ethics of duty is universal and foundational in form and so whatever duty applies to an individual will apply to anyone. In this way it contrasts with the particularism and hermeneutic nature of virtue ethics. If virtue ethics has an important role for emotional motivation and partiality, then an ethics of duty is based purely on reason and impartiality.

One of the cornerstones of duty ethics is the notion of autonomy; it is *obligatory* to respect patient rights grounded in the recognition of their autonomy. A more modern, and arguably sophisticated notion of trust, recognizes that autonomy is the necessary precondition for a genuine form of trust. This has consequences for:

1   The doctor–patient relationship.
2   The *ideal* informed consent ritual.
3   Patient rights, such as the right to know and the right not to know.

The doctor–patient relationship

In terms of the doctor–patient relationship, a more adequate basis for trust requires patients to be on an equal footing with professionals, which involves being better informed and less dependent. This fundamental equality between doctor and patient grounds autonomy of deliberation and action for the patient: the only trust that is well placed is given by those who understand what is proposed, and who are in a position to accept or refuse in the light of that understanding. This marks a shift from an asymmetrical and dependent paternalistic relationship where the virtuous doctor infantilizes the patient to an interdependent and equal relationship where the patient has certain inalienable rights.

The ideal informed consent ritual

The precondition for informed consent is autonomy and the opportunity to refuse or to consent to treatment. In this way 'informed consent is a modern clinical ritual of trust' (cited in O'Neill, 2002), thus embedding a properly institutionalized respect for patient autonomy. Ideally what we see is a relationship between equals – the patient being empowered by information that they can fully understand and freely deliberate upon, arriving at a decision to refuse or to give consent to treatment.

Patient rights, the right to know and not to know

Patient autonomy also embeds patient rights. For example, this has relevance in the right to know/not to know debate which has particular relevance to genetic medicine. The right to know our genetic constitution may well have a probabilistic impact on our future health as well as those we are related to. However, we also have the right not to know, as knowing the nature of disease and risk may, in certain cases, threaten a sense of well-being.

At the heart of the right to know/not to know is patient autonomy; where being informed about consequences of a genetic test (through genetic counselling perhaps) allows the patient to be empowered to make certain choices beneficial to their personality type that is, whether one is risk averse or not (Chadwick, Levitt and Shickle, 1997). This is a controversial area, not least because there is often a clash between competing rights: that is, while the right not to know is related to the right to privacy and self-determination, implementing such a right may pose significant risk if it seriously affects those we are related to.

Because genetic medicine has relational consequences in terms of inherited disease, principles that uphold *naïve* autonomy, become increasingly questionable. As such, genetic medicine poses questions for a notion of autonomy that champions individualism, over and above a new ethic of solidarity (Knoppers and Chadwick, 2006), which opens up a responsibility to those to whom one is genetically related – it invokes the need to consider others not just ourselves.

Whereas autonomy maybe a cornerstone of medical ethics in healthcare, it is important to understand:

- What is meant by autonomy and how this may militate against or foster a sense of trust?
- How we can ground autonomy in duty ethics?

What is meant by autonomy?

Autonomy can be interpreted simply as independence. Yet, as O'Neill (2002) points out, if autonomy is a matter of independence then, it is easy to see how it plays havoc with relations of trust, since independent people may be self-centred, selfish, lacking in fellow feeling and solidarity with others. Once autonomy is simply interpreted as independence from others' views and preferences, we have little reason to believe that the potentially trusted person has an interest in maintaining a relationship with the truster. In short, once autonomy is interpreted as *mere* independence the tension between autonomy and trust is predictable.

Furthermore, autonomy understood as individual independence is likely to maintain nothing more than the *illusion* of challenging professional authority in that an autonomous decision within the ritual of informed consent is nothing more than the right to refuse a treatment that has been championed by professionals in the first place. This leads to a less optimistic view of the informed consent ritual, where professionals either inform their patients *until* they consent or are secure in the fact that the limited right to refuse is nothing other than a costly exercise, where there are few or no other options of treatment (O'Neill, 2002).

Less optimistically speaking, informed consent may become a fig leaf to legally protect professionals from litigious patients – rather than attending to the true ethical demands of the ritual (Beauchamp and Childress, 2001). To be ethically rigorous, informed consent requires a genuine dialogue between physician and patient, where information is presented in accessible way, so as to empower the patient to make an *authentic* choice. For informed consent to be meaningful therefore, the attending physician needs to be impartial, preserving the *autonomy of the patient's will* to make meaningful choices for *their* health and well-being.

One way of developing a more ethically liberating account, that avoids the pitfalls of autonomy as independence (that supports an unhelpful individualism) has been to develop a notion of 'principled autonomy' – expressed in action whose principle could be *adopted by all others* (O'Neill, 2002).

Principled autonomy, rights and duty ethics

A way of grounding a richer concept of autonomy (principled autonomy) has been through the notion of rights justified by an appeal to Kantian duty ethics (O'Neill, 2002). Traditionally human rights, such as in The United Nations Declaration of Human Rights of 1948 started off as a mere declaration and only gained political force through subsequent ratification of member states. Yet while serious respect for individual autonomy was politically legitimated, the deeper philosophical justification of why rights should be universally enforceable was missing. However, some philosophers have seized the opportunity to ground the legitimacy of rights beyond the voice of political authority alone, by underpinning rights with the notion of duty and universal obligation.

One advantage of grounding rights in human obligations rather than human goods is that there is an *obligation* on us to secure such rights – as a necessary requirement on us to act on our obligations so that those that should *receive,* do. This means being circumspect about what we identify as a human right. This makes human rights more than simply aspirational and voluntary (O'Neill, 2002). So, instead of having an impossibly idealistically right to universal human health, for example, that is unattainable, it is at least possible to have a human right that makes it obligatory to *deliver a certain level of healthcare.* Whilst there are good arguments to ground human rights in human obligations, such arguments are only plausible if we can ground arguments for human obligations. This is about the pragmatics of the possible in context rather than universal definitions of rights attainment.

Having identified the need for obligatory acts, we ourselves need some sort of mechanism to legislate what should and should not be obligatory. This can be found in Kant's so called *Formula of Autonomy* – one of (many) versions of the Categorical Imperative that states: 'choose only in such a way that maxims of your choice are also included as universal laws in the same volition' (Guyer, 2006). Autonomy in this regard can be thought of as a form of universal self-legislation. It is a distinctive constraint or requirement in the form of a test – the formula of autonomy where principles of action *could* be chosen by all. That is to say, *principled autonomy* requires actions whose principle could be *adopted by all others.*

Strengths and weaknesses of Kantian duty ethics and principled autonomy

Principled autonomy has a number of strengths that makes it a robust and trustworthy mechanism for securing a morality:

1 As already mentioned, Kantian duty ethics often leads to morally binding obligations that must be fulfilled toward others.
2 Principled autonomy is a version of autonomy that places constraint on any self-centred desire and inclination.
3 Principled autonomy is based on the universalizability of Reason that is non-contradictory. Note it is worth distinguishing Reason with a capital 'R' from reasons – where the former is more than a mere reason or explanation for something but a fundamental Reason that upholds the internal coherence or consistency for upholding it. One feature of this is that it is supposedly self-contradictory to will

something that is un-Reasonable in the first place. Put positively, our ability to keep and receive promises for example, depends upon the general compliance of keeping promises. If we were to break promises sufficiently often or to will breaking promising as a universal law, then there would be no such thing as promise giving or promise breaking, because no words could any longer have the required force. Any consideration of universalizing the imperative or principle, 'Let me, when hard pressed, make a promise with the intention of keeping it' is un-Reasonable because lying promises are self-contradictory. That is, we could will the lie, but we could *not* will the universal law to lie, for in accordance with such a law there would be no promises possible at all (Blackburn, 2001).

4   The universalizability and impartiality of principled autonomy means that it is structured to be egalitarian and socially just. True universalizable principles lead to people being treated fairly and consistently.

In short, Kantian duty ethics is trustworthy because it attempts to secure moral certainty.

Having summarized the strengths of the Kantian position, we now examine its weaknesses:

1   There is the difficulty with motivation in the Kantian position, as Kant would have it that we need to do what is morally right and not what we are necessarily inclined to do. However, this may not be a fundamental problem since Kant is not denying certain virtuous behaviour that is more motivated by inclination he is simply denying that this has a moral dimension. For him morality is only expressed in what can be universalized as human obligation. Beneficence – doing good for others – is something that we can do after we attended to any prior moral duty that the situation demands.

2   Arguably the more serious criticism questions whether Kant's principled position is wholly supportable through an appeal to Reason alone. For example take a person who is against the whole business of promising. Why shouldn't they undermine the institution from within by giving false promises – with one of their aims being the breakdown of trust and cooperation? Naturally, a nice or prudent person would not have such a goal. But, if Kant appeals to such virtues, *any purely formal appeal* to Reason to ground his theory vanishes – we only have a reason not to make lying promises, not a

Reason (Blackburn, 2001) Of course Kant's moral philosophy is more complicated – not least because he makes a strong appeal to the goodness of the will in orientating his moral philosophy, at which point any special pleading on behalf of Reason as founding duty is exaggerated, as without the goodness of our will Reason is insufficient (by itself) to guarantee morally commendable behaviour.

Duty ethics, trust and healthcare

Having examined *some* of the major strengths and weaknesses of the Kantian position, we now specifically apply any appeals this may have to healthcare.

1 Duty ethics recognizes the principled autonomy of the patient, which, if authentically taken account of in an informed consent ritual for example, can transform the whole dynamic of the doctor–patient relationship, putting it on a more equal footing and deepening a sense of interpersonal sense trust.
2 Duty ethics through the notion of Human Rights can be grounded in a set of human obligations. These can be translated in a further sub-set of patient rights to health provision that we are morally obligated to deliver. This is not an aspirational appeal to perfecting our well-being, but a moral necessity founded in universal Reason. The role of moral necessity in biomedical ethics makes duty ethics a more trustworthy foundation for healthcare.
3 Duty ethics is both impartial and universalisable, making it an ideal candidate for justifying a just and trustworthy healthcare for all.
4 Because duty ethics is structurally related to the notion of rights, it can be universalised and politically legitimated through charters and declarations at various levels of relevance, that is, not only are they international, like the declaration of Human Rights, but they can be made relevant in more specific healthcare contexts that champion patient rights. This is quite different from a voluntary professional code of conduct like the Hippocratic Oath, which is more aligned to the virtue model of healthcare, because it obligates professionals to treat patients with fundamental rights. In actual fact, the two models in healthcare can be thought of as complementary, it is just that the duty ethics model has more moral and political and legal force.

The difficulty with Kantian duty is that for all it formal legitimateness it still relies on the goodness of the will. This makes it as impotent as virtue ethics in preventing malevolent or poor practice. Even though duty ethics takes account of the symmetry of power between medical professional and patient, there is little that can be done by those determined to abuse this. While this is somewhat offset by using it to philosophically legitimate a political system of human rights, which can be enforced legally, there are still no guarantees that rights are easily enforceable.

Both virtue ethics and duty ethics (in the Kantian mould) are plausible candidates for the challenge of *interpersonal trust* in healthcare. One way of overcoming the limits of interpersonal trust that depends on personal motivation (to some degree) and the goodness of the will, is to take a consequentialist approach to systems of healthcare. Here 'duty' is located in the justice and efficiency of 'utilitarian' systems that are aggregative and that often uphold the principle of the greatest good for the greatest number. Whilst utilitarian systems instil a kind of systematic confidence in the delivery of healthcare, distinguishing between priorities – that is, between major and minor interests – it is based on a different form of trust, one that is aligned to the notion of accountability.

On an interpersonal level this may be illustrated by Hardin (2006) and his encapsulated interests view of trust. By this he means 'the right intentions on your part as a person we might trust are to want to take our interests (or possibly our welfare), as *our* interests, into account in *your* actions' (Hardin, 2006). That is, the right intentions only become clear once we have relevant knowledge of the reliability of someone's character to hold our interests as their own so that we can trust them. This knowledge can be said to constitute our degree of trust or distrust. In other words, the degree of trust or distrust becomes a matter of the reliability of someone's character, demonstrated perhaps, by some direct knowledge of their competence, or by indirect knowledge of the reputation that they have.

This depends on an overly rational view of trust that is largely consequential and utilitarian in nature. That is, we need to 'know' what someone's interests are before we can ever hope that they may also encapsulate 'our' interests as theirs, limiting trust to verifiable behaviours that necessarily align to our own agenda. This tends to underplay the view that trust is to some degree or other always a risk, often based on intuition, emotion or a 'gut' feeling and, not necessarily always about furthering our interests, as if they are (un)problematically and neatly encapsulated by another.

In some situations we may indeed knowingly make calculations about whether the interest of another and our interests might be mutually inclusive and reinforcing. Indeed this often happens in our relationships with those we know and even with strangers. A good example of this is in relation to 'organizational politics' where a person might regularly work out how alliances might strategically find common ground with others to secure their position, career, and so on. However, our point here is that this rationale, which focuses on being purely calculative and instrumental in our decisions about who to trust and who to distrust in life, does not do justice to the full range of considerations about trust. Hardin's work is thus useful but incomplete in its account. People use more than instrumental decisions, they also make decisions about trust which are intuitive, emotionally driven and to various degrees 'blind'.

On the level of systems, consequential or utilitarian views of duty are about making healthcare more publicly accountable.

On the positive side accountability is a way of shoring trust in systems, procedures and institutions that interpersonal trust cannot be expected to deliver because of its over-emphasis on people and the goodness of their character or will. Accountability changes the emphasis from trust in inter-subjective relationships to inter-objective systems, where people are to be held to account to certain prioritized *outcomes* that deliver procedures and targets that are already secured in some form of consensus about what constitutes 'good' healthcare. This is an important shift of emphasis, because while virtue and duty ethics (to a lesser degree) depend on the 'goodness' of motivation to deliver trustworthy healthcare, accountability is essentially about *distrusting* such personal motivations *per se*, requiring behaviour to be accountable to acceptable norms that are publicly safe and acceptable.

This is a central point and tension for us to consider in this book and we return to it in Chapters 7 and 8. In this chapter and in Chapters 2 and 3 we have looked, quite properly, at the need to focus on the subjective and inter-subjective aspects of trust in healthcare and in human life more generally. However, the enormity of the modern globalized world with its complex systems that are built and justified by those running and partaking in them (like healthcare), demand that we have to go beyond the personal. The macro-social and political aspects of trust lead down the path of understanding the conditions under which we might reasonably *distrust* what we encounter in life. Once the latter conditions for distrust come into play the danger is that they then undermine the quite reasonable grounds for continuing to trust. This leads to a paradox to be considered more in Chapter 7: by setting up systems to reduce risk, we might then negate the ordinary human requirements for people to act in good faith (in this case as patients and their paid carers).

Basically, the dilemma is this: while accountability shores up public transparency in professional standards, systems and outcomes, it can become overly dominant eroding interpersonal trust within professional circles and between professionals and patients. This is because accountability is necessary when interpersonal trust fails, as is evidenced by the plethora of Public (health) Inquiries which hold rogue medical professionals and teams to account when trusting in them (and their methods) spectacularly fail. The difficulty with Public Inquiries is that they are mechanisms that are put in place *after* public confidence has been eroded. This perpetuates the dual myth, that systems of accountability, no matter how well designed, can, on the one hand rebuild trust, stamping out all malign and/or unacceptable practice and, on the other hand, deliver a healthcare system that is ultimately perfectable (see Chapter 8).

Having examined in depth two models of ethics and their relationship to trust in healthcare, we now turn to outlining integrated models of ethics.

Outlining integrated approaches to ethics and trust in healthcare

In reality, modern healthcare systems, like the NHS, have elements of both models (virtue and duty ethics); the history of the NHS for example, has allowed an 'ad hoc' growth of both, accountability being the most recent addition and virtue being the most ancient of the three.

So far we have explored philosophically orientated models on which trust in health care could be based. In fact, the actual model that is in existence does not conform to either philosophical ideal so far formulated.

Take the doctor–patient relationship for example; what actually exists in the NHS is a consumerist relationship, one that is typified by voluntary contractual obligations that recognizes autonomy in the ritual of informed consent as a way of preserving individual preference. In other words, the obligation of a doctor to a patient comes into existence through the negotiation of consent which implies a voluntary contractual obligation that the doctor, as well as the patient, must enter into. However, because the bias is on patients getting what they want, one of the consequences of the consumerist relationship between doctor and patient is that the responsibility of decision-making passes from doctor to patient. While the doctor is still empowered to refuse if the treatment may result in harm (or it may not obviously benefit them), the social role of the doctor, either as an agent of virtue, or as a principled agent whose duty is to what is in the very best for their patient (as they see it), is greatly diminished. What this model fails to take into account is the relationship of care that already exists – the duty to treat or the duty to care that the professional has by taking on the social role of healthcare professional in the first place. In sum, a strong account of interpersonal trust that exists in both the virtue and duty model of healthcare no longer exists. The void of weakened interpersonal trust has been filled by systems of accountability, where health care practitioners are more and more accountable to systems that are designed to minimize harm and maximize patient choice.

Summary

This chapter has discussed:

- The virtue ethics model in relationship to trust and healthcare.
- The duty ethics model in relationship to trust and healthcare.
- The integrated approach to ethics, trust and healthcare.

CHAPTER 5

Social Aspects of Trust

Introduction

This chapter extends some of the arguments and descriptions we offered in Chapters 2, 3 and 4 and discusses them in their social and cultural context. Accordingly, we start with some general points about inter-subjectivity, which is the level of the 'micro-social'. By the end of the chapter we will be discussing matters at the 'macro-social' level. The chapter then has three aims.

First we will argue that non-calculative aspects of trust, trust as an end in itself, and *both* positive and negative aspects of dependence are all important for understanding healthcare. Yet the main emphasis in discussions of trust in social sciences, and particularly around notions of risk, tend to be on the calculative aspects of trust and on the *negative* aspects of dependence. The focus is primarily on the *risk* of losing power or some other present or desirable aspect of the person's sense of self. For example, within the context of healthcare, patients risk being abused or neglected or they risk that they might lose control over their lives, when submitting themselves to the decisions of professionals. In addressing these debates we will first offer a brief conceptual discussion that tries to primarily focus on non-calculative aspects of trust, trust as an end in itself, and positive aspects of trusting, and will draw on an additional set of notions about relational autonomy, principled auton-omy, care, recognition, respect, and solidarity.

Second, we will try to understand why it is negative (rather than positive) aspects of trust that are dominant in the current academic and political debates. Here we will discuss how different social domains and societies, more generally, can be associated with specific interpretations of autonomy, solidarity, belonging, trust, risk, and how such assump-tions remain for long periods of time relatively stable and unchallenged within their respective cultures. Drawing on examples from the UK, we will focus on the notion of risk, in particular, as it has acquired a central place in understanding and describing the complexities of everyday life, the challenges to governing the NHS, and the dilemmas associated with the restructuring of the state.

Third, we will discuss the implications of these questions for our understanding of relationships within the health system and the debates about changes in the NHS.

Trust as positive and negative dependence

Discussions of trust often tend to make the assumptions that (a) we trust because we do not have better options available and that (b) trust is primarily motivated by self-interest. Thus, we rely on others only if and when we cannot rely on our own efforts, abilities and knowledge. This could be because we do not have perfect information about others and the future (Giddens, 1990) or because the world is too complex (Luhmann, 1979). Further, trust could be instrumental and strategic. It could allow us to improve our chances for success *vis-à-vis* those who do not have access to trustworthy others, have poorer information or are more hesitant than us in taking risks.

However, the act of trust puts us in a vulnerable position. Doctors could be negligent in dealing with confidential information. Nurses could be malicious and deliberately inflict harm. Hospitals might be dirty and they could expose us to risk of infection. The vulnerable position of trusting could put our well-being at risk. This is because with any new personal environment come new risks and in those new contexts others might behave in an untrustworthy manner. They might put their own, rather than our, interests first or express their interest at our expense. Vulnerability here is an outcome of acting on trust. In a sense, when we trust we are taking a risk or gambling; it is rather like placing a bet (Sztompka, 1999, Baier, 1994).

Such understandings of trust would only be valid if we assume that individuals are separate, unitary, and have only or primarily conflicting interests. Individuals here are imagined as rational actors, who pursue their own interests, while the interests and feelings of others are assumed to only be important inasmuch as they may have an impact on individual utility.

While the utility model of trusting others has its merits, it is also partial and so potentially misleading. Individuals could *also* be viewed validly as moral and social beings, whose emotions are inseparable aspects of their decision making. To reiterate, to what extent is it realistic to think that our sense of connection with others is both externally and internally sanctioned through values, norms and ethical principles? Is it plausible to think about attachment and dependence on others as only a necessary social evil? To what extent are attachment and dependence basic human needs?

The ambivalence of whether we should be attached or not leads to a dilemma: we are either vulnerable in our attachment and dependency on others or invulnerable and immune from attachments that may lead to disappointment and failure to trust others. However, an over-reliance on ourselves as the only trustworthy agents, leads to increasing social isolation and subsequent physical, emotional and mental hardship. The positive aspect of dependency and attachment as necessary social reality are associated with human well-being and human flourishing (Honneth, 1996). Non-utilitarian arguments for exchange through gift giving, sociality and solidarity have been widely discussed in social sciences (by, for example, Durkheim, 1992; Mauss, 1970; and Smith, 2002).

When re-framed in this way, the emphasis is not on vulnerability as an outcome of trust but trust as an outcome of vulnerability. That is, part of being human is to make ourselves vulnerable through risking love, cooperation and solidarity with others. If we cannot do this, we risk not being fully human and damaging our mental health and well-being. While in some circumstances we can be vulnerable *because* we trust, we can also be vulnerable if we do *not* trust. It is undoubtedly risky, but riskiness carries with it many potential benefits to actualise our potential as human beings.

Trust is an ambiguous concept because it can be *both* instrumental and calculative – for example, I trust you because you have been reliable in the past in encapsulating my interests – *and* inherently, blind, emotionally intuitive and risky. For example, I make myself vulnerable by trusting you because if I don't I will never actualize my full potential. While these may represent different kinds of trust, where the latter is a form of interpersonal trust which is more blind and mostly associated with the closer relationships we form with significant others, they are not mutually exclusive forms of trust. In the more affective and intuitive form of trust, often found in close personal relationships with partners and family, dependence and attachment is highly desirable. It does not necessarily lead to anxiety and is not motivated by instrumental rationality. Instead, it could be seen as a *positive dependence*. That is where dependence is sought after not as a pathological need or path to vulnerability but because as social beings it is natural for us to need intimacy and share the company of others.

If interpersonal trust has a certain character in human relations characterised by independence (rational and calculative trust), it also has a particular character in more intimate human relations characterized by positive dependence (affective, intuitive trust). To add to this complex picture, in interdependent human relationships, in good friendships or in ideal relationships between responsible persons, trust may be more about rational and affective mutuality.

In this sense, the richer, complex and ambiguous nature of trust can be thought of as having for our purposes three main aspects (these are explored in many of our chapters):

1 We need to hold in mind that trust is both personal and interpersonal. It can be thought of as *both* an individual characteristic (involving motives, and feelings) *and* as a transaction between people.
2 Trust is a window into other important dimensions of human existence, especially power, risk, autonomy, interdependence, solidarity and care.
3 Trust is one lens to view current changes in the restructuring of the healthcare system.

All three points indicate that trust is invariably bound up with *social relationships*. It is not something that only happens in the minds of individuals – and even when the latter is the case, the inner lives of those individuals consider and include those around them past and present.

Having established our broad case for complexity and ambiguity, we now turn to specific implications of these three main points.

Autonomy and the embeddedness of trust in social relationships

Our cultural assumptions about autonomy tend to be associated with independence, which is primarily seen as something good and desirable, and therefore, having to rely on others could, following such an assumption, be seen as a compromise or infringement of our freedom.

In other words an unavoidable dependency of healthcare may compromise a taken for granted autonomy (as independence), leading to forced dependency and possible shame and embarrassment. It might jeopardize our self-respect. Such assumptions of autonomy as independence could be associated with the process of growing up, which entails growing away from the rituals of dependence, especially related to feeding and excretion: our dignity and self-respect as adults is derived in part by leaving those rituals in the past.

Most of us most of the time want to enjoy health and avoid the role implications of sickness. Generally we prefer *not to have* to consult medical professionals. This is more than escaping the recognition of the pain, anxiety and impairment of our injuries and ailments. The reality of sickness, if it is denied to others, creates loneliness in suffering. However, this denial is not just an intra-psychic process; it is also an interpersonal stance. It involves a daily struggle to prolong the self-respect and autonomy that is part of adult life. In this sense caring could be seen as an infringement of autonomy or a process of infantilization (Giddens, 1998, cited in Chattoo and Ahmad, 2008).

Our cultural assumptions are not necessarily consistent across different social fields. For example, we tend to believe that economic exchanges are primarily motivated by profit and that economic relationships can be well understood as calculative and focused on self-interest. Drawing on such assumptions it becomes possible to define trust as a game where rational actors are carefully selecting their next move for the sake of maximizing personal gain. However by contrast, trust in healthcare that involves emotional dependency and loss of independence is not like a rational or calculative form of trust.

Of course the emotional dependency and loss of independence that we find so difficult to cope with in the West may be experienced differently in other cultures. It could be hypothesized that in cultures where autonomy as independence is less important and where care giving flows through closely knit communities and families, access to healthcare may not provoke the same shame and embarrassment. For example, in China and India, there is a generational interdependence, where it is quite natural to be looked after by family, society and/or healthcare systems (if one can afford it).

In our culture there is more ambivalence in our attitude to ill health and dependency. For instance ill health is often seen as a form of bad luck and is often experienced as some sort of personal failure. For example, obesity and heart disease are often perceived and portrayed as shameful because 'we have somehow let ourselves go' and 'have failed in maintaining our individual autonomy and self-respect'. It seems that western society is fundamentally split in its attitude to healthcare; between a negative sense of dependence on the one hand and autonomy as a positive form of independence on the other hand. Maybe our cultural challenge is to tolerate the ambiguity of dependence because it involves accepting our vulnerability and accepting that others will care for us anyway. Perhaps we are better off thinking of ourselves as interdependent rather than independent or dependent.

Taking this point further, it can only ever be relative – for example most of our actions, even when fit and healthy rely on others creating supportive opportunities. We cannot turn on the light if a whole raft of people and processes are not there to ensure the electricity supply. Our ability to enjoy the sense of independence is embedded in the material circumstances that surround us and it has to be understood in relational terms. Some form of dependence is unavoidable: we can only be independent in some respects and not simultaneously in everything.

For example, delegating responsibility to patients can in some cases be welcomed as this would make doctor–patient relationships more equal and would also give the patient a better understanding and control over their condition. However, this would not always be desirable. Thus, while reliance on professionals could reduce our independence in one aspect of our life, it could also increase our options in our life more generally. Indeed, Luhmann (1979) argued that trust is an important mechanism through which we can extend our capacity to handle higher levels of complexity. Rather than dependence on others limiting our autonomy it can also act to extend that autonomy. A good example here is when disabled people depend on personal assistants to allow them to maximize independent living.

Another reason for not reifying independence as an aspirational ideal, is that not all of us are equally equipped to be independent. That is, many might be ill and forcibly dependent on heath care, while others might not be able to take full advantage of the healthcare system provided. Social class and educational attainment in this respect are important factors in whether people take full advantage of the opportunities afforded by the healthcare system. For example, social class could be an important factor in understanding why some people might be more deferential to professional authority and more sceptical about the recent health policy emphasis on patient choice and responsibility (see Chapter 7).

Independence is not just about individual autonomy; it is also a relational concept – that is in independence from something. In this respect individual autonomy is also relational autonomy (Mackenzie and Stoljar, 2000); capacity for choice, reflexivity and self-direction is both enabled and constrained by available social relationships, practices and institutions (Chatoo and Ahmad, 2008).

For example, trusting patients to take more responsibility for their health also involves confidence in the enabling or disabling features of the social, economic and cultural context in which they live. These conditions vary substantially between individuals and between groups. Some social contexts provide the background for social habits that are highly contested: cigarette smoking, for example, which is seen as both unhealthy in the long term and anti-social by some and an immediate source of well-being, solidarity and comfort by others. It is little surprising that those with more positive reasons to be alive – that is, those that may be better educated with fulfilling jobs and who have more reason to do what is in their long-term interest – will take up healthy habits more readily.

Therefore, when assuming that changing patient lifestyles or adopting wider self-management practices are matters of choice and personal commitment, there needs to be a shift in our understanding that at least recognises that some choices are culturally embedded to stave off boredom, ennui and despair. Trust in independence and individual choice and responsibility is overrated – as is, in part recognized in the NHS, whose stop smoking campaigns involve getting help and group support to quit. Trust in individual independence and autonomy can be exaggerated, reducing the fact that we are *already* culturally embedded and habituated to act in certain ways that resist common sense. Emphasizing individual choice and responsibility too much, courts failure to change public health attitudes by 'victim blaming' and misses the point that many people require a wide range of strategies to change unhealthy habits – not least, group support from their peers.

Individual autonomy and principled autonomy

Some aspects of the above discussion on autonomy and their implications for healthcare are well illustrated by O'Neill's (2002) notion of principled autonomy, which we introduced in Chapter 4. O'Neill distinguishes between *individual autonomy* that is related to the autonomy of the self, person, individual, from *principled autonomy* that is related to autonomy of reason, ethics, willing, and principles. *Principled autonomy* requires that we act *only* on principles that can be principles for all. In this sense autonomy has a social and relational dimension as well as an individualist one. It implies that we should be wary of defining good healthcare using consumerist principles, where 'choices' become overly dependent on patient preference.

Whilst autonomous consumerism in healthcare does not necessarily conflict with the professional duty to provide the best care, they do make strange bedfellows. Consumerism tends to favour individual autonomy at the expense of principled autonomy and thus can create tensions about what we mean by 'choosing the best care available'. Professional values based on principled autonomy rather than individual autonomy, tend to prioritize communicative over instrumental action (see Brown, 2008b, on doctor–patient relations).

Whereas a respect for individual autonomy may be a necessary and minimal condition to earn a patient's trust, it may not be a *sufficient* condition to offer them trustworthy care. That is to say respecting individual autonomy secures individual freedom, that is all. This may be empowering, in the sense of respecting (and not harming) someone's capacity to choose, but it may still fail to ensure prudent choices which may benefit a patient's optimal healthcare and well-being. Principled autonomy universalises what is in the best interest for all patients *per se*, protecting them from an individual autonomy that is blind to the best possible outcome (given that *all* patients should receive the best care available). Also, unrestricted individual autonomy may be harmful if it risks the social freedoms and roles of others. For example, giving one patient all that they ask for may disadvantage other patients in a budget-capped service.

This indicates two, often confused, notions of personal liberty in modern societies. In the first we are free from constraint – *freedom from* and in the second we are free to make prudent choices – *freedom to be*. The latter will arise via, for example, a respectful dialogue with healthcare experts who then enable the patient to make wise choices. People who are counter-dependent (they avoid experts at every point they can in life or oppose their advice at every turn) are denying themselves the freedom to be. What is pre-empted is a true ethical endeavour of collaboration between patients and professionals.

For example, by promising radical consumer choice (freedom from constraint) one may be inhibiting an optimal freedom to be as healthy as one can, which in part relies on a professional judgement to safeguard choices that are always in the best interests for all patients *per se*. In other words, safeguarding principled autonomy is not the same as giving licence to individual autonomy without restriction.

Recognition, positive dependence, and trust as a need

We will now continue exploring what we call trust as a positive dependence in relation to the notion of recognition. The discussion of recognition has two aims here: first, debates around recognition offer additional arguments for looking at trust as a need and second, it offers an entry point to a discussion on the role of self-esteem, self-respect, intimacy and solidarity in relation to trust.

Trust implies, in some ways, the recognition, respect and acceptance of others. This is more than just an external account of trust *vis-à-vis* someone's reliability or competence, and involves existential, ethical and political dimensions to the debate around trust.

It could be argued that full human flourishing is dependent on the trustworthiness of 'ethical' relations, especially love, respect and dignity, established through the struggle for recognition. In this sense, recognition is not a luxury or a mere courtesy that we owe other people, but a vital human need (Taylor, 1992; Anderson, 1996). Honneth (1996) argues that the possibility of the development of a fully autonomous and individuated person depends on the development of self-confidence, self-respect and self-esteem. Studies in psychology confirm that human beings have a psychological need for recognition, and that its denial might lead to damage for life (see Chapter 3). Recognition of our autonomy cannot be achieved through unilateral demands. It has to be acquired inter-subjectively, that is, by giving and receiving recognition:

> Even though we may objectify ourselves through labour by producing objects, objects are not capable of reflecting back to us our conception of ourselves as subjects, having some degree of freedom and responsibility. Only other persons, also subjects and having some degree of freedom and responsibility, can do this. (Sayer, 2005a: 56).

If recognition can secure the freedom of another, it can also undermine it. This could be illustrated in relations of unequal power, and could in very broad terms be associated with what Hegel calls the 'Master–Slave relation' (Hegel, 1977). Yet, as Alexander Kojève explains when a relationship is reduced to only its power constituent recognition becomes meaningless:

> The relation between Master and Slave ... is not recognition properly so called ... The Master is not the only one to recognize himself as master. The slave also considers himself as such. Hence, he is recognised in his human reality and dignity. But this recognition is one-sided, for he does not recognize in turn the Slave's human reality and dignity. Hence, he is recognized by some one who he does not recognise. And this is what is insufficient – what is tragic – in this situation ... For he can be satisfied only by recognition from one who he recognises as worthy of recognizing him. (Kojève, 1969: 19).

Relationships between patients and health professionals are unequal in terms of their respective health-related knowledge and skills. However these inequalities are differently expressed within malign and benign forms of medical paternalism. In benign medical paternalism, the doctor may well have regard for their patients, but will be unable to recognize that they may be able to make competent health choices for themselves. In other words, the recognition is partial but predominantly one-sided, the patient recognizes the authority of the doctor but the doctor does not fully recognize the patient.

In the case of malign paternalism (see Chapter 6), clinical professionals recognize neither the humanity and dignity nor the authority of those under their care. Moreover, because 'the patients' or 'subjects' of medical experiments have been deceived or coerced or both, the patients or subjects cannot possibly assent or consent to what is being done to them. In this sense, malign medical paternalism is a double blind form of non-recognition – the doctors do not recognize the patients in their authority or their humanity, nor do the patients recognize the doctors and their true intentions.

We can here ask what is the type of recognition on which relationships of trust are, could, or should be built within the healthcare system? Is the recognition of one's humanity and dignity sufficient, can they be undermined by the organization and governance of health systems? How do these relationships differ when they are applied not only from the perspective of the professionals towards the patients, but also from patients towards professionals, as well as between health professionals? In order to address these questions we will first draw on a distinction between unconditional and conditional recognition, before looking at how this distinction can help us understand relationships within modern healthcare systems and the NHS as one specific example of such a system.

Unconditional and conditional recognition

Unconditional recognition is a deep form of recognizing others in their full humanity and is related to the possibility of unconditional love and deep empathy for others that are fundamentally like us, in their vulnerability, dignity and capacity to suffer. Unconditional recognition operates in the acquisition of self-respect and is not exclusive but inclusive, in that it is given regardless of another's difference – whether this is expressed in terms of age, race, mental/physical ability or sex. Unconditional recognition supports both the justice of non-discrimination on the one hand and the love of unconditional positive regard on the other hand. By contrast, conditional recognition has to be earned. It is granted depending on the moral and other qualities, behaviour, and achievements of others and is necessary for them to acquire self-esteem (Sayer, 2005a).

For example, a professional who operates consistent unconditional recognition would treat all patients exactly the same, independent of their condition, age, sex, race, class, ability to pay, and so on. By contrast, conditional recognition would be manifest if these factors introduced differential attention and respect into the caring relationship. Patients and relatives who defer obsequiously to professional action without question and buy gifts for staff are signalling that conditional recognition may well operate and that unconditional recognition is precarious in complex care systems.

We feel empathy and compassion when faced with the suffering, vulnerability and violations of the dignity of fellow human beings. Health professionals are regularly faced with situations that arouse such sentiments. This is in the nature of their work. One of the most important ethical aspects of care-giving is directed at ensuring the respectful treatment of patients that does not jeopardize their dignity. Health professionals may express appreciation for the patients' ability to cope with pain or with their capacity to change their lifestyle and improve their condition. However, such an evaluative aspect of the doctor–patient relationship is likely to be of only secondary importance. Thus, hospice care for the dying places much effort in ensuring that particular needs are met to maximize personhood, when the patient has a dwindling existence.

If the act of dying means the patient can no longer ensure their own dignity and respect, then others, more able, might do their best to offer it in compensation. This is an example of how the recognition of the humanity of others, at its best, endures until death. Our capacity to want a dignified end for others, not just for ourselves, points to this deep impulse for the need for recognition. Our ability to accept that recognition requires trust in others is a risky existential position. This is why some of us defend planned euthanasia for ourselves because we wish to pre-empt such a risk. If we see examples of people with undignified deaths where unconditional recognition was absent, we also might risk that fate.

We expect respectful treatment of our bodies even *after* our death (see Chapter 6 on the case of Alder Hey). This is because the body is not only a focal point of suffering but is also an important symbol of our dignity. Self-respect is most intimately related to the body and to our control over it. Such control is partially lost when we are ill and need to allow external intervention on the part of health professionals. Most extreme experiences of humiliation, however, are related to unwarranted attempts to gain control over a person's body, as these are most destructive for one's practical relation to self. This is regardless of the intentions that might be behind such attempts (Honneth, 1996: 132). This is more than the need for recognition of rights or acceptance and belonging.

While the experiences of patients are mostly characterized by degrees of attenuated unconditional forms of recognition (affected by practitioner preferences and prejudices), recognition in relationships *between health professionals* is mostly conditional, that is, dependent on achievement and personal qualities. The recognition of our personal qualities (for example, friendliness, integrity) is likely to be equally rewarding for us, regardless of whether such appreciation comes from patients or colleagues. However, the recognition of our professional achievements is most rewarding when it is on the part of *our peers*.

The dilemma of love between strangers and state paternalism

A profound implication in what we have just argued is that love may be the real driver and touchstone of healing relationships. Rooted as it is in the traditions of kith and especially kin care (and within that especially benignly preoccupied parental care) healing as an act of love now finds itself in a new social context. We are now typically in a world of complex impersonal care systems, where unconditional recognition is constrained but still present as both possibility and requirement. Kith and kin relationships vary in their presence to augment or replace impersonal healthcare systems.

One scenario is that the impersonal logic of healthcare systems will simply obliterate unconditional recognition. Another scenario is that state paternalism for the health of populations over-rides individual recognition (as in mass childhood immunization). Elsewhere we find such mass management of a healthy order favouring the needs of some at the expense of others, such as, the removal of public nuisance by the use of mental health law. (These and other examples are discussed in Chapter 6.)

Another prospect is that our need for unconditional recognition may leave us sentimentalizing healthcare and craving a one-dimensional image of it in our cultural production and consumption; hence the idealization of A&E activity in popular dramatic representations. In different ways all these scenarios reflect a failure of adult democratic engagement about the complexities and challenges of healthcare.

More subtly, and implying large variations in the quality of care relationships, the impulse of unconditional recognition in impersonal settings is shaped by the emotional idiosyncrasies of patients and staff. One way of understanding this is the psychoanalytical expectation of transference and counter-transference in the relationship. Each party brings in unconscious needs which are played out in each new relationship, whether the party is a carer or being cared for. Overlying these psychodynamic aspects of the relationship are socio-cultural factors such as race, class, age and gender which might compromise both mutual empathy and mutual trust. These also make animosity possible (for example, the white racist patient who resists and resents treatment from a black worker).

Thus, we now have impersonal systems populated by caring scenarios between strangers, not kith and kin. Moreover, care systems are now offered to whole populations (as in the NHS) or selectively to large paying populations (as in the USA). As a consequence, the unconditional recognition of individuals is tempered logically and inevitably by the need for routines of discrimination and prioritization (for example, waiting lists or triage in A&E departments). In payment-based systems the rich have rapid access to choice but the poor do not and they are reliant on a safety net of emergency care.

What has emerged then is the variable supply of treatment to populations containing variegated need; a scenario which has become the focus of substantial political and ethical contestation. Once we ask and answer the question 'who is more deserving?', then undifferentiated unconditional recognition for all has to be modified by some version of differentiating justice.

The modification of unconditional recognition in complex systems, driven by political and economic necessity has three implications in modern societies compared to those which relied on small, parochially provided kith and kin relationships.

The first is that we must simply take on trust that a whole range of technical and professional resources are reliable. The second is that our individual need for care competes with those of others. There is a need to trust in equality and justice which is differentiated on a basis of evaluated need. The NHS employs a form of interest utilitarianism where major health interests outweigh minor health interests. This is most evident in A&E where the most serious cases are given priority following triage but it operates in other healthcare sub-systems albeit less evidently at times. This utilitarianism is demanded by resource constraints and leads to rationing of healthcare in one way or another.

The third is that those caring for us begin and to some extent must remain strangers. This requires us to trust an ethical imperative that strikes a correct balance between distant respect and familial love. If the professional is too distant then this is experienced as cold and even cruel. But patients cannot expect reciprocal obligations (as would happen in families) from medical staff because such obligations are naturally partial and biased towards those one is intimate with. This is why the training of healthcare professionals now requires a careful consideration of 'boundaries': intimacy has its limits and its rules of engagement in healthcare settings.

Perhaps, most importantly, professionals cannot express their own neediness in relationships with patients. This is partly about the need to maintain appropriate boundaries – which might seem at odds with loving kin relationships. However, it is also in a modified form a reproduction of those kin relationships. For example, medical paternalism is a variety of kin relationships where parallels can be legitimately drawn.

Parents are not supposed to put their needs before those of their children and there is the universal incest taboo. The version of this in professional care is when erotic relationships ensue between patients and their paid carers. What in the family would be child sexual abuse in the context of modern healthcare becomes therapist sexual abuse – one form of professional malpractice. Thus we can see how in modern healthcare non-erotic care for others can be reproduced in an honourable way which aims for unconditional recognition for another's care. The notion of 'duty of care' reminds us that non-erotic love for those we care for as parents or as professionals is an ongoing ethical requirement.

Solidarity, belonging and identity

Our discussion of trust as positive and negative dependence, and as related to autonomy, and recognition has, so far, mostly dealt with relationships on the interpersonal level. Here we are going to extend these discussions to our broader relationships in society and our place in it. Within this context, relations of trust are also closely related to notions such as solidarity, identity and citizenship. In turn these are a function of the character of the state. For example, authoritarian states, which intimidate and manipulate their citizens into compliance, will be less permissive of free citizens and their communal expressions of solidarity than liberal states. This is why libertarians of left and right are suspicious of state power in both free market and socialised forms of political governance.

In sociology and anthropology, positive dependence has been recognized as a necessary precondition for the existence of society, where the non-instrumental, symbolic, aspects of exchanges are fundamental for the social bond (Mauss, 1970; Durkheim, 1992). Thus, we may feel affection, moral responsibility and commitment towards larger groups of people constituted of unknown and unknowable individuals, what Anderson (1983) called 'imagined communities'. Imagined communities would most notably refer to the nation, but would also include any other (usually) large group in which membership is not reproduced through face-to-face relationships. Our feelings of emotional attachment towards members of such imagined communities and sense of commitment and responsibility to their perceived objectives and needs could have different degrees of strength that could include readiness for the ultimate sacrifice of one's life. We might be particularly prone to identify with imagined communities which resonate with our identities (based on say race, gender or political ideology).

The nature of our relationships towards the members of abstract imagined communities have many resemblances to emotions and commitments that we have towards family and friends, and which could go beyond the expectation for others to act in our interest (see Gilson, 2006). Indeed, thinking about citizenship as social citizenship, the type of citizenship on which the welfare state is based, is only possible through a degree of sense of belonging that goes beyond a calculation of interests for individuals and is more like that which Durkheim called 'moral community' (we will further discuss this notion in relation to professional groups in Chapter 7).

This does not imply that all communities are moral communities (not even predominantly), but that the nature of the existing bonds could be different and that this would have implications for our sense of identification with it as well as for the stability of the community over time. A community based primarily on interests could only sustain a minimum level of obligation between its members. Social stability and reproduction requires the presence of a degree of generalised trust (Giddens, 1990) among its members. This is both in terms of the reliable functioning of its institutions (system integration) and in terms of their legitimacy. The latter would be strengthened if we feel that our interests and identity are recognized in the way in which these institutions are set but also if we feel a sense of belonging and self-identification with the community (social integration).

Trusting the social order is a two-way process. We legitimize and perpetuate its existence but through which process we are also recognised as members of a society and acquire a sense of belonging. The latter has implications for understanding the changing role of the state and the state policies in relation to healthcare restructuring. Indeed, citizenship is increasingly moving away from social citizenship in advanced capitalist societies with unavoidable implications for both the extent and actual form that healthcare provision takes.

In the case of Britain, with its NHS free at the point of need, social solidarity is invested via the state in a collective form of healthcare provision. However, the integrity and continuity of the system is only possible inasmuch as this specific form of solidarity persists over time. There are no such guarantees and indeed some forms of inequality (and thus suggesting a more nuanced understanding of solidarity) were already present in the way the system was set up. Thus, for example in relation to the NHS:

- From the outset some aspects of care were means-tested, such as optical care.
- Private medical practice has been tolerated from the outset.
- GPs have not been directly salaried in the main but have operated as small entrepreneurs, in a constant negotiation for more payment from the state.
- Economic scarcity drives a wedge between rich and poor patients. Apart from private practice allowing richer patients to have quicker consultations and more treatment options, this outcome also occurs in any mixed economy of healthcare. For example, there has been a recent controversy about top-up co-payments for drugs not approved by the National Institute of Health and Clinical Excellence, which would ease the fiscal burden on the NHS but would also differentially favour those able to pay.
- The general population may demand care at the time of need but is not always willing to provide the central taxation required to ensure that provision. Patients tend to underestimate the real costs of care and cost with their right as a citizen to a standard of perceived service. Thus some voters seem to want to 'have their cake and eat it': they may want a fully comprehensive NHS for all, but are not prepared to underwrite that ambition by paying more tax.
- Healthcare now offers a mixture of responses to a wide continuum from immediate life saving to elective cosmetic procedures. It is a moot point about which of these are real, rather than constructed, needs. But however we define points on the continuum, clearly healthcare resources are devoted to those rich enough to afford elective procedures for quality of life-enhancing procedures that are not really necessary to avoid immediate death or prolong life. Healthcare activity in the private sector is skewed towards quick throughput expensive procedures at one end of the continuum. However, the education of those practising is paid for in whole or part by general taxation (depending on the society), so the poor will make contributions to forms of activity denied to them as individual consumers of healthcare.

These points are made at this stage to indicate that healthcare mirrors our wider socio-political attitudes about social solidarity. In the USA, where individualism is highly favoured and solidarity distrusted much more than in Northern Europe, they have created a form of healthcare which mirrors this difference. Critics of changes in the NHS point out that we are drifting towards US cultural values of atomised individualism. Critics of the US healthcare system argue for a drift in the opposite direction (or in the case of current Republican opposition they are complaining about that drift). Thus, our healthcare systems do signify our state of social solidarity and the tensions surrounding citizenship as personal freedom and citizenship as interdependence.

Trust in a 'risk society'

In the discussion of autonomy earlier, we argued that by linking the notions of trust and risk we are making assumptions about the nature of interpersonal relationships, individual motivations and needs. In this case, risk is the outcome of our engagement with others; it is through putting trust in others that we are opening the possibility of such risks. The notion of risk has another dimension that is also important for understanding trust. It is about a description of the world around us, about solidarity and our relationships with generalised others, and our place in society. Thus, we can distinguish between trust and risk as aspects of all cultures and societies and the specific form that trust takes in a society that describes itself as a 'risk society'. In the latter case, the complexities of its present (which may, but does not necessarily have to, be more challenging than those in other societies or times in history) are primarily expressed through the notion of 'risk'.

A 'risk society' is a society that understands trust primarily in negative terms, that is, as a form of risk. Our trust in society and social systems manifests in how socially secure we can make perceived cultural and societal *insecurity*. This manifest insecurity, or lack of trust, has been theorised by Beck in terms of 'risk', Furedi in terms of 'fear', O'Neill in terms of 'anxiety', and Douglas in terms of 'danger'. We now look at these implications for healthcare.

Discourses on risk have been very visible in academic and policy debates and some authors have suggested that at present we are living in a society dominated by risk (Beck, 1992). There is, however, a change in the nature of risks that we face. Beck (1992) argues that contemporary risks are predominantly man-made and are related to the misuse of technology, technological failures, and unintended and unforeseen consequences. The advances in science and technology as well as the closer global interconnectedness have created new types of hazards, such as pandemics and environmental disasters, which cannot be contained in time and space. The existing systems for prevention and response, mainly created by states, may not be adequate in response to such risks. However, other commentators have cautioned that the extent and novelty of global risks should not be overly exaggerated. Such risks are not entirely new. Also there are many aspects of our lives that have become much more secure and predictable, compared to previous generations. In this sense it can be argued that the main change is in terms of our *perceptions* of the existing risks.

Thus, Furedi (2005) argues that we live in a culture of fear, while O'Neill (2002) suggested that contemporary society is dominated by feelings of anxiety. Perceptions of risk, so prevalent in contemporary society, do not necessarily reflect risk that is 'out there' but rather are culturally specific and the question has to be 'how safe is safe enough for a particular culture' (Douglas, 1992: 41). There are two closely inter-related but analytically separate aspects of this question that are related first to cultural orientations, and second to the institutional structures within which they are embedded.

Douglas (1992) argues that the question to be asked is not whether the society in which we live is more or less exposed to risk but rather, which risks are visible and which ones are invisible; and who is scrutinised and blamed for failures. Definitions of risk and danger are important mechanisms for inclusion and exclusion, for building and enforcing boundaries between groups and for keeping internal order. In this sense, the ways in which a specific culture perceives risk and attributes blame is an indication of first, how this culture understands its environment, and second (and related to the latter) reflects its internal structure and degree of openness to outsiders.

Drawing on Thompson (1982), Douglas distinguishes between four ideal types of cultural orientations, or what she called 'myths', about the predictability of nature. These are: nature is capricious, nature is fragile, nature is robust and nature is only robust within limits. Each of those 'myths' is represented by a picture of a ball in a landscape:

1   *Nature is capricious* corresponds to a fatalist view of the world where what comes next is unpredictable and therefore theorizing about it is of no use (the ball could roll in any direction on the plane). (See Figure 5.1.)

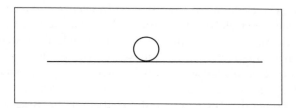

Figure 5.1 *Nature is capricious*

2   *Nature is fragile* is a view where there is a very tender equilibrium and only the smallest change could disrupt it with dramatic consequences (the ball could roll down from the top of the mount in any direction). (See Figure 5.2.)

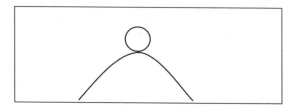

Figure 5.2 *Nature is fragile*

3   *Nature is robust* is a view where the equilibrium can only be disturbed temporarily but the tendency is for stability to be re-established quickly. (See Figure 5.3.)

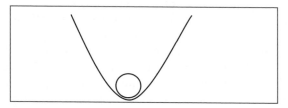

Figure 5.3 *Nature is robust*

4   *Nature is robust within limits* is a view where equilibrium would be quickly re-established as long as the changes are not too extreme and do not pass a breaking point. (See Figure 5.4.)

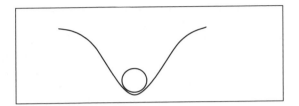

Figure 5.4 *Nature is robust within limits*

In the context of health and healthcare provision, individual and broader cultural beliefs and attitudes could vary in relation to questions such as, what is the risk to good health, and whether bad health is predictable and controllable? Thus, some people may think that good (and bad) health is inherited and/or that it is dependent on supernatural forces. Such beliefs could be associated with scepticism of individual, social and professional capabilities to avoid and deal with risks ('nature is capricious'). In this case trust and confidence would be irrelevant, and it is only hope and faith that could provide some sense of control. In contrast to the sceptical outlook on health some people may believe that there are no real risks to their health ('nature is robust'). For someone who believes that nothing will ever go wrong with their health, questions of risk and trust are less important because they are fully confident in their own invulnerability.

The two other ideal types of attitudes to risk that Mary Douglas discusses – 'nature is fragile' and 'nature is robust within limits' – are more nuanced. Thus, we may believe that many things around us pose potential risks to our health (nature is fragile), and therefore we may feel that we need to be constantly aware of these risks, try to avoid them, and/or put in place mechanisms for dealing with them. Trust here is very important. However, because we believe that risk is an ever present companion in our lives, the people and institutions around us need to be constantly reassessed and tested in order to give us confidence that the tender balance between good and bad health will remain intact.

Finally, we may believe that although there are potential risks to our health, those risks are only triggered under specific circumstances (nature is robust within limits). Thus, most of the time we would not worry about risks to our health and would only become concerned with the trustworthiness of health-relevant institutions and people when there are cases of failure outside of what we think is acceptable or normal. While the above examples are primarily referring to individual attitudes they could also be attributed to cultures, and it is the latter that is the main focus of the original argument.

Douglas further argues that while all of the above orientations are present in all cultures some tend to be dominant. For example, if we believe that at present we live in a 'risk society' this would correspond to a belief that 'nature is fragile' (Figure 5.2) (or 'nature is robust within limits' as in Figure 5.4, but where we have reached the tipping point). However, cultural orientations may differ not only between societies but also *within* societies, where different 'myths' could be dominant in relation to our health, the economy, and politics, for example. That is why, depending on which society or specific social field we are interested in, we can encounter different cultural orientations nested into each other. For example, 'risk society' (nature is fragile) could be a dominant overarching theme, but this could be combined with a belief that the economic world is chaotic and unpredictable (nature is capricious), especially in a time of crisis, and that we can have a great deal of control over our health (nature is robust within limits).

Douglas argues that which belief is dominant in societies could, to an extent, be related to the social environment (and institutional structure) and more specifically the types of restrictions that it puts on the autonomy of individuals. Douglas uses two dimensions, grid and group, in order to distinguish between types of social environments. The first one, grid, is about the degree of structuredness of society, where the higher the degree of structuredness the less scope there is for negotiating individual options. The second dimension, group, is about the degree of inclusiveness of the group. The two dimensions can be represented in Figure 5.5.

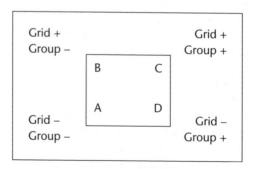

Figure 5.5   *The two dimensions of grid and group*

Thus, low level of internal structuredness and weak group boundaries (ideal type A in Figure 5.5) could be associated with a high level of individual autonomy. Such a culture would have an affinity with a 'nature is robust' view and would tend to encourage entrepreneurial activities. High level of internal structuredness and weak group boundaries (ideal type B in Figure 5.5) could be associated with a culture that would have affinity with a 'nature is capricious' view and would tend to encourage withdrawal and scepticism about the possibility to influence the world outside. High level of internal structuredness and strong group boundaries (ideal type C in Figure 5.5) could be associated with a low level of individual autonomy. Such a culture would have an affinity with a 'nature is robust within limits' view and would tend to encourage belief in the effectiveness of regulation and hierarchical structures. Low level of internal structuredness and strong group boundaries (ideal type D in Figure 5.5) could be associated with a culture that would have affinity with a 'nature is fragile' view and with communitarian beliefs.

In other words the internal structure of a group would have affinities with questions of solidarity and individual responsibility, and this in turn would have some affinity with the beliefs that its members have in relation to risk. In this way beliefs about risk to health would have some affinity with questions such as: What are the limits of solidarity within a group? What are the boundaries of the group? To what extent is one's health individual responsibility or the responsibility of all members of the group? We can use the two aspects of Mary Douglas's argument as a heuristic device for exploring some plausible links between attitudes to health-related risks, social structure, and existing institutional arrangements.

Starting with the latter, we can look at the different organization of healthcare provision, insurance and payment in the United States and United Kingdom. In the United States health is assumed to be an individual responsibility and therefore paying for healthcare is also an individual responsibility, while buying health insurance is voluntary and privately paid for. Provision of healthcare services is primarily carried out by private providers. In contrast, in the UK, payment, insurance and provision under the NHS is primarily offered by the state, within a system that is providing universal access. This is on the premise that health is a public good and that it is a responsibility that all members of society collectively have for each other.

Following Douglas we can argue that the more individualist health system in the US has some affinities with the weaker group boundaries, and the real or imagined belief in the low level of structuredness of society, where opportunities are deemed to be equally open to all. If this was the case, then belief that 'nature is robust' is a useful coping strategy within a context where there is little external help. In contrast to the US, the more solidaristic system in the UK can be associated with stronger group boundaries, and the acknowledgement of a highly structured social system (for example, level of inequality and social mobility). Such social structure could have stronger affinities with a 'nature is robust within limits' attitudes to risks.

While these arguments are making only very tentative links between highly abstract categories within an abstract model, and very specific examples, they are useful in demonstrating the critical potential that the arguments advanced by Mary Douglas have. Her analysis and conceptual frameworks offer productive avenues for asking relevant questions about actual and perceived risks, and their relation to the organization of social relations and the logic of different institutional levels (some of those, particularly around the role of the state and different types of governance, we will discuss later in this chapter and in Chapter 7).

Thus, there is no perfect match between institutional structure, cultural orientations, and actual events. Indeed, we are often surprised by actual events as they may not correspond to what we might have expected. If we believe that the environment is predictable and controllable any sign of the opposite would create anxiety, and could lead to demands for introducing mechanisms to re-establish the equilibrium and prevent future failures. Furthermore, specific expectations could differ between different social systems (such as, health and economics), while there could also be a disparity or a temporal lag between cultural orientations and existing institutional structure. For example, the public ethos of the NHS may have been undermined by the promotion of entrepreneurial values and the introduction of performance indicators in the past twenty years.

Douglas links cultural orientations with social structure and the broader environment: beliefs, expectations, reality, etc.; so that risk is not explained purely as being out there and life becoming riskier (or not) or as purely socially constructed and in the minds of individuals. Following her analysis we can distinguish between different aspects of contradictions and tensions, which might arise between, for example, cultural orientations and institutional structure (expectations based on cultural orientations and actual events). However, before looking at such tensions we are going to look at the cultural and institutional tendencies in contemporary Western society.

Individualization, globalization, solidarity and trust

Modernity has favoured the restructuring of relationships across space and time, loosening the social bonds and obligations to the society in which we live (Giddens, 1992; Beck and Beck-Gernsheim, 1995). Given that the ascribed bonds of traditional society have been lost, living in modern societies is often experienced as a tension between individualism and solidarity, autonomy and reliance on others. While these themes have been central to the discussion in this chapter, here they appear as an aspect of a historical process referring to a broad social and cultural transformation that defines our present more generally. This tension is experienced on the personal level but is also implicated in the ways in which our society is organized politically, and includes questions about identity, solidarity and political representation. The state has been a central arena for negotiating different interests, identities and solidarities, and the nation-state where representation is ensured through democratic participation in the formal and informal aspects of the political process, as a specific form of state, is the one with which we are all most familiar.

Looking at our present and more recent past it has been argued that there has been a tendency for withdrawal from active participation on the part of citizens both from the formal political process and from the informal sphere located between the family and state, referred to as civil society. This tendency of withdrawal, in turn, has led to the weakening of social institutions that would otherwise have created different levels of solidarity and trust, bridging the social sphere of our intimate relationships with highly abstract societal systems in national and supranational institutions (Putnam, 2000). Moreover, there has been a 'hollowing out' of the state, and a weakening of its commitment to social welfare, in favour of a redefinition of citizenship with a stronger emphasis on personal responsibility (Jessop, 2008).

States have less control of the security over their own territory, risk now being perceived in terms of: the vagaries of global market; the state of the global environment; the risk of global terrorism and pandemics that threaten all citizens across the globe. Individual identities are free floating and complex, no longer wedded to locale or even necessarily nation-states, challenging the very notion of solidarity and the trust this inspires in respect to community.

For example, many of our rights, including our rights to health and well-being, are guaranteed by institutions outside of the nation-state, such as the EU, where there is a broader sense of citizenship and solidarity in play. The challenge to the state is not only global in a geographical sense, but it is also global in the digitalization of human health by way of the genetic code, where new forms of trust in technologies that promise the power of genetic knowledge and health for us all ameliorate health risks that were once thought intractable. In this way DNA databases provide a new form of solidarity of information where citizens are linked to each other by their biology rather than their geography and or immediate family (see Rose and Novas, 2003; Rabinow and Rose, 2006; and Rose, 2008). In sum, the meaning and boundaries of society that were, in the past, predominantly associated with the nation-state, have become increasingly more complex with the onset of globalization.

On the one hand, individualization can be seen as a challenge to social order that gives us a sense of security. Indeed, Misztal (1996) suspects that the increased interest in issues of trust has to do with the erosion of solidarity and cooperation in complex modern societies. On the other hand, the weakening social bonds also mean liberation of individuals from oppressive forms of belonging and obligation to communities and states, empowering individuals to have more control over their own lives and making their own history (Giddens, 1992). Thus, we return full circle to the tension between personal freedom and interdependence in civil society, where different kinds of trust compete in institutions that are increasingly independent of place and state.

Returning to our earlier discussion of types of orientations to risk, it could be argued that we are witnessing an institutional and cultural shift. This is towards what Douglas (1992) associated with low level of internal structuredness and weak group boundaries, high level of individual autonomy, and a cultural affinity with a 'nature is robust' view (ideal type A in Figure 5.5). This is a useful perspective from which to explore some of the tensions between cultural orientations and institutional structure, and expectations based on cultural orientations and actual events.

To what extent has the cultural orientation moved towards entrepreneurial culture around healthcare? Also, if such a shift has occurred, to what extent has this been in different social systems? It could be argued, for example, that there is a strong attachment to the more solidaristic ethos of the NHS and therefore a strong resistance to entrepreneurial and managerial mechanisms on the part of professionals and patients. So, while an institutional shift has taken place, this is not necessarily the case on the level of cultural orientations. It could also be the case that within the context of healthcare such tendencies are only temporary and state policies could be seen as pendulum-like moves between regulation and de-regulation (Turner, 2001).

The 'risk state'

Earlier we noted that we live in a 'risk society' (Beck, 1992) associated with a 'crisis of trust'. There is an emphasis in such a position on the claim that risks have increased objectively and that our subjective responses of fear mirror this increase. By contrast, O'Neill (2002) argues that contemporary society has developed a 'culture of suspicion'. This places more of an emphasis on changes of view not on the changes of external factors, real or imagined, that warrant them. Thus the tension between Beck and O'Neill suggests that we might conceptually uncouple a putative increasingly risky world from our increasing collective need to minimise risk.

Thus from O'Neill's perspective, claims that there is a crisis of trust can be associated with an unrealistic search for a state of complete risk elimination. This reflects a process of the 'denaturalization' of risk and uncertainty as part of life (Honkasalo, 2006). In times when life was typically 'short and brutish', death and disease were imminent for most people and so risk was normalized and accepted fatalistically (as 'God's will').

With increasing secularization, increasing longevity and expectations of increasing quality of life, we can now make disease and death deferrable risks. Once these prospects are raised then we become suspicious of *anything* that might jeopardize our health and well-being. 'War' is declared on risk, whether the latter is terrorism, illicit drugs or cancer. The new cultural expectation of risk-elimination creates a discourse in which there is an infantile fantasy that these wars can indeed be won. Morbidity can be prevented and reversed by our own personal tactics of survival. Being healthy and living beyond the average become moral imperatives and political expectations; and this is where two groups of expectations in our current times co-exist and might at times come into conflict. Health is not only a matter of moral effort it is also a political expectation of experts. Dependency on our individual efforts and dependency on experts co-exist to cure sickness and ward off death.

In the latter regard, full certainty and, by implication, trust is to be restored through 'transparency' and 'disinterested expert opinion'. For example, informed consent has replaced presumed consent (especially following the Alder Hey scandal noted in Chapter 6) as a principle guiding relationships with patients. Yet, questions such as, how much information is sufficient, how should it be communicated, how much resource should be spent on the process, remain open and their answers are not self evident (O'Neill, 2002).

Furthermore, references to '*expertise and scientific uncertainty*' assume the possibility of external, absolute 'objectivity' devoid of stakeholder and normative perspective/bias. This might be highly unrealistic and often takes place at the expense of potentially more fruitful avenues for dialogue and building trust between different stakeholders (Dunn *et al.*, 2008).

This now poses a problem for both healthcare organizations and the states, which develop policies to legitimise those organizations. How do they find ways to respond to such expectations, regardless of how unrealistic demands for absolute transparency and predictability might be? Adopting discourses and policies of risk management could be seen as responses to such expectations. Indeed, Wilke argues that contemporary states could be defined as *risk states*, inasmuch as they are promising to protect their citizens from a wide range of unpredictable risks (Jessop, 2008).

Bauman (2004) offers a narrower definition of states being preoccupied with security – that is, the 'security state'. This is in contrast to the *social state*, for example, the main objective of which is to extend welfare rights to all its citizens. The risk discourse offers the security state a common language to refer to a set of diverse relationships, which in turn makes the development of centralized communication and governance procedures easier. However, the problem with the risk discourse is that it may legitimize and reinforce unrealistic or at least questionable expectations. Can all hospital-acquired infections be prevented? Will patients never die on the operating table during routine surgery for non-life threatening conditions? Will the healthy-lifestyle individual never die before their time? Can the state invent mechanisms of accountability to eliminate risk from healthcare systems?

One particular response to heightened risk awareness is the growth of *audit culture* (Power, 1997; Strathern, 2000) and the adoption of audit as a state and organizational strategy of dealing with risk and with heightened risk sensitivity. This is a specific form of governance ('super-accountability'), which makes it more difficult to attribute blame on the state but is instead transformed into a set of procedural issues. Thus failures can be attributed to individuals or to institutions (incompetence, corruption, and so on), which in turn reduces the threat of destabilising the broader social order.

In this way, increased surveillance (transparency, accountability) is compatible with withdrawal of state responsibility; or at least buffering systems can be put in place between governments, which develop healthcare policy and the professionals who populate healthcare in practice. A number of organizations are currently present in Britain to fulfil this buffering role (which we list in Chapter 7) and arguably, official public inquiries into 'health scandals' have a similar role (see Chapter 6).

The very existence of these statutory regulatory bodies and assembled inquiry teams in such large numbers and meriting such vast amounts of public money indicates that healthcare systems cannot be left alone and trusted by politicians to simply function and deliver optimal care. Part of this is about cost-effectiveness or *financial probity*. But there is more political advantage to the state than this alone. Extensive highly funded mechanisms of accountability are *processes of surveillance* to check that policy is implemented in practice. This allows the state to partially *withdraw its responsibility* for the well-being of the population by clarifying many aspects of the duty of care of *agents of the state* (health service employees in this case) or its autonomous sub-systems. In the case of the NHS this currently means NHS Trusts.

This clarification denotes the partial devolution of state power from politicians to practitioners and their direct local employers to look after those in need (*parens patrie*). One outcome of this process is that state-imposed processes of audit reinforce a cultural expectation of risk elimination. It is not so much that investigation exposes inadequacy (which it does, because nothing is perfect in life) it also talks up the 'expectation gap' for the public in healthcare (Power, 1997). It suggests that finding fault over and over and more and more will somehow lead eventually to a risk-free system. Instead of an honest democratic *dialogue* about what is feasible in healthcare, with its limited resources, technical limitations and human frailties, we find ourselves with an audit culture *monologue*. This names and shames and recommends authoritatively from its state-funded position of power. Democracy and a grown up debate about risk and trust in healthcare is once more stymied.

Citizens and the state

In the midst of these recent dynamic social forces, both the nature of citizenship and the organization and powers of the state are changing. These concerns contribute to restructuring the nature of citizenship, the relationship of state and citizen, and they have an impact on public policy developments. Political strategies are at least to some extent reflections of the structure of society and the expectations of citizens. What then are the responsibilities of the state to its citizens and what should citizens expect from the state? It could be argued that a process of individualization is challenging the ideals of solidarity perpetuated by the founding principles of the NHS, for example. Entrepreneurial culture also means individual responsibility, which translated into citizen–state relations tends to prioritise the citizen as a tax payer rather than the citizen as a member of a moral community.

This point in relation to healthcare is particularly salient. After all the highest demand comes from those on the outside of the labour market, whose concrete tax contributions proportionally are very low (obstetric care, paediatric care and healthcare responses to chronically sick adults of working age and retired people). This is why from the tradition of the UK, where the healthy and able-bodied workers pay for all in society to have access to healthcare, the US system appears so iniquitous and offensive. In the latter system those outside the labour market, who are also statistically the sickest and most vulnerable, are the very ones least able to pay and so access healthcare. Also, there is a related tension between the solidaristic ethos of care at the point of need and the capacity to pay for it. This is especially problematic in the light of common public health challenges and their financial costs – where smoking, obesity and alcohol abuse, for example – take a toll on being able to pay for the ideal of the NHS.

The introduction of consumerist principles in healthcare is one demonstration of that; while consumer rights could be seen as positive in empowering patients, one counter argument could be that this empowering is taking place within a specific framework, where the focus is purely on the individual. In principle, this could work well in the economic domain but, even there, social critics like Barber (2007) note that consumer capitalism generates products that people do not really need and panders to infantile needs, at the expense of psychological and political health in civil society. This demonstrates that the 'logic of the market' is fundamentally flawed. 'Market principles' may ensure good outcomes for producers and consumers if objective and depersonalised economic criteria are used. But if we operate other criteria about our well-being and quality of life then we arrive at a different evaluation.

This could lead us to question consumerism as a promising pathway to good healthcare and good health. Drawing on our earlier discussion we could argue that good health is maintained and restored via interpersonal relations and demonstrations of care, affection and respect are often an integral part of healing and well-being. The obverse is true: pain and social, not just individual, suffering is bound up with social and economic relationships and cannot be simply managed away by consumerism (Bourdieu *et al.*, 2002). The atomized individual consumer of healthcare poses many challenges to the delivery of a complex form of healthcare. Not least, is consumerism an adequate solution to the delivery of optimal quality healthcare, and is it wholly ethical?

The introduction of managerial practices and definitions of risk in the health system can be related to assumptions of calculability and thus undermining trust in professionals. This undermines interpersonal trust where risk is evaluated through everyday lived encounters between professionals and their patients. Moreover, the traditional biomedical approach to health work reduces the complexity of the lived experience of suffering to a narrow notion of pain and risk to be understood as skin-encapsulated aetiology and pathogenesis. In contrast, a broader agenda has been developed in the social sciences, particularly around the notion of *social suffering* (Kleinman, 1988, 2008; Bendelow, 2006; Wilkinson, 2006).

The increasing power of the state for control over the governance of the healthcare system seems to go against the trend for state withdrawal (Harrison and Ahmad, 2000). Further, the drive towards growing surveillance of doctors, medical staff and the NHS would appear to be at odds with the drive towards the introduction of self-care, care in the neighbourhood, and care by relatives who sometimes need to learn very complicated procedures in order to be able to provide assistance. Here the competence and reliability are subsumed under 'attachment', 'intimacy' and 'care'. The difference between the medical professional and the 'home carer' is their different relationship to the state – the regime of their responsibility is differently generated.

It could be hypothesized that adaptation of states involves strategies that differ across different social fields. In this way healthcare may be sheltered from a broader tendency from withdrawal from healthcare support. Yet given the emphasis of responsibility to the tax-payer this means bureaucratization and focus on the introduction of accountability principles. A related feature of government commitment is its distancing from immediate involvement in healthcare through the introductions of indirect mechanisms of control; agencies, committees, special investigations and so on (see Chapter 7). At a time of crisis they can take up a substantial part of the blame while also ensuring a small-scale, and localized, rather than a systemic crisis of trust.

The simultaneous drive towards highly formalized systems of accountability for professionals and the relatively unaccountable non-professional carers creates a splitting apart of care regimes. On the one hand, there is confidence in impersonal mechanisms that regulate professionals within systems of trust that shore up super accountability. On the other hand, there is the ever present interpersonal trust in kith and kin relationships. The upshot is that accountability-centred confidence is in the ascendancy in modern healthcare, at times undermining interpersonal trust.

There are two closely interrelated aspects of the changing relationship between state and citizens that have an impact on the reorganisation of the healthcare system. The first one is that states are increasingly withdrawing from their commitment to welfare provision and are moving away from a weaker version of social rights, where entitlement is related to need rather than a reward for contributions (Turner, 2006). And the second aspect of this change is the increasing preoccupation of societies and governments with risk noted earlier (Douglas and Wildavsky, 1982; Giddens, 1990).

This version of social rights excludes certain individuals with mental health problems defined as an unacceptable risk to society that cannot be trusted to act as free and fully responsible citizens. Risk and diminished responsibility provide an ongoing justification for the use of state compulsion to incarcerate certain individuals against their will.

Some of the points we make are universal and timeless (for example, the role of relationships in maintaining health and in healing sickness). But some of the points highlighted by us suggest that our willingness to trust healthcare practitioners and healthcare systems are closely bound up with a new cultural landscape of risk elimination. This landscape is increasingly secularized, consumerist in character and unrealistic in its aspirations about risk elimination. How unrealistic this is remains a matter of reflection and debate for us all; we offer our view in Chapter 8.

Summary

- Trust can be understood as both a positive and negative form of dependence. This dependency can be explored from a number of conceptual frames and can be analysed at different societal levels.
- Trust may be secured through individual and principled autonomy.
- Trust is borne out of an affective as well as rational relationship and can be grounded in the struggle for recognition. Recognition has positive and negative aspects and can be conditional as well as unconditional.
- At the societal level trust is related to the concept of solidarity and how this shapes what citizens might expect from healthcare.
- At the societal level trust is the corollary of the risk society. The social anthropologist Mary Douglas has theorised different forms of structures of society where risk or danger play various roles. This may have implications for different models of governance in the health service.
- There is an important relationship between solidarity, trust and citizenship. How one understands this relationships is significant in the modelling of different kinds of health service.
- Accountability is a form of trust in systems and plays an important role in the health service where different professional bodies and

committees have set up accountability mechanisms to increase confidence in various sectors.
- There are different levels of trust in operation – namely basic trust, interpersonal trust and systems of trust (accountability) that relate in complex ways within healthcare.

CHAPTER 6

Framing Trust in Healthcare through Case Study Analysis

Introduction

The emphasis in previous chapters was to look at trust from multidisciplinary and interdisciplinary perspectives, peppering our discussion with examples from healthcare where appropriate. We now reverse the emphasis in our discussion, putting various kinds of case studies that say something important about trust in healthcare first. There are three reasons for this

1 We bring together a range of case studies that say something about trust in one place.
2 We provide a strategic device to bring some of our analysis together in one chapter.
3 We reverse the emphasis in approach, by headlining cases rather than theory.

Whereas in previous chapters we grouped our analysis of trust in fairly complex ways, largely depending on the perspective – that is, ordinary language discussions of trust, and disciplinary aspects on trust that illustrate previous chapter headings – we group the case studies in fairly simple ways, in terms of their significance and impact. There are two reasons for this. First, there is no ready and easy form of classification of case-study material that illustrates one conceptual analysis over another. The case studies illustrated in this chapter involve multiple readings of how to understand trust in healthcare. Second, we want to avoid any forced distinctions that overlay the richness of the case study material.

We group case studies in the following terms, for these reasons:

- *Medical scandals*: so-called because they have had such an impact that they have led to international declarations and codes of conduct (for example, the Nuremberg code that followed the revelations of the medical experiments perpetrated by the Nazi and Japanese officers/doctors on prisoners of war during the Second World War). They have arguably had a considerable historical impact on trust in healthcare, even though they are very much historically backgrounded in respect to more contemporary national scandals that have more clearly shaped the parochial and current norms of healthcare. For this reason we also include a number of national scandals: so called because they have had an impact on the national stage and official investigations are said to be necessary as they are in the public interest. Here we examine Tuskegee in the USA and Alder Hey, Bristol, and Shipman Public Inquiries in the UK. In our section on medical scandals and trust, we concentrate on clear *breakdowns* of trust, looking briefly at what this teaches us and how it has historically been rebuilt and reframed.
- *Medical controversies*: so called because they tend to pose more controversy rather than scandal, offering particular challenges to trust in healthcare. Examples we include here are childhood vaccination, end-of-life care, genetic medicine and mental health law. Medical controversies are less obviously about clear breakdowns or failures in trust, and more subtly about *uncertainties* that highlight current and future challenges for trust in healthcare.
- *Routine breakdowns*: so called because it is easy to overlook the everyday challenges to the breakdown in trust, through stories of neglect and poor care that are readily available on patient websites for example. Moreover, routine breakdowns also illustrate our personal anxiety and insecurities around hospitals that often escape any official record, but are nevertheless corrosive in respect to a dependency and compliance that is taken for granted in the role of inpatient. Because trust in healthcare generally gets a lot of high profile journalistic coverage its effect can be overblown. This can hide some of the more mundane and everyday breakdowns that can easily be overlooked by over-emphasising the dramatic.

Since there is so much case study material out there, this chapter cannot hope to illustrate all that is relevant (especially those that are most current). The aim is to create a fair cross section of examples that cross reference to our commentaries in previous chapters. Because of the strategic purpose of this chapter in bringing together much of the analyses of the cases in one place, the actual discussion of cases will illustrate a more elaborate form of analysis than previously attempted.

Medical experiments, scandals and trust

In this section we examine the medical 'scandals', initially dealing with three case studies of international and historical notoriety (Box 6.1) and then moving on to more recent examples from the NHS in the UK (later in Box 6.2).

Box 6.1   International medical experiments

Nazi war experiments and the Nuremberg code

After the Second World War, trials of war criminals were conducted before the Nuremberg military tribunals. They lasted from October 1946 and finished in April 1949 and involved indictments of all those who had been enrolled by the Nazis to participate in war crimes and crimes against humanity. Whilst crimes against humanity (genocide) were treated separately, war crimes were connected with plans and enterprises involving medical experiments without subjects' consent, upon civilians and members of the armed forces of nations then at war with the German Reich.

In the course of these, subjects were coerced into horrific medical experiments, which inflicted torture, pain and disease. They entailed shocking, wounding, maiming, infecting and killing those forced to participate. The chief scientific purpose of these medical experiments was to provide information that would benefit the German armed forces. They included: high altitude, freezing, mustard gas, sulphanimide and other experiments designed to glean information that would benefit the German war machine. For example, between about March 1942 and about August 1942 experiments at Dachau concentration camp were conducted to investigate the limits of human endurance and existence at very high altitudes (up to 68,000 feet) in low-pressure chambers where high-altitude conditions could be successfully duplicated. The experiments were to benefit the German air force, and inflicted grave injuries and many deaths on those who

---

were subjected to being placed in a low-pressure chamber (cited in Beauchamp and Walters, 2008).

Tuskegee syphilis study

The Tuskegee study, which remarkably took over 40 years to be exposed (1930–1972), tracked 399 African-American men with syphilis. It was premised on a gross deception about the true nature of syphilis and the fact that it was treatable (see Pence, 1995). Participants in the study were deliberately misled about what medical condition they had and what the purpose of treatment was. The scientific *raison d'être* was to have a deeper understanding of the natural history of syphilis, promising better knowledge of the course of the disease and to inform more efficacious future treatments. With these ends in mind, the Tuskegee Institute in cooperation with the United States Public Health Service (USPHS), saw an opportunity to observe (rather than treat) men who had syphilis of several years' duration (cited in Beauchamp and Walters, 2008).

The Milgram experiment

This experiment at Yale University was described in Chapter 3 in some detail (Milgram, 1963). It involved health volunteers who believed that they were taking part in an experiment about a memory task but they were duped into administering what they thought were electric shocks to subjects (who were secret confederates of the experimenter). It was thus a cruel hoax, with many of the volunteers being distressed by what they were doing (a few dropped out in protest, once they thought they were inflicting serious pain). In Chapter 3 we also reported the objections offered by Erich Fromm about the extrapolations made from this experiment to ordinary life situations.

Analysis

Talk of the Nazi war experiments, the Tuskegee syphilis trial and Milgram experiment may now seem passé. However, in the light of more contemporary medical scandals, all three have had a significant historical impact on how we expect healthcare to function as a trustworthy institution, not least because all three are examples of malevolent cultures that have deeply challenged what we take for granted in a healthcare setting. Generally we are acculturated to believe that in the latter, patients are treated benevolently and are not maltreated, that all patients are equal and that those experimented on are not cruelly deceived or duped.

Arguably, the Nazi war experiments, the Tuskegee syphilis trial and the Milgram experiment at Yale, have been notorious enough, in their different ways, to be labelled as forms of 'medical scandal'. Strictly Milgram's was a psychological not medical experiment, as he did not use real patients but the white-coated scientific authority of the experimenter offered an important link for our purposes here about horrendous acts carried out in the name of scientific authority in clinical settings. Below we note that its legacy is also, for this reason, more ambiguous in guiding current ethical practice. A feature that unites the three is that they have had an international impact. They have led to changes in research governance arrangements and their notoriety has meant that these cases are often referred to beyond the communities and countries of their origin.

Having briefly looked at some of the broader commonalities between the three case studies we now look at them individually.

The Nazi war experiments

The Nuremberg trials between 1946 and 1949 revealed a number of serious and obvious flaws in the treatment of prisoners of war and 'undesirables' in medical experimentation by the Nazi and Imperial Japanese army officers. The first and most obvious is that medical experimentation is not necessarily benevolent and benign. The Nazi medical experiments (as well as those perpetrated by the Imperial Japanese against the Manchurian Chinese between 1932 and 1945) were heinous and cruel acts that purposely inflicted a great deal of pain and suffering, often leading to death or grievous injury. Prisoners of war and/or undesirables – who were considered racially inferior – were *mere* means to supply information that would benefit combatants of the German and Japanese war machines.

There are a number of levels at which trust in healthcare was abused. Most obviously, it was an abuse of the doctor–patient relationship, established at the level of interpersonal trust. In other words, the 'virtuous' doctor that takes an oath to do no harm (see Chapter 4) could not practice experimental medicine on prisoners and undesirables in the Nazi death camps without courting danger. Many doctors in these camps purposely inflicted harm on patients and those who tried to alleviate it in small ways had to do so covertly. It was simply a matter of routine to damage, injure and kill 'out groups' in order to glean information for 'in groups', thus perverting the virtues associated with medical practice (see Chapter 4). This was not only an abuse of interpersonal trust, it was also an abuse of self-trust in the integrity that is necessary to call oneself a 'doctor' in the first place.

However, this was by no means straightforward. While malign camp doctors perpetrated heinous crimes on prisoners of war and 'racial undesirables', they often behaved kindly and decently to kith, kin and fellow nationals (Dimsdale, 1980). This was so much so, that if their professional help were needed in this different context, then their doctoring skills and virtues of character to alleviate harm would have been impeccable. To confirm these double standards about those warranting compassionate medical intervention, the Nazi period also witnessed 'involuntary euthanasia' for life 'devoid of meaning' (those with mental and physical disabilities). From our perspective now, this created a seemingly bizarre paradox: Jewish patients were *not* killed because they were considered to be unworthy of inclusion in a programme of medical ministry (Burleigh, 1994; Lifton, 1986). This highlights that, pre-Nuremberg, medical ethics existed but they were not applied universally to all human beings. Nazi doctors could inflict pain on some and murder others with an apparently clear conscience and in a subjective state of what they considered to be complete professional integrity.

The Nazi period also highlighted something important about a form of malign trust in systems and procedures that become routinized, in what Arendt (1963) called the 'banality of evil'. With the latter, those that carry out unspeakable pain and suffering do so in a form of blind obedience to certain norms where 'outgroups' are routinely maltreated and killed. This is connected to what we have called, elsewhere, 'followship' (see Chapter 3), where those acting cruelly are doing so by following a kind of accepted 'group think' that this is acceptable and necessary for attaining some form of perverted notion of a higher good.

If the breakdown of trust can be analysed at different levels that involve different kinds of trust, the rebuilding of trust at Nuremberg in healthcare after the War, involved a number of clear outcomes that are at the background of some of the taken-for-granted norms we recognize today. For example, the Nuremberg Code established the important principle of 'voluntary consent', which is the historical forerunner of what we now know as 'informed consent'. Voluntary consent helped safeguard the fact that the means of experimentation do not justify the ends. Ironically, the Nazi war experiments mined a lot of useful data and knowledge about human injury, infection and endurance. However, this knowledge does not in any way justify the means to which it was obtained. Not only did Nuremberg establish a moral basis for medical experimentation, it provided its legal enforceability through international law. It signalled a significant watershed with the past, where moral codes of conduct had been internally regulated by medical professionals through covenants and oaths, which could be applied arbitrarily to some patients and not others at the discretion of doctors.

Tuskegee and Milgram

The big difference between Nazi and Japanese war experiments and the Tuskegee and Milgram experiments is that, while the war experiments involved the transparent coercion of people into experiments, the Tuskegee and Milgram experiments relied on deceiving its participants. Whilst these are clearly different ways of abusing trust in healthcare, they are both malign forms of trust that lead to different kinds of damage. In the case of Tuskegee, this led to African-Americans being deliberately misled about the true state of their health, with the result that the participants in the syphilis trial were prevented from genuinely knowing what they had, thus preventing the procurement of knowledge and early more effective treatment.

In other words, Tuskegee was based on a form of significant medical neglect that had serious psychological and physical consequences, that is those duped into participation were angry at being lied to on racial grounds and had to contend with symptoms that could no longer be treated effectively, once syphilis was well established in the later phases of the condition. This denied the African-American group the knowledge, choices and early treatment that they needed. If the outcome of Tuskegee represented psychological and physical harm, then Milgram marked a psychological abuse in experimentation. In the case of the Milgram experiment, participants were psychologically rather than physically abused, as for all Milgram's barbarous appearances, it was purely a cruel hoax, which uncovered some interesting features about what we have called 'followship' (see Chapter 3). Like coercion, deception is an abuse of trust. Deception is the antithesis of honesty, which is an essential ingredient in any interpersonal form of trust (see Chapter 2).

While the Tuskegee syphilis trial was clearly a form of deception, it was not straightforwardly malevolent in the way one person may get pleasure in hurting another (sadism) or in treating people as straightforward inferiors/non-persons (the Nazi experiments). What is important to understand in the Tuskegee case is the cultural context of abuse – in the Southern States of America between from the 1930s and well into the 1960s and 1970s, African-Americans were seen as 'lesser' than 'whites'. Unlike, the Nazi war experiments, where eugenics and prejudice also featured, the intention was less straightforwardly malevolent, in that prejudice was affected by misplaced paternalism. That is, the paternalistic rationale for keeping uneducated black men in the dark about their condition was that they were 'like children' and had to be protected from any genuine knowledge about their condition.

'Bad blood' became a euphemism to cover up the true label of their condition: syphilis. What is interesting is that this mirrors old-fashioned medical paternalism, where the doctor knows best and infantilizes their patient thus denying autonomy to make self-determining choices. While such views about illiterate black men held by those managing the syphilis trial led to malign consequences, this did not necessarily follow from malevolent intentions. That is, prejudicial views about blacks hooked into and exacerbated a more general problem with the old-fashioned medical paternalism – denying any voice or choice (see Chapter 4).

Finally in this section we can note that because the Milgram experiment did not involve patients, but healthy volunteers, its legacy has been less clear cut than that of Nuremberg and Tuskegee. Whereas now medical experimentation with patients ethically precludes deception, the latter remains common in psychology experiments, leading some to defend this outcome on grounds of legitimate knowledge production and others to argue that it should be deemed unequivocally unethical (Baumrind, 1985). The unease of the second, dissenting, group reflects the stricture of the 1964 Declaration of Helsinki, which stated that 'In research on man [sic], the interest of science and society should never take precedence over considerations related to the well-being of the subject.' This principle from the World Medical Association has still not been adopted by professional psychological bodies internationally (World Medical Association, 1964).

Having concentrated on experiments that have had an international impact, we now turn to well known national Public Inquiries, that have been set up in the wake of relatively recent medical scandals in the UK. These are summarized in Box 6.2.

Box 6.2 National public inquiries, medical scandals and trust

The Shipman Inquiry (Smith, 2002; Smith, 2003a, 2003b; Smith, 2004a, 2004b)

Harold Shipman was a GP and the UK's worst serial killer, murdering 215 patients under his care. He graduated from Leeds University Medical School in 1970. Five years later he joined a GP practice in Todmodern, West Yorkshire, where he was caught unlawfully obtaining Pethidine to which he was addicted. He was probably killing elderly patients by the late 1970s and was nearly caught in the act by a district nurse in 1989 when he was a GP in Hyde, Greater Manchester. In 1993 when Shipman set up a solo practice in Market Street, Hyde, where there were more opportunities to kill elderly patients. In 1998 Shipman was finally arrested for the murder of Kathleen Grundy. Between joining the single-handed practice in 1992 and finally getting caught in 1998, his killing rate rose dramatically. In 1997 alone he killed as many as 37 patients. When he was arrested for killing Mrs Grundy and badly forging a will, which raised the suspicions of her lawyer daughter, Angela Woodruff, Shipman was killing at a rate of once every 10 days. The public inquiry into the murders concluded that by this time Shipman was 'no longer in touch with reality' (Smith, 2002). Two years after his arrest in 1999, Dame Janet Smith led that inquiry into the Shipman case, publishing three reports between 2001 and 2003 – the remaining two reports were published after his suicide in 2004.

The Bristol Inquiry (Kennedy, 2001)

A public inquiry was launched into the treatment and care of babies undergoing complex heart surgery at the Bristol Royal Infirmary 1984–1995. The abnormally high death rates among babies at the hospital led the parents of the children who died, or were brain damaged in or after heart surgery, to want to know why. The lead government health minister at the time, Frank Dobson, announced a Public Inquiry in June 1998 led by Professor Kennedy. This followed a separate inquiry by the GMC which had found Bristol surgeons to be guilty of serious professional misconduct.

> *The Alder Hey Inquiry* (Redfern, 2001)
>
> Another Public Inquiry, about research practices at Alder Hey Children's Hospital, Liverpool, was implemented as it emerged that, in 1999, whole organs and organ systems had been removed from recently dead children without the proper consent of their parents. This led to parents burying their children incomplete, without knowing that they had been systematically stripped of their organs. The inquiry was headed by Lord Redfern QC and is sometimes also referred to under that name.

Analysis

The common thread in all these UK medical scandals – Shipman, Bristol and Alder Hey – is that they all went to Public Inquires. These are independent bodies that are set up if serious breaches of accepted practice (in this case healthcare practice) come to light and their investigation is deemed to be in the public interest. Their remit is to examine breakdowns of trust at all kinds of levels, to both review and re-establish acceptable norms of practice. In doing so, their function is curiously reactive, that is, they tend to be established after a very serious incident or set of incidents, where trust has *already* broken down. In other words they are restorative mechanisms that tend towards re-establishing public confidence, even though arguably they are, as it were, 'closing the stable door after the horse has bolted'.

While such mechanisms are very analytically thorough in identifying how various kinds and levels of trust have broken down, they are primarily concerned with learning about systems of accountability that regulate the individual and their relationship with others. While this ensures some public transparency and confidence with recommendations about new checking policies for the future, it does so by actively doubting individual professionals and their interpersonal and self-regulating relationships with colleagues. This 'leaving nothing to chance' approach to new policies and procedures is thus at the (further) expense of a form of self-trust that individuals have in themselves, and interpersonal trust, which teams of professionals have in each other. While accountability in systems is important, it can become a form of 'hyper-' or 'super-' accountability that damages and erodes trust in the self and others (see Chapter 7).

This leaves Public Inquiries open to the charge that such a balance is wrongly placed and that their recommendations perpetuate the myth of a perfectable utopian healthcare system. Having made some general comments that draw some broad similarities between the public inquiries of interest, we now analyse them individually.

The Shipman Inquiry

The Shipman case involves a breakdown of trust at three identifiable levels. First of all, it illustrates a breakdown in basic or *self-trust* in Shipman's psychological state to be able to practice medicine. Individuals like Shipman can manoeuvre themselves into positions of power over patients where they may grossly abuse the trust invested in them. Because Shipman resisted any formal psychiatric and psychological investigation, it is difficult to say what motivated him to murder elderly patients under his care. Any deeper investigation into his state of mind was thwarted by his suicide in 2004. Whatever his motivation, the basic or self-trust doctors need to have in themselves in order to treat all patients benevolently was missing in Shipman.

Interestingly, the Shipman case is by no means unique, if one takes a careful historical look at other rogue professionals. From a contemporary perspective this is evidenced by Beverley Allitt, a specialist nurse, who was diagnosed subsequently with 'Munchausen's syndrome by proxy' and who murdered four children under her care (http://www.angelfire.com/fl5/ikill4attention/). Moreover, there was the rogue pathologist, Professor Van Velzen, who, while he did not kill, was arrogantly unrepentant after carrying out distressing and improper postmortems on children without parental permission in the Alder Hey case (see Redfern, 2001).

Second, the Shipman case illustrates a deliberate abuse of *interpersonal trust*. That is, Shipman engineered himself into a position of being able to kill at will, by eventually ending up in a single-handed GP practice and purposely inveigling his way into people's confidence. Interestingly, even after Shipman had been charged with murder, there was a group of people who had confidence in his doctoring and organised a campaign to defend him. This was partly because Shipman's *modus operandi* was to kill a certain group of people – elderly and vulnerable patients. It was also partly because Shipman had so successfully exploited the paternalistic image of an old-fashioned doctor that spent time with patients and listened to them.

Indeed, he deliberately went out of his way to cultivate an image of an 'old-fashioned doctor', so that he could kill elderly patients. While he might have cared for some, it was a cover for his more nefarious practices. In other words he cynically abused traditional medical paternalism in order to commit murder. Whilst this was blatantly an abuse of interpersonal trust, it was a malevolent and cynical abuse of a trusted relationship that is almost always benevolent. What was so shocking about the Shipman case was that it highlighted our taken-for-granted trust in the integrity of a doctor's mission to preserve life and treat it with reverence.

Third, while the Shipman case is more obviously about the trustworthiness of the individual and interpersonal integrity, it is also an account about shoring up *systems of accountability* to stop such abuses happening again. In other words in the third and fourth Shipman reports (Smith, 2003b and Smith, 2004a), presided over by Dame Janet Smith, there were recommendations that tightened up procedures that might detect another Shipman. For example, the third report picked up on the issuing of death certificates by simply stating 'natural causes' (that allowed Shipman to evade the notice of coroners altogether).

This third report called for: radical reform of the coronial service; medical coroners to work with judicial coroners; revised certificates to be completed for all deaths; the General Medical Council to impose on doctors a duty to cooperate with the certification system; random and targeted checks of certificates; and deaths possibly due to medical error or negligence to be investigated by the coronial service. The subsequent fourth report tightened up the legislation on controlled drugs (the latter allowed Shipman easy access to morphine without being accountable). Thus whilst starting with an investigation into a highly deviant individual, the Inquiry was a springboard to rule on systemic trust (see Chapter 7).

There are a number of features that mark out Bristol and Alder Hey public inquiries from the Shipman Inquiry – some of which are more obvious than others. First, they marked a breakdown of trust that occurred in secondary as opposed to primary care. Second, they were abuses of trust that were less nefarious in nature – in that patients were not intentionally murdered. Third, while the breakdown of trust involved incompetent, insensitive and arrogant individuals, the problem lay more in malfunctioning teams and dubious cultures, which enabled some rogue individuals to practice. Having noted these differences between Shipman and Bristol and Alder Hey, we now turn to individual analyses of the latter two.

The Bristol Inquiry

At the beginning of the report of the Public Inquiry into children's heart surgery at the Bristol Royal Infirmary 1984–1995, there is a clear opening statement about the locus and nature of the problem:

> The story of the paediatric cardiac surgical service in Bristol is *not an account of bad people. Nor is it account of people who did not care, nor of people who wilfully harmed patients.* It is an account of people who cared greatly about human suffering, and were dedicated and well motivated. Sadly, some lacked insight and their behaviour was flawed. Many failed to communicate with each other, and to work together effectively for the interests of their patients. There was a lack of *leadership* and *teamwork* [emphasis added]. (Kennedy, 2001)

That is, it was not so much a problem about malign individuals *per se*, but an account of failing cultures and systems of trust. The result was a paediatric cardiac service (PCS) that led to around one-third of all children who underwent open heart surgery receiving less than adequate care. Between 1991 and 1995, some 30 to 35 more infants died after open-heart surgery in the Bristol unit than might have been expected had the unit been typical of other PCS units in England at the time (Kennedy, 2001: 2). The summary and subsequent recommendations to rebuild trust reflect this.

The Alder Hey Inquiry

The scandal at Alder Hey on Merseyside concerned the improper removal, retention and disposal of infant body parts, without proper parental consent. This practice was also prevalent in Bristol and was not confined to these two hospitals alone. (This indicates a wider cultural problem at the time in paediatric medicine.) The central figure in the Alder Hey scandal was Professor Dick van Velzen. He was the head of the foetal and infant pathology unit at the University of Liverpool and honorary paediatric pathologist at Alder Hey. Whilst he was held to be largely to blame, it also involved the practices of colleagues under his leadership.

The dubious practices of the pathology unit were exacerbated by institutional factors. These included: the difficult relationship between the University and Alder Hey; a lack of clarity with regard to coroners' procedures; and the way in which the hospital dealt with the affair once it was discovered. Also, individual misconduct manifested itself in a culture of paternalism within the medical profession. This entailed parental consent being discounted and undervalued at Alder Hey. While there are many differences between these two cases, there is insufficient space to go into them in any depth. However, it is worth identifying some broad similarities (Redfern, 2001).

Some common threads between Bristol and Alder Hey

Both Bristol and Alder Hey Inquiries focused on institutional and cultural problems, more than on individuals *per se*.

- *Trust at the level of the institution – poor leadership, incompetence and poor communication*. At an institutional level at Bristol, it was a system of hospital care that that was poorly organized and was beset by uncertainty of how to get things done and who should take charge. This was complicated by it being a split site, with insufficient facilities and staff. At Alder Hey there was a period of institutional denial and responsibility. This was exacerbated by poor communication of the news of improper organ retention to parents. This was further complicated by an ineffective and complex relationship between Liverpool University and the NHS Trust at Alder Hey.
- *Trust at the interpersonal level – incompetence, collusion and deception*. At Bristol there was collusion between professionals who were unwilling to look at their performance in relation to other specialist centres. This exacerbated the problem of inadequate professional standards in paediatric cardiac surgery. This resulted in deception and dishonesty in communication with parents. At Alder Hey there was collusion between van Velzen and his staff, who failed to comply with proper post-mortem procedures and therefore fell short of expected professional standards. This led to deception and dishonesty, with parents of children being lied to about post-mortems carried out. Both Bristol and Alder Hey resulted in a less collusive culture, where procedures like consent (informed consent) were significantly tightened up in the wake of the Inquiries.
- *Trust at the individual level*. At both Bristol and Alder Hey individuals were named and shamed. However their underperformance or

unethical behaviour was embedded in a larger context that had to do with institutional and systems failures.

- *Trust, incompetence and blindness to unethical behaviour.* Unethical behaviour and incompetence was allowed to thrive in cultures that promoted an uncritical medical paternalism. However, unethical behaviour was less about intended harm and more about a form of ethical blindness. At Bristol there was blindness to under-perform-ance and its consequences for patients and their families. This is also true at Alder Hey, where many did not understand how it was possi-ble to harm the grieving process through improper post-mortem procedures. The culpable clinicians seemed unable to appreciate that harm to others in healthcare can still occur after the death of an indentified patient.

Having examined medical scandals and trust, we now turn to a similar exercise in the examination of medical controversies.

Medical controversies and trust

Whereas the last section on medical scandals concentrated on clear breakdowns of trust through malevolent practices, such as murder, gross neglect, incompetence and deception, mistrust through medical contro-versies has more to do with uncertainty, perceived risks and ambiguities rather than clear breakdown and failure. Examples are now summarised in Box 6.3.

Box 6.3   'Good death', genetic screening, childhood immunization and mental disorder

A good death

The idea of a 'good death' has attracted much attention in the litera-ture and the media. Schneidman (2007) lists the following optimal criteria for a good death:

1   Natural: a natural death, rather than accident, suicide, or homicide.
2   Mature: after age 70; elderly yet lucid and experienced.
3   Expected: neither sudden nor unexpected; some decent warning.

---

4 Honourable: emphasis on honorifics; positive obituary.
5 Prepared: a living trust; pre-arranged funeral; some unfinished tasks to be done.
6 Accepted: willing the obligatory: gracefully accepting the inevitable.
7 Civilized: attended by loved ones; with flowers, pictures and music for the dying scene.
8 Generative: to have passed the wisdom of the tribe to younger generations.
9 Rueful: to experience the contemplative emotions of sadness and regret without collapse.
10 Peaceable: with amicability and love; freedom from physical pain.

Genetic screening

The Nuffield Council on Bioethics defined genetic screening as:

> a search in a population to identify individuals who may have, or be susceptible to, a serious genetic disease, or who, though not a risk themselves, as gene carriers may be at risk of having children with that disease. (1993:3)

Screening may be a form of 'secondary prevention', aiming to detect disease in pre-symptomatic individuals, in order to provide more effective treatment in the early stages of disease, or 'primary prevention' aiming to identify risk factors or carrier states.

The oldest are Wilson and Jungner's ten principles for genetic screening (1968). Whilst these have, arguably, been superseded by more 'modern' reformulations – Cochrane and Holland's seven criteria (1971) and Cuckle and Wald's eight principles (1984) – Wilson and Jungner's original insights are still relevant and in use today.

Wilson and Jungner's ten principles are:

1 The condition sought should be an important problem.
2 There should be an acceptable treatment for patients with a recognized disease.
3 Facilities for diagnosis and treatment should be available.
4 There should be a recognized latent or early symptomatic phase.

5   The natural history of the condition, including its development from latent to declared disease, should be adequately understood.

6   There should be a suitable test or examination.

7   The test or examination should be acceptable to the population.

8   There should be agreed policy on whom to treat as patients.

9   The cost of case finding (including diagnosis and subsequent treatment) should be economically balanced in relation to the possible expenditure as a whole.

10 Case finding should be a continuous process and not a 'once and for all project'.

Mass childhood immunization

This topic remains contentious because it entails medical interventions which are imposed on healthy bodies without consent (permission is given by parents not the recipient of vaccines). The logic is that public health is more generally protected by reducing infection via 'herd immunity'. The contention only exists because vaccines contain an iatrogenic risk (if they were always proven to be totally safe in all circumstances then no concern would be expressed by those criticising their use).

Mental disorder, trust and risk

Whether or not they display insight into their behaviour, people with mental health problems cannot be trusted to follow rules and fulfil roles in a reliable manner. They have broken an implicit social contract about interpersonal reliability. Consequently, they pose a risk to social order and economic efficiency. It is a matter of constant debate about the extent to which each patient can be accountable for their actions when this contract is broken. In most developed countries there is so-called 'mental health legislation' which devolves powers of the state to medical personnel and allows them to remove, without trial, the liberty of people who are deemed to be mentally disordered.

Analysis

The concept of a 'good death', innovations in public health and the control of mental disorder are case studies that bring forth the problem of uncertainty, risk and ambiguity in what may be perceived as trust-worthy and taken for granted norms in healthcare. Lack of trust, in these case studies, has a completely different contextual significance than those we have labelled 'medical scandals', since in the latter cases there is an unequivocal breakdown in trust. In short, what unites these case studies are the concepts of uncertainty and risk and what challenges this poses for trust in healthcare. Having looked at the broad theme of what unites the cases, we now examine them individually.

Is a 'good death' a utopian aspiration?

There are a number of assumptions about what trusting in a good death is that have been summarized above: natural; mature; expected; honourable; prepared; accepted; civilized; generative; rueful and peace-able. Having said this, there is a lot of uncertainty about the trustwor-thiness of a 'good death' so described, largely because it is difficult to see how and why such seemingly straightforward criteria of a supposedly good death should apply. Not only does this obfuscate the actuality of many different deaths, it also denies a plurality of meaningful kinds of death.

To problematize the trustworthiness of a good death so conceived it is worth examining most of the criteria listed. For the sake of convenience we group the criteria into existential, social and practical expectations.

The assumption that a good death should be accepted, expected, rueful and peaceable connect to a series of existential concerns about death that are not in the least straightforward. Take the idea that death should be accepted: that is, willing the obligatory and gracefully accept-ing the inevitable. Well, such an attitude very much depends how stoical we are and what fears and beliefs we have about death. If we are of a stoical disposition, we may accept the fear of death with equanim-ity. In the words of Marcus Aurelius:

> Fear of death is fear of what we may experience. Nothing at all, or, something quite new. But if we experience nothing, we can experi-ence nothing bad. And if our experience changes, then our exis-tence will change with it – change but not cease. (Aurelius, 2004: 133)

However, such equanimity in the face of death is something that we can by no means take for granted. That is, while a Stoic may be able to reconcile the equanimity of not knowing, the experience of nothingness is very frightening for anyone who has lived a life of remembering only something (experience of some sort). Moreover, the experience of something new after death is also little consolation, especially if one believes that one is judged (in the hereafter or in the next life) by the acts and habits one has chosen and been conditioned into in this life. It seems like a death of acceptance is not so trustworthy – the more one contemplates what acceptance entails.

The next existential assumption that is highly questionable is the concept of an expected and mature death. The existential truth is that underlying the veneer of permanence – bolstered by advances in medicine, lifestyle and nutrition – is the actuality of impermanence.

Death stalks all of us unexpectedly, through careless accident, misfortune (accidents that involve other people's mistakes) malign intent, war, and/or underlying and undetected disease. While statistically we may expect to live to a mature old age that may approximate the national average, the fact is that many of us just don't, simply because we have not accepted the real possibility of impermanence.

Another existential assumption involves the idea of peaceable and rueful death. While some of us with strong religious beliefs for example, may be able to find comfort and peace at the end of life by holding on to the thought that we may be going to a better place, many of us will find little consolation in such beliefs. However, it is also perfectly reasonable to 'rage against the dying of the light', as Dylan Thomas would have put it.

The assumption that peaceable death is also a rueful one – where we somehow contemplate a series of appropriate emotions – sadness, regret (without collapse) – is wholly dependent on the circumstances and beliefs we encounter at the point of our death. Fighting for our lives may be appropriate when there is still some hope of survival, even if we may be facing, in fact, the prospect of an inevitable death.

Finally, the idea that death should somehow be natural is also questionable and uncertain. While of course no one wishes to be murdered or have an accident, there are other circumstances where a 'natural' death might be impossible. This is especially true in cases of terminal illness where the quality, rationality and dignity of our lives is eclipsed by the prospect of facing a continued biological existence through advanced medical technologies in a specialist care unit. Whatever opinion we have about assisted dying, it is often involves technologically assisted death that is far from natural. This may be welcome to some of us and not to others, depending on how long we want to live and under what circumstances we want to carry on living. For some of us who may want a dignified death, where our rationality to choose human ends is preserved over and above continued biological existence, a natural death may be difficult to achieve. This is especially vexing in cases of active voluntary euthanasia, where the dignity to end a human life may come at the expense of our continued biological existence. Voluntary euthanasia is illegal in the UK, even if the Director of Public Prosecutions recently softened the law on prosecution of those who enable the terminally ill to die – providing their motivations are compassionate and align to perceived wishes and interests of those wishing to end their lives prematurely.

If there are existential uncertainties about the prospect of the ideal of a good death, there are also social and practical ones. For example, the idea of a peaceable death, also involves the ideal of a pain-free death. This is a very modern conception of a good death. The aspirational ideal of a good death, in times past, had been about the ability to die with honour – that is, to endure pain, and to die consciously in full integrity of one's values and what one believed in. This has shifted, in modern times, with advances in medical technologies and the promise of a pain-free death. Where once we might have placed our trust in the heroic ideal of an honourable death, we now place our trust in the dignity of a pain-free death.

There is, however, a shadow side to the trust we place in the ideal of a pain-free death. First, there is the problem of actually achieving it, and second is the more pernicious problem of the price we have to pay for it. This is because heavy duty pain medication clouds lucidity of consciousness. In other words, pain free often comes at the expense of a compromise. In reality, trusting in the ideal of a painless death, may obfuscate another ideal of dying consciously and naturally. In reality then, trusting in a good death may be an acceptable compromise between the two. Such a delicate compromise may involve further decisions about the ideal place of death and how the dying should be best cared for.

Another criterion of the good death is the idea of civilized and honourable death. By civilised, what is usually meant is having one's loved ones around one with homely and familiar surroundings. Trusting in a civilized death involves an expectation about where one is going to die. Statistically speaking, most people that die in Britain, die in hospital – whether or not they are receiving care in an intensive care or high dependency unit. This fact alone is at odds with the expressed wishes of the majority. The latter would prefer more personalised care in a hospice, with an increasing number wishing to die at home. Again, the reality of where people are dying, does not match where they would, ideally, like to die. Furthermore, not everyone wants to die in a 'civilized way' with family and friends around them. Perversely, dying can be more difficult in the company of loved ones, unless both parties feel totally comfortable and accepting about the other's predicament.

There are further ideals about honourable death, by assuming an emphasis on a positive obituary. Although, this is an aspirational ideal, it simply does not always meet the reality of someone's death. That is, not everyone who dies was a good person. While it is impolite to talk ill of the dead, it is also inauthentic to eulogize and speak positively of the dead, when in fact they might have been quite awful when they were alive. Rather than being falsely positive about the deceased, it might, on occasion, be better to say as little as possible.

The final aspect of trusting in a 'good' death is about the assumption that one should be prepared. This can mean a number of things: creation of a living trust; prearranging a funeral; making a will; finding closure on unfinished business and before the terminally ill are unable to communicate their wishes, attending to an advanced planning directive.

Fenwick and Fenwick (2008) argue that one of the most impenetrable barriers to a 'good death' is unfinished business. They say that reconciliation is a necessity in the sense that everybody has the opportunity to say 'I'm sorry' or 'I forgive you' or 'I love you'. This is not only so that the dying person can let go in peace but also that those left behind can have a guilt-free parting. Of course, this is an ideal, and there are many deaths that leave unfinished business, mostly accidentally but sometimes purposely.

The other topic worth discussing further is advanced care planning. Advanced care planning has been receiving growing interest in policy circles (for example, Department of Health, 2003; 2006) and has been spearheaded by public and patient groups such as Help the Aged and Age Concern. Advanced Care Planning (ACP) is a means of setting on record the views, values and specific treatment choices of those living with serious, progressive conditions, future proofing as it were, the ability to communicate wishes to others. ACP can be understood as an umbrella term under which different aspects of decision-making about

future care and treatment can be made, for example, instructional direc-
tives (like advance decisions), nomination by proxy and the setting out
of general values and views.

There is mixed evidence about the acceptability of ACP among seriously ill and dying patients. For example Martin *et al.* (1999) in a study
involving 140 HIV-positive patients reported that ACP helped them
prepare for dying by facilitating and strengthening their relationships
with loved ones and preparing them to face death. Horne *et al.* (2006)
looked at the views of people affected by inoperable lung cancer in
Rotherham (UK) and found a certain resistance to the spirit of ACP. For
example, she found that older men, had the desire to dwell in the present and not dwell on a 'gloomy' future, to trust the doctor (doctor
knows best) and to be guided by medical opinion and finally had a
desire to plan for death but not dying.

Thus while ACP may be a sensible ideal, the way it is received as an
ideal, very much depends on understanding social preferences and
how they are constructed within their particular cultural frames of
reference. In other words, while ACP may be a worthy aspiration for
what it means to trust in a good death, we need to be flexible in its
application, especially considering that there will be significant resistance to it in certain communities, where people's values do not align
to its purpose.

To conclude, the idea of trusting in a good death is both existentially
and socially complex, where there are noteworthy and significant
exceptions to any aspirational ideals we may generally hold. Having
looked at the issue of whether or not we can trust in the notion of a
good death, we now turn to new technologies and the trustworthiness
of genetic screening.

Is the utopian ideal of robust screening criteria trustworthy?

Genetic screening has offered a means to advance the predictive power
of medicine. Again, as was the case in the analysis of the concept of
'good death', there are a number of criteria in genetic screening that are
supposed to make the technology reliable and trustworthy. We reiterate
the Wilson and Jungner's screening criteria and problematise their trustworthiness.

The condition sought should be an important problem.   There is a hidden
complexity in defining the 'importance' of a problem, a difficulty that

Wilson and Jungner recognize. The most obvious criteria that may help define importance are prevalence and risk: that is, genetic conditions with the highest prevalence per head of population and the conditions that pose the highest risk to both health and well-being. The 'importance' of the condition incorporates both quantitative and qualitative elements of evaluation, both of which are sufficiently complex to make decisions about screening problematic.

Take the concept of prevalence, for example. The vast majority of genetic disorders are very rare. Nevertheless, collectively they are quantitatively an important public health issue. In a population survey, Baird *et al.* (1988) found that 5.5 per cent of the population would develop a genetic or part genetic disorder by the age of 25, and 60 per cent in a lifetime, when common disorders with multiple gene predispositions are included. Thus what might initially seem a minority matter, as an aggregate genetic disorder, affects the majority of the population.

Gene or birth frequencies are the primary objective measures of importance, followed closely by evaluations of the serious health risk a defective gene or combination of genes actually poses. Post *et al.* (1992) have helped clarify 'importance' by attempting to clarify seriousness or severity of genetic diseases. They suggest three important dimensions: the degree of harm to health if the disease occurs; the patient's age at onset (early onset considered to be more severe than late onset); and the probability that people with the gene will develop the disease (penetrance of the gene). Such factors become key factors in the viability of the genetic screening programme.

There should be an acceptable treatment for patients with a recognized disease. To paraphrase Wilson and Jungner, of all the criteria that a screening test should fulfil, the ability to treat the condition adequately, when discovered, is perhaps the most important. One of the key problems with screening is that screening technologies that may identify a genetic problem and disease are far in advance of many effective clinical treatments for those individuals affected. While it is hoped that gene therapy may provide the opportunity for effective treatment or even a cure, it is still very much in its infancy. Gene therapy is a therapeutic procedure in which 'healthy' genes are intentionally inserted into cells using vectors (vectors act as transporters and protectors of therapeutic genes).

There should be a suitable test or examination. Having a suitable test or examination is not as simple a matter as it seems. There are a number of controversies of a technical nature, which make devising a suitable test difficult. One such difficulty arises from the nature of some diseases where it is not always possible to make a distinction between those individuals where the disease is present or absent even when there is a so-called 'gold standard'. For many conditions there exists a continuous distribution of variables, such that at one extreme, individuals appear diseased, while at the other they appear 'healthy'.

The test or examination should be acceptable to the population.   There are a number of competing ways of assessing whether an examination should be 'acceptable', with one way not necessarily mapping onto another. For example, there may be good clinical utilitarian reasons, in which the net utility (benefits) for testing is demonstrably clear to the testers. However, this may not sit well with *individual* wishes and motivations of those being tested. In the latter regard we find a range of stances from 'risk lovers' to those who are 'risk averse'.

This makes a difference to *hypothetical* questions about perceived benefits of screening and actual dilemmas that arise when one is *actually* faced with the possibility oneself. For example, prior to establishing mass carrier screening for cystic fibrosis, survey results suggested that the demand would be high. However, when an *actual* offer of screening was made, the uptake was considerably lower than expected, even amongst families at high risk of the genetic disorder, many individuals chose *not to know*.

This leads to an ethical controversy about the right to know and the right not to know, first cited by Chadwick *et al.* (1997), strictly in terms of risk lovers and those that are risk averse. The right to know seems to be based on a different psychological aspect of trust than the right not to know. That is, the right to know, is about *external* trust, trust in the 'objective' outcome of events, where certainty and reliability are in question. The right not to know, however, is based on an *internal* trust (or what we have called 'self-trust'). This is not so much based on the need for external certainties, but on our capacity to have hope in the future or, indeed, have faith in being able to deal with whatever outcome life has in store. This leads to alternative ways of dealing with predictive testing.

Take, for example, an asymptomatic person with a parent affected by Huntington's Disease, where there is a 50 per cent risk of developing the disease. Such a person may either prefer knowing and having the *uncertainty* about their fate removed or not knowing and having the *hope* that being asymptomatic will remain an open possibility for as long as they live or at least as long as possible. The latter is probably more unusual because it requires a self-trust that can never secure certainty that a test could (within reasonable probabilistic limits). The right not to know relies on an internal trust generating hope in a long-term future and or, faith – in terms of existential faith rather than wishful thinking. This allows one to face up to the very real possibility of one's own difficult death in the short- to medium-term future. This discussion connects to notions of self-trust and ontological security which founds it (see Chapters 4 and 3 respectively).

In conclusion, genetic screening and testing involve complex decisions which problematize the seemingly trustworthy principles on which genetic screening is based. While it would be too simplistic to say that genetic screening principles are therefore untrustworthy, the reasons for and against are often open to controversy, and need to be carefully interpreted on a case by case basis.

Can parents trust orthodox mass childhood immunization (MCI) policy?

Concerns about MCI are not new; they date back to the nineteenth century (Durbach, 2000; Beck, 1960; Porter and Porter, 1998; Spier, 2001). Today it is a routine and taken-for-granted public health policy but which is still faced with opposition from some parents, who distrust it for a number of reasons (Simpson *et al.*, 2001; Streefland, 1999; Rogers and Pilgrim, 1995).

- First, they fear that the health of their child might be compromised by the intervention from short-term anaphylactic reactions or from long-term neurological disabilities: the problem of iatrogenic risk.
- Second, they fear that the long-term integrity of the immune system of the growing child might be compromised by the aggregating impact of several vaccines: the problem of health being undermined developmentally.
- Third, they fear that iatrogenic risks will not be recognized and dealt with honestly by healthcare professionals and politicians, when and if vaccine damage emerges: the problem of warranted compensation being avoided by government.
- Fourth, they are concerned that drug company profits compromise fair and reasonable risk assessments: the problem of distorting commercial interests.

- Fifth, they note that informed consent is being denied to the individual at risk (the child), who at the time of the intervention is healthy and not a patient: the problem of stricture from medical ethics about informed consent and non-malificence being ignored.
- Sixth, they are concerned that government encouragement and financial rewards (for example, by meeting practice targets for immunization coverage) subvert the motivation of healthcare professionals (such as GPs and practice nurses) to be honest about competing risks for particular children: the problem of medical credibility and practitioner conflict of interest.

Thus parents who avoid compliance with this policy exhibit a form of 'situated rationality' and hold the view that professional communications represent propaganda not honest accounts. Moreover, their concern is with risk to an individual, whereas public health policies are concerned with collective risk, which generates a different rationality about 'herd immunity'. A stand off then ensues between professionals with their campaigns to maximize compliance and doubting parents with their suspicions about propaganda and vested interests. A spiral of distrust then emerges, with professionals arguing that parents are neurotic or feckless and the latter arguing that medical experts are being dishonest about iatrogenic risks and that financial considerations sustain and amplify that dishonesty. MCI is a good example then of how what seems to be a straightforward offer of health policy progress soon becomes contentious because of a lack of public trust (Taylor-Gooby, 2002).

McKeown, Dubos and Illich, introduced in Chapter 3, have also been critical of immunization on two other fronts, one empirical and the other political. First, they argue that the overall global downward trend of infectious diseases in the past century has occurred by and large because of improved sanitation and access to clean water and nutritious diets. Some non-medical technical changes have also contributed to this trend (for example, the risk of tetanus infection declined as the motor car replaced the horse, with its faeces as a common source of the disease). Second, and implied in the first point, a bio-medical focus may divert our political attention from the social sources of risk to health. An emphasis on the individual's proneness to infection may mystify the picture about the collective risk some populations are differentially exposed to because of their lack of access to clean water, good sanitation and nutrition. The latter require political interventions to reverse poverty and risk-exposure and such needed reforms can be shelved if a bio-medical fix, such as MCI, is on offer.

Our concern here is not to prove one way or the other whether mass childhood immunization should be seen as a good or bad public health policy (each reader will have their own view). Instead our emphasis is on the practical implications accruing from the stand off between mainstream professional opinion (supported by government officials) and that held by dissenting parents. That spiral of distrust is now part of our healthcare landscape.

Dystopias and mental disorder

Having examined the trustworthiness of utopias (about primary prevention, screening and a 'good death') we end by looking at dystopias of mental health and how this threatens trust. Those who are controlled using legal measures are typically those who are psychotic or 'personality disordered' and are deemed to be a risk to self or others. Simply to exhibit symptoms of madness or personal dysfunction such as hearing voices or having strange beliefs is not enough, it must have some social consequences – all psychiatric crises are social crises. Thus the trustworthiness of some people who are deemed to be mentally disordered is a focus for those of us who are sane by common consent. The unpredictability or lack of competence to conform to role-rule relationships arouses distrust, wariness, contempt and fear in others. These reactions then extend to prejudice and social rejection. A medical diagnosis for a mentally abnormal state removes responsibility from the patient but it also jeopardizes their right to be respected and socially included – it discredits them.

If people with mental health problems pose a real or imagined risk to social order and the well-being of others, it is also true that they have been at constant risk of unwanted and harmful treatments (Pilgrim and Vassilev, 2007). The priority of responding to the rights of the mentally 'normal' has ensured that those who are deemed to be mentally abnormal have been exposed disproportionately to treatments that are often life-diminishing and occasionally life-threatening. Moreover, much of mental health work is concerned with surveillance of behaviour and risk assessment and risk minimisation. These processes often preclude true patient-centredness in mental health work. If the healthcare system is not responding to the expressed needs of patients (rather than a defined need suggested by professionals or the expressed needs of third parties), then *ipso facto* they will not trust services or those who work in them.

Another consideration is in relation to the capacity of services to generate mental health gain from the patient's perspective. The point here is that whereas third parties might consider that continued detention is a good enough definition of the success of 'care' for detained patients; the latter will be more interested in their freedom from restraint and of a reduction in those symptoms which distress them. If service contact leads to an experienced *deterioration* in mental health, then the patient will lose confidence in those offering them treatment.

Another point to note in this section relates to the trustworthiness of treatments (whether they are imposed and so resented or are anxiously sought and gratefully received). Biological treatments (drugs and electro-convulsive therapy) have well known adverse effects and so elicit an understandable wariness in their recipients (Moncrieff, 2008). This negative reputation of biological treatments has led to frequent calls for the availability of talking treatments. The assumption is that the latter are benign and carry no risks. However this is not the case. At the hands of incompetent or abusive practitioners, they cause harm to patients (in the professional literature these are called 'deterioration effects') (Lambert, 2007).

Turning to those who never enter the psychiatric system, they may be its indirect beneficiaries. The central logic of so called 'mental health legislation' is to define the conditions under which identified patients are lawfully restrained, detained and treated without the normal due process of a trial. Consequently, those who are offended, frightened or inconvenienced by the actions of those deemed to be mentally disordered find immediate but not always indefinite relief from psychiatric detention. Psychiatry operates to resolve those social crises emerging from mental abnormality. But non-users cannot depend on the coercive wing of the state run by medicine (psychiatry) to permanently remove mental disorder from their midst. This leaves them with the anxiety that it will reappear to offend, perplex, inconvenience or frighten once more. They cannot trust the psychiatric profession to make 'false-negative' decisions. And because patients themselves cannot be sure that professionals will avoid 'false–positive' decisions, then psychiatric professionals may be the target of permanent distrust from *all-comers*.

The final point to note on this topic is that non-users are sensitive to the possibility that the civil rights infringements acceptable to them in the response to mental disorder should not be applied unfairly. After all, they may thus become a personal casualty of that potential injustice. This fear of 'unfair detention' was the main preoccupation of the general public at the turn of the twentieth century. Since then part of the legal paraphernalia of mental health legislation has been about 'safeguards' to protect the sane from psychiatric detention. This anxiety leads to the construction of two populations, those 'deserving' forced psychiatric admission and treatment and another group who are inappropriately dealt with. The boundary between the two is contested and so there is another dimension to trust that this implies: who can be trusted to put the sane and insane in the correct category?

Routine breakdowns of trust

Stories about breakdowns of trust in healthcare tend to concentrate on the dramatic; medical scandals and controversies by their very nature attract media attention and headlines. However, we recognize that there are many more routine stories that are often neglected, when talking about challenges to trust in healthcare. It is to this, often neglected, set of stories that we now end in summary in Box 6.4.

Box 6.4 Routine breakdowns of trust

Patient complaints, fear, anxiety and insecurity

There are many stories of neglect and poor patient care that are readily available on patient websites and that represent the less dramatic breakdowns of trust experienced from the perspective of patients. However, there are also everyday examples of our unrecorded personal fears and anxieties that are less about breakdowns in trust and more about challenges to trusting in hospital care.

Dependency and wrong-headed assumptions about professional care

Because patients are often vulnerable and dependent when they come into hospital they misplace trust in a service that many professionals cannot, realistically, be expected to offer.

Professional fears about patients and breakdowns and challenges to trust

Many patients either ask too much from medical professionals, or simply behave badly and unpredictably. As such, professionals – especially in hospitals – have grown wary and distrustful of some patients.

Analysis

Patient complaints, anxiety and insecurity

Readers can consult websites such as *Patient Opinion* and *NHS Choices* and find a range of anonymized views from patients about their experiences of the NHS. These are probably more telling than accounts provided under the more formal mechanism of the complaints procedure in the NHS (which are constrained by the prospect of a quasi-legal style of dispute and fears of recrimination for vulnerable patients and their relatives). The accounts on these web-based systems reveal that patients seem to offer compliments and complaints in roughly equal measure. Moreover, even complaints often concede good aspects of care as well, reminding us that the experience of care is not a black and white matter.

The negative aspects of care reported particularly emphasize interpersonal aspects, such as rudeness and a lack of compassion, which understandably create hurt and offence. At other times a loss of dignity created by the impersonal mechanics of hospital routines are highlighted. In more extreme cases patients complain of unnecessary pain and suffering created by healthcare interventions. Often the above are by no means dramatic stories but cumulatively they become significant and might be common enough to erode general confidence in an overstretched NHS.

The other issue that is worth noting concerns patient anxiety, often brought on by going to hospital and exacerbated by being dependent and vulnerable. Such anxiety about hospitals is not only prompted by a lack of trust in others but is also, more significantly, indicative of a lack of self or basic trust in oneself and one's ability to recover and mend. This is connected to our discussion of ontological security (see Chapter 3): it reflects our perceptions about security in ourselves in-the-world. Ontological insecurity manifests in hospitals especially, because it is here that we are most dependent on others whom we can only have faith in – since our knowledge of our own health status and prognosis is limited by a lack of specialist knowledge. Also the unfamiliar and impersonal nature of hospital settings is a threat to our sense of a confident place in the world. Hospitals demand routines which are inherently impersonal and these are enacted by staff, whom patients, at first at least, encounter as strangers. This creates the conditions, which are the inverse of a 'homely' environment.

Dependency and wrong-headed assumptions about professional care

As noted elsewhere (Chapter 3), dependency in times of sickness or injury leads to challenges in our trusting relationships with others. In some cases we are reduced to being highly dependent, in the manner of having our basic needs met, just like an infant. This is challenging because vulnerability in this sense is often a regression to some earlier state that as adults we can easily resent. This makes caring for patients in vulnerable states a tricky business. At the other extreme, dependency can be actively sought, patients often unconsciously manipulating professional staff to have their basic needs met. Most seriously, this manifests as Munchausen's syndrome, where patients deliberately inflict harm on themselves to attract attention. Interestingly, if patients' trust in professionals can be damaged or broken, then so can professionals' trust in patients.

Professional fears about patients and breakdowns and challenges to trust

Finally, there is the problem of irrational and aggressive patients who behave so badly that professionals lose trust in their capacity to be reasonable. This is most evident in A&E departments, where notices are placed, very visibly, warning patients of the consequences of unacceptable behaviour. So, as well as attention-seeking individuals, who might be labelled malingerers, there is the challenge to routine, everyday trust, through unacceptable patient behaviour. Given that many incidents leading to admission to A&E departments are alcohol-related, there is a disproportionate probability that admitted patients may act in an anti-social manner, compared to the general population (Pirmohamed *et al.*, 2000; Waller *et al.*, 1998).

Having briefly looked at some examples of routine breakdowns and challenges to trust, we now briefly conclude.

Summary

- We have attempted to reverse the emphasis on our earlier disciplinary analysis and bring the case study centre stage.
- From a case study perspective we have grouped trust in healthcare through the frame of medical scandal, controversy and the routine breakdown of trust.

- Medical scandals (international and national): these have included case studies that show unequivocal breakdowns in trust and subsequent efforts to rebuild trust, through, for example the public inquiry (in the national UK context).
- Medical controversies: these have included case studies that have highlighted risk and uncertainty in trusting healthcare.
- Routine breakdowns and challenges to trust: these have included examples of an everyday nature where trust in professionals and patients comes in to question.

CHAPTER 7

Trust in Systems

Introduction

Much of this book has been about the immediate face-to-face sense of trust, which renders the concept both a personal and interpersonal matter. However, people also embody group interests and they operate in a supra-personal context. This final chapter focuses on the latter, without losing sight of the personal and interpersonal dimensions of trust, and also discusses 'pubic confidence in healthcare'.

As an example of the link between the personal and contextual aspects of trust, we trust professionals because, as experts, they are competent to address our complaints. However, we also expect them to subscribe to certain ethical and moral standards, and we would expect them to be honest with us and act with integrity. While the latter can be seen as personal qualities of *individuals* they are also values that healthcare professionals internalize as an integral part of their belonging to a professional *community*.

In this sense, trust in the honesty and integrity of individuals is 'personal' only in as much as it is encountered within a healthcare context, where trustworthiness is embodied by *particular* individuals who stand for *many*. We noted in Chapter 1 that Hardin prefers to make a distinction between trust in individuals and *confidence* in systems. However, we retain the notion of trust for both because persons embody the norms of the systems they come from in terms of current routines and historical expectations. Note that trust in persons here does not necessarily imply familiarity (although it does not necessarily exclude it either) but either way it is clearly bound up with our confidence in the functioning of expert systems and professional groups.

While personal and professional ethics are difficult to separate, as they are embodied in individuals, it is nevertheless useful to keep them analytically separate for discussion. However, the broader point here is that depending on the way we frame our question about trust, trust in persons and trust in systems could appear to be contradictory, complementary, or in a state of tension. It is therefore useful to identify different perspectives, within which we could explore the distinction between trust in persons and trust in systems. Here we will suggest four different aspects.

- *Trust reflecting degrees of familiarity.* We can look at a change from the predominance of relations of familiarity within immediate localities towards relationships of interdependence with unknown others dispersed across distant locations and mediated by abstract systems. This is therefore a transition from specific familiarity to general confidence (Luhmann, 1979, 1988; Giddens, 1990; Seligman, 1997).
- *Trust reflecting change.* Specific descriptions of changes in healthcare over time also throw into relief the question of trust. In recent decades government and the professions have sought to re-shape healthcare (or resist those changes). Both changes and resistance to them have reflected new regimes of governance (see below) which entail questions of power, economic efficiency and the quality of the patient's experience. Descriptions of these shifts over time implicate new attempts to improve trust but, in doing so, to some extent they also inevitably express *distrust* of the regime to be replaced or reformed.
- *Trust in different levels in the system.* Trust in persons and trust in systems is also a way of exploring the interdependencies of relationships on the micro (interpersonal) and macro (system-institutional) levels. Here trust in systems could be discussed in relation to the specific expectations that different stakeholders can have from a set of institutional arrangements that constitute the healthcare system. These expectations are different from the expectations that we have from individuals, they follow different logic and lead to different types of contradictions. We trust persons and systems differently.
- *The role of trust in forms of healthcare governance.* Trust in persons and trust in systems could also be discussed as two alternative mechanisms of regulation of the relationships within specific healthcare systems – in other words different modes of *governance.* They could be related to different principles of organization, assumptions and cultures. The meaning of 'system' here is related to a specific form of governance, that is highly formalized and bureaucratized as opposed to governance where informal relations are equally or even more significant than formal rules and regulations.

This chapter will address all of these interweaving emphases by focusing on the British NHS – though many of the arguments below could be applied with caution to other healthcare systems.

Trust in a changing healthcare system

The 'crisis of trust' in the NHS, especially following the well-publicized 'scandals' discussed in the earlier chapters, has become a prominent discourse in the media and a serious concern within the medical profession. The 'crisis of trust' is often associated with a subsequent increased government emphasis on the introduction of accountability and transparency principles (Davies and Mannion, 1999; Alaszewski 2002).

This government-led drive towards the introduction of accountability principles in healthcare has been opposed by many professionals (though not all them, especially those co-opted to govern the local implementation of service protocols and audits). It has been argued by its critics that a shift towards principles of formal accountability is missing the point about interpersonal trust. Those resisting this shift consider that trust in their historically tested ethical conduct and autonomy, directed towards the interests of their patients, has been unreasonably displaced with counter-productive consequences. Those with a cultural history of being trustworthy are now being publicly distrusted and so are coming to resent and resist this change in status and reputation (Thomas and Davies, 2005; Kolthoff et al., 2007). When power is imposed from without, resistance is an option (Foucault, 1990). In turn the resistance is met with more demands for accountability in the light of non-compliance and so a spiral of distrust is created between practitioners and their managers.

The cultural shift in healthcare has not been limited to matters of governance. There have also been challenges to professional dominance in relation to the production, consumption and interpretation of health-related knowledge. Not only do non-professionals now claim a stake in these matters, there has been increased managerial and research interest, for example, in lay epidemiology and self-care. This has involved a complex realignment of relationships between professionals and patients, professionals and managers, professionals and policy makers, but also policy-makers and citizens. It has also led to changes in the internal structure of the healthcare professions and even the structure of the state.

Improving trust by this alteration of power and control in the relationship between the state and professionals has meant that the interests, experiences and concerns of patients and the general public are either mediated by the state or by representatives of professional bodies. Consequently we cannot be confident that we truly understand the unmediated views of patients and citizens. The shift to a focus on lay understanding, patient-centredness and service-user involvement has still been mediated by healthcare professionals and their managers.

What professionals consider to be patient-centred activity may or may not coincide with that of the lay people they claim to understand and paternalistically represent. A good cultural example of this currently in the NHS is when GPs claim a particular mandate to understand and represent 'their' patients' interests within Primary Care Trusts. It is likely that patients, professionals and government, would tend to have different interests, priorities, and understanding of quality, which would also reflect on what they would understand by a 'trustworthy healthcare system'. Thus although trust has been a driver in recent alterations in the power relationship between the state and professionals, it has not necessarily delivered alterations in trust from a lay perspective. True lay democracy is still awaited in the NHS.

Stakeholder perspectives on service quality

The trustworthiness of the healthcare system can be assessed on the basis of different aspects of quality. Donabedian (2003) distinguishes between six main aspects of quality:

- *Effectiveness:* the degree to which improvements in health now attainable are, in fact, attained.
- *Efficiency:* the ability to lower the cost of care without diminishing attainable improvements in health.
- *Optimality:* the balancing of improvements in health against the cost of such improvements.
- *Acceptability:* conformity to the wishes, desires and expectations of patients and their families.
- *Legitimacy:* conformity to social preferences as expressed in ethical principles, values, norms, mores, laws and regulation.
- *Equality:* conformity to a principle that determines what is just and fair in the distribution of healthcare and its benefits among members of the population.

Different aspects of quality are often in contradiction with each other and they could be perceived as more or as less important by different stakeholders. Take the tension between acceptability and equality. If we become ill, we expect to receive the best treatment that is available. We would like to get a second opinion for a complicated procedure and would want to make sure that the diagnosis and the treatment are appropriate. However, the use of some of the diagnostic equipment could be expensive. Thus one of the questions that could be asked is whether the additional information that will be gained justifies the additional resources that will be spent performing such tests.

In a system where patients pay directly for care this difficulty is solved by simply charging patients for all the procedures wanted by the patient or identified as possible by the professional. However, in a state-funded system there is a need to prioritize. The additional money and staff time that would be spent on such tests could (from the perspective of value for the majority) be better used to help other patients where the same amount of resources would proportionally make a bigger difference. Decisions on priorities also need to be made in terms of which of the treatments that are currently available are to be funded by the state. In these cases the principle of optimality is in direct contradiction with what is acceptable and desirable by the patients and with what can be achieved by healthcare professionals.

While we, as patients, are primarily concerned with how we are treated when we need professional help, the way in which healthcare professionals relate to us is also dependent on constraints that could be imposed by other stakeholders (such as managers and policy-makers). For example, we may believe that our illness requires more of the doctor's time than the time actually allocated during an appointment. However, there could be constraints on that time imposed by the number of patients the doctor has to examine and treat and the administrative and other duties that have to be met each day.

Further, different stakeholders are likely to have different priorities. Thus, considerations of the optimal use of resources (efficiency) and value for money (optimality) would be less important for users than they would be for managers. Professionals would be primarily concerned with the effectiveness of treatment and the process of providing care. By contrast, users would be primarily concerned with the extent to which the process and outcomes of the treatment meets their expectations. If we take the example of mass childhood immunization (see Chapter 6) it makes lots of sense on the population level, as it offers a cost-effective solution to disease management, and therefore would be supported by politicians. However, at the personal level, parents would be more interested in the threats and benefits to their *particular* child.

System stability despite inner tensions

Thus, the meaning of 'quality' is multidimensional and different aspects could be associated, to a variable extent, with the priorities and interests of different stakeholders. However, while on the micro level there are always ongoing power struggles between different stakeholders (for example, between doctors and managers, managers and government, and so on), at the macro level, healthcare systems tend to be relatively stable over long periods of time.

System stability is constituted around a constellation of institutions, and cultural practices. It is based on a specific set of knowledge, accepted and normalized procedures for acquiring, applying and evaluating such knowledge, and so on. More generally, system stability involves the normalization of a broad set of cultural practices and an institutional framework within which different stakeholders operate and strive to achieve their priorities, and in relation to which they stage their power struggles. Thus, for example, certain power disparities, such as between doctors and nurses, are normalized and, while power struggles are still taking place, they are not challenging the overall logic and functioning of the system.

Relative system stability could be achieved around different models of power distribution with either stakeholders having equal say, or alternatively, one or more stakeholders being dominant. Rowe and Calnan (2006) develop a matrix of high/low trust (here understood as stakeholder trust in professionals) and high/low state control, and distinguish between five models of governance of the healthcare system. These are: market, management, bureaucratic, shareholder and professional models (see Figure 7.1).

The professional model, which was associated with self-regulation and autonomy of professional groups, was put in place when the NHS was first created. However, it was already challenged in the 1990s when the Conservative government healthcare reform initially focused on the creation of an internal market, where self-governing units were expected to compete with each other for patients and funds. The latter model was however short-lived and was soon replaced by a new public management model, where devolved operational units worked under

Figure 7.1 *Matrix of high/low trust and high/low state control*
Source: Adapted from Rowe and Calnan (2006).

strategic central control, while performance was determined against centrally defined targets.

The shift from stakeholders to consumers

In the late 1990s, during its early years in government, the Labour administration favoured a stakeholder model in which health action zones and primary care groups encouraged active stakeholder engagement, communication and decision-making. Rowe and Calnan (2006) further argue that the later shift of Labour government policy towards a managerial and choice-focused governance model was mainly motivated by the need to be able to report improvements in quality. Thus, accountability was among the main reasons for introducing financial and clinical governance mechanisms and for moving away from the stakeholder model. The central role of accountability is consistent with a growing preoccupation of contemporary states with identifying and providing safeguards against risks, as well as the need to efficiently communicate to the public the presence of such mechanisms and the efforts made on the part of governments to control risk. We discussed this point in Chapters 5 and 6.

We will further discuss the different models of governance later in this chapter. In the following part of the chapter we will primarily focus

on two of these models: the professional and the government dominated, management model, because they have been historically most
significant for the NHS. Also they are diametrically opposed alternatives
in the discussions around 'crisis of trust', 'trust in systems' and 'trust in
persons' that were mentioned earlier in the chapter.

Professionally led governance: a culture of trust in persons?

The NHS was established in 1948 and until the middle of 1970s there
were very few major intra- and inter-organisational changes. The relationships between the main stakeholders (a term not even used then)
also remained relatively stable over the whole period. However, the
distribution of power and responsibility between them was highly
unequal. It was the medical profession that took a leading role in almost
all aspects of healthcare provision: from the creation and validation of
medical knowledge, through establishing guidelines for its implementation, giving and taking away licenses to practitioners, as well as all
major decisions related to the management of healthcare organizations
(Allsop, 2003; Allsop and Saks, 2003). Not only did medical interests
dominate those of patients, it was also unequally distributed between
the different professional groups. Thus, Turner (1995) distinguishes
between dominant and subordinated professions within the healthcare
sector, where doctors are more powerful than other professional groups.

   This aspect of medical dominance ensured that the daily politics of
healthcare were led by doctors and thus the 'allied professions' and
nursing had a knowledge base deemed to be partial, secondary and a
diluted version of medical knowledge. Resonances of this remain today
but are less clear cut now as these other professions have sought greater
autonomy. That seeking of autonomy reflected a distrust of a simple
dependency on medicine but it also signals that professional action is
self-interested and not necessarily orientated to patient care. Tensions
in healthcare 'tribalism' are time consuming and may imply actions,
which could undermine, rather than enhance, optimal care from the
perspective of patients.

   Whether power is held unilaterally (as it was with traditional medical
dominance) or it is shared by several parties, this potentially diverts
healthcare from purely patient-centred aims. However, being in a powerful position does not necessarily mean that power will be abused or that
those who have less power are necessarily worse off because of that fact

alone. Being in a position of power often comes with the requirement to continue earning it and a responsibility not to abuse it. When others trust professionals it puts a strong pressure on them to be trustworthy. This is in order to gain the respect and recognition of patients and to gain social (from society) and professional status (from peers).

For example, the scandals related to malpractice in the NHS, discussed in Chapter 6, led to serious concerns among members of the medical profession and these could not be simply explained as a fear of a possible loss of privileges. In contrast, if we feel that our actions are monitored and that our trustworthiness is constantly put in question then we may start acting accordingly, that is, either disregarding the interests of others or deliberately acting against them. We learn to 'cover our own backs' as a priority in our work. In this sense, trust and trustworthiness are not simply static attributes that could be attached to specific groups or individuals. They reflect *dynamic processes* within cultures; just as the exercise of power might divert professionals from satisfying the expressed needs of patients at times, so too with managerial controls and their provocation of resistance.

Until the 1980s, the self-regulation and autonomy of the professions were paralleled by a high level of trust on the part of the other main stakeholders. Thus patients (not then 'users', 'customers' or 'consumers') expected to be treated effectively and with care, while the government, expected professionals to use the available resources in a responsible and efficient manner. This system of trust relationships that was centred on the healthcare professional was often exemplified by the close interpersonal relationship between them and their patient. This was expected to be long-term, personal, intimate, face-to-face, one-to-one, and in the confines of the professional office, a scenario of special mutuality (O'Neill, 2002).

Furthermore, while clinical professionals, formally speaking, had a high level of control over the functioning of the healthcare system, the actual relationships within organizations between doctor and manager, for example, were not so much of confrontation and imposition of authority, but were rather relationships of divided responsibility. Doctor–administrator relationships in that period could be described as constituting a stable policy community (Salter, 2003), that is, a community where relationships were based on common understandings, language and values, and decisions were taken within an ethos of informality and cooperation. Managerialism has been the norm for so long in the NHS that it is easy to forget that until the mid-1980s it was *administered* not managed.

These broad set of relationships could be referred to as 'a culture of trust' where patients and government trusted the professionals with setting priorities and implementing them, while professionals responded by acting in a trustworthy manner. Differences in setting priorities were settled within an ethos of cooperation both on the macro level between professional bodies and government and on the micro level between professionals and managers within organizations. The stability of such relationships was built on the assumption that the professionals belonged to what could be called a *moral community* (Durkheim, 1992). The dominant position of professionals was not used purely in order to protect and extend their privileges. It was also oriented towards improving the well-being of others.

Moral communities or interest groups?

In pre-consumer days, when the NHS was administered not managed, professional groups could be discussed from two different and not entirely mutually exclusive perspectives as *moral communities* or as *interest groups*. It is a common observation that professionals are Janus-faced, suggesting that at different times they operate in both modes. Analytically we can still think about the same distinction, despite power relationships now tipping away from professionals towards service managers after the mid-1980s. We can still think of the professions as *moral communities,* where certain ethical and professional standards are an integral part of belonging to the profession and adhering to them is an important aspect of individual self-esteem, as well as for peer and social recognition.

These principles are deemed to be internalised, their application is mostly left to the practitioner, and are reinforced through professional organisations and the relationships of trust within and without the professional group (Evetts, 2006). The ethical and professional standards distinguish professions from each other but they also give each of them different places in the normative order of the state. In the case of healthcare professionals we would expect them to be competent and honest, and to act with integrity and care (discussed in Chapter 2). Nevertheless healthcare professionals similar to other professional groups also have their own interests and would want to protect them. As a consequence, the way that they practice and evince trustworthiness, and react to accusations of its failure, become political not just ethical matters for the professions. Whilst the Durkheimian view emphasized professionals operating for the greater good as a trustworthy moral community, Weberian sociologists of the professions have been far more critical about interest work.

Thus, the professions can also be seen as interest groups that are competing for status, income, and for increasing their influence over other professional groups (Johnson, 1972; Larson, 1977; Evetts, 2006). The mechanisms through which professional groups can achieve such objectives are embedded in an institutional structure state recognition. While debates about the current restructuring of the healthcare system is often presented as a power struggle between the healthcare professions and the state, here it is worthwhile pointing out that the two are also closely interconnected.

That interconnection is not new. It is even older than the NHS. For example, the state has always relied on professionals to act as their agents, in matters such as public health measures and mental health work, sickness certification, and so on. In return, governments in their formation of health policy and legislation have afforded professionals special forms of influence. More specifically, the power of the professions could be protected and enhanced through control over the process of the formal recognition of other professional groups (thus also controlling the legitimacy of their practice and the status of their knowledge), control over the production of knowledge (for example through funding) as well as defining the very meaning of (useful, adequate) knowledge and the criteria through which knowledge becomes scientific.

For example, groups such as practitioners of alternative medicine have for a long time been refused professional status. Here positions of power are closely related to the definition of what constitutes legitimate knowledge. This is a good example of the ways in which judgements about trust in healthcare are bound up with professional power. Doctors define what is trustworthy on behalf of patients and prospective patients, by their power to define what knowledge is legitimate and which practitioners can deploy that knowledge. This culture of medical control over knowledge has been disrupted recently through the introduction of competence-based forms of governance and manpower planning (the knowledge and skills framework).

Notwithstanding this recent shift to competence-based forms of working, as well as the general tendency in (late) modern societies for disrupting the link between the 'experts' and their 'moral authority' to guide our decisions, the medical profession can still presume and evince a proxy authority for patients' rights and expectations of trust in systems. As we argued earlier, drawing on the work of Giddens (1992), trust in abstract, expert, systems does not have an alternative in modern societies – the immediacy of familiarity can now only play a very small role in organising societal relationships.

However, earlier in this chapter we argued that trust in systems also refers to different governance models that establish different types of balance between stakeholders and make different provisions for their responsibilities and accountability. Regardless of the specific governance model, healthcare professionals are the most obvious repository for patient expectations. However, more distant and so less visible and accountable interests also influence this process. For example the drug companies influence medical practice and education on a regular basis and so shape what is deemed to be optimal clinical routines, which patients passively receive.

In Chapter 5 we also noted the ways in which healthcare commissioners now shape practice beyond the consulting room. It is worth noting at this point that whatever objections can be raised legitimately about professional dominance at least, as far as practice is concerned, trust in clinicians can be ascertained by direct 'face work'. While the 'ideal type' of the family doctor (where familiarity and continuity play a very important role in doctor–patient relations) is increasingly unlikely (given the increased mobility of people and the restructuring of the provision of health services), patients still, in most cases, need to make appointments, see clinicians, and make their personal judgements.

By contrast, the trustworthiness of drug companies and healthcare commissioners is not brought into an equivalent arena of personal evaluation by lay people during the face work of clinical encounters. Currently the shadowy status of these distal sources of power renders them both untrustworthy and unaccountable objectively. Whether they incite subjective distrust will depend on experiences of patients and their willingness to be critical rather than blindly confident in the competence and intentions of professionals. The over-emphasis in policy and in media debates on the trustworthiness and accountability of health professionals tends to shift our attention and the policy debate away from the interests and the power of private capital in shaping access and relationships within the healthcare system.

Returning to the apparent stand-off between the healthcare professions and the state (their main employer), professional groups play a key function for the operation of the latter. The two are enmeshed, not in opposition, much of the time and this is regardless of the specific governance model that is dominant in any country or at a specific time period. For example, the actions and advice of clinical professionals make a contribution to the health of the population. They also are given extended state power to regulate who can work or go to school or, in the case of some with mental health problems, even retain their liberty. Historically the medical profession has also determined who might enter or leave a country at its borders.

This devolved state power is called *parens patrie* in legal terms, which indicates that the state and its agents typically take on the role of a parent and that all citizens should trust them. This cultural legacy about governments is a very powerful basis for professional paternalism and for trust in systems being defined and operated *on behalf of patients* rather than expressed directly by them. The professional power to *define* trustworthiness trumps the simple expression of trust by patients, while the introduction of mechanisms of formal accountability does not necessarily give more voice to patients, but rather shifts the power towards governments (and away from professionals).

The two governance models implicated here, professional and managerial, make two different assumptions about the nature of professionals as either a moral community or as an interest group. In contrast to the moral community perspective we have the professional and managerial models. These models lead to different analytical concerns. In the case of the professional model – where there is more overlap with the moral community – there is interpersonal trust, trust-worthiness, cooperation and responsibility. In the managerial model any analysis must contend with notions of interests, power, status and conflict.

Which of those two models is more appropriate for the regulation of the NHS is in part, but not exclusively, dependent on whether we believe that healthcare professionals resemble more a moral community or an interest group. However, there are examples that would support both interpretations. As we noted earlier, when referring to the professions as 'Janus-faced', these roles are not mutually exclusive. From the perspective of users, healthcare professionals and organizations are *in most cases* perceived to be trustworthy. However, this is not always the case and professional bodies have been widely criticized for mostly taking the side of their members and for a tendency to only change if under external pressure. Also the public may expect a professional regu-latory body to permanently bar members guilty of malpractice but this is a rare event. Most are suspended for a defined period and prescribed training and supervision, before returning to practice.

One of the examples of how the understanding of professional ethics is changing is that in the past professionals were expected to refrain from making disparaging remarks about their colleagues, while more recently it is suggested that it would be unprofessional *not* to alert the appropriate authorities for unethical conduct of colleagues. Further, ethical conduct in the past was mostly focused on relationships between professionals and more recently have become much more patient centred (see Stone, 2003). The latter examples would tend to support the perception of the healthcare professions as closed interest groups, whose aims and priorities do not necessarily coincide with those of other stakeholders, such as users and the government.

Here we argue that in order to understand the position that the healthcare professions occupy in relation to other stakeholders, we need to look at the complex interdependencies in these relationships without reducing them to *either* relations of trust *or* relations of power. Both trust and power work simultaneously on different levels of these relationships: this is a 'both–and' not an 'either–or' scenario.

As we argued in earlier chapters, part of the complexity in understanding trust is that it, as well as other closely related notions such as power, risk, familiarity, confidence, as well as distinctions, such as trust in persons and trust in systems, refers to interrelated, but different processes. Trust and power can stand in contradiction but they can also reinforce each other. The balance of these relations also changes over time and currently the dominant governance model has shifted away from the professional-led model. The latter was characterised by high levels of trust in the professionals, and within which informal relationships were present on all levels of the healthcare system and were instrumental for its good functioning.

Government-led governance: a culture of trust in systems?

In Britain, the more recent form of healthcare governance is primarily state-led and organized around principles of formal accountability (Smith, 2001; Calnan and Rowe, 2006). It is characterized by trust in formal systems and leaves little space for informal negotiation. However, the changes are much broader and while describing this change as a shift from 'trust in persons to trust in systems' is informative, it is also incomplete. In addition, as we argued in the beginning of the chapter, such trust-based descriptions are also embedded in the discourses of change of only two of the three key stakeholders: the state and the healthcare professions. Patients are largely left out of the picture in a context in which British healthcare has simultaneously been *both* marketized *and* bureaucratized.

One of the ways to describe the changes in the NHS since the 1980s is as a large scale process of change in terms of:

- how scientific knowledge is produced and who is allowed to interpret and apply it;
- the extent to which healthcare professionals, organizations and institutions are presumed to be trustworthy (both on the part of users and government);
- the extent to which professionals have had the power to take decisions in terms of priorities in health-related issues.

These changes have also challenged the existing balance between the main stakeholders and can be described in terms of the declining autonomy and governing powers of the medical profession. This can be seen in, for example, the introduction of different forms of control to its clinical role, the increasing powers being given to managers, as well as a tendency towards increasingly intensive external scrutiny of medical standards and practices. The use of surveillance of the adequacy, competence, and effectiveness of the work of clinical professionals both intensified and was implemented by external bodies. These are now constituted by different stakeholders, such as user groups, managers and politicians, not just clinical staff (Harrison and Ahmed, 2000; Harrison and Smith, 2004).

Here is a list of some of the main state-sanctioned bodies responsible for risk minimization (and by implication trust maximization). The details are taken, at the time of writing, from the websites of the organizations involved:

- The *General Medical Council*: 'registers doctors to practice medicine in the UK. Our purpose is to protect, promote and maintain the health and safety of the public by ensuring proper standards in the practice of medicine' (GMC website). In the early 1980s the GMC was constituted by 97 members out of which 50 were elected from members and 47 were appointed by the Privy Council acting on behalf of the government out of which there were 7 lay members. In 1997 the GMC consisted of 104 members and 25 of them were lay people, while since 2003 there were 35 members out of which 14 were lay people.

- The *Care Quality Commission*: 'We regulate care provided by the NHS, local authorities, private companies and voluntary organizations. We aim to make sure better care is provided for everyone – in hospitals, care homes and people's own homes. We also seek to protect the interests of people whose rights are restricted under the Mental Health Act.'

- The *National Institute for Health and Clinical Excellence*: 'produces guidance in three areas of health: public health – guidance on the promotion of good health and the prevention of ill health for those working in the NHS, local authorities and the wider public and voluntary sector; health technologies – guidance on the use of new and existing medicines, treatments and procedures within the NHS; clinical practice – guidance on the appropriate treatment and care of people with specific diseases and conditions within the NHS'.

- The *National Clinical Assessment Authority*: 'We lead and contribute to improved, safe patient care by informing, supporting and influencing organizations and people working in the health sector.'

- *Council for Healthcare Regulatory Excellence*: 'the health professions' watchdog. Our primary purpose is to promote the health, safety and well-being of patients and the public. The Council for Healthcare Regulatory Excellence is an independent statutory body covering all of the United Kingdom. It is answerable to the Westminster parliament. It was established by parliament in 2003 to ensure consistency and good practice in healthcare regulation.'

- '*Local Involvement Networks* (LINks) aim to give citizens a stronger voice in how their health and social care services are delivered. Run by local individuals and groups and independently supported – the role of LINks is to find out what people want, monitor local services and to use their powers to them account. LINks will be established in most areas between April 2008 and September 2008. Each local authority (that provides social services) has been given funding and is under a legal duty to make contractual arrangements that enable LINk activities to take place.'

- *Parliamentary and Health Service Ombudsman*: 'We carry out independent investigations into complaints about UK government departments and their agencies, and the NHS in England – and help improve public services as a result.'

- *The Health Professions Council*: 'We are a regulator, and we were set up to protect the public. To do this, we keep a register of health professionals who meet our standards for their training, professional skills, behaviour and health. We currently register over 180,000 professionals from 13 professions.'

- *The NHS Litigation Authority:* 'The NHSLA is a Special Health Authority (part of the NHS), responsible for handling negligence claims made against NHS bodies in England. In addition to dealing with claims when they arise, we have an active risk management programme to help raise standards of care in the NHS and hence reduce the number of incidents leading to claims. We also monitor human rights case-law on behalf of the NHS through our Human Rights Act Information Service. Since April 2005 we have been responsible for handling family health services appeals and in August 2005 we acquired the further function of co-ordinating equal pay claims on behalf of the NHS.'

- *The Audit Commission:* 'is an independent watchdog, driving economy, efficiency and effectiveness in local public services to deliver better outcomes for everyone. Our work across local government, health, housing, community safety and fire and rescue services means that we have a unique perspective. We promote value for money for taxpayers, auditing the £200 billion spent by 11,000 local public bodies.'

- *The Health Protection Agency:* 'is an independent organization dedicated to protecting people's health in the United Kingdom'. It does this by providing impartial advice and authoritative information on health protection uses to the public, to professionals and to government. It combines public health and scientific expertise, research and emergency planning within one organization. It works at international, national, regional and local levels and has many links with many other organizations around the world. This means that they can respond quickly and effectively to new and existing national and global threats.

This extensive though not comprehensive list is current and so re-formable. It gives a sense of the state-prescribed sub-systems of accountability trying to encourage confidence in healthcare. The workings of these organizations are part of the current cultural land-scape of practitioners. For example, the 'revalidation of doctors is a set of procedures operated by the GMC to secure the evaluation of a medical practitioner's fitness to practise as a condition of continuing to hold a licence to practise. Revalidation's purpose is to "create public confidence that all licensed doctors are up to date and fit to practise".'

Another common organisational process on that landscape is the norm now of annual appraisals which 'regularly record an assessment of an employee's performance, potential and development needs. The appraisal is an opportunity to take an overall view of work content, loads and volume, to look back on what has been achieved during the reporting period and agree objectives for the next. Appraisal by one's peers and clinical mentors is currently part of educational supervision and employer career monitoring, but will, in an amended form, be part of a reaccreditation (or recertification) and revalidation process.'

Thus it is obvious that the recent history of healthcare has accumulated an aggregating set of bodies and processes, which are aimed at encouraging or insuring trust in systems. There are two closely interrelated trust questions that we can ask in relation to these changes. First, who can be trusted to decide on the *priorities* for the quality of healthcare? Second, who can be trusted to *regulate* the healthcare system?

The very existence of such a wide range of bodies and processes can be interpreted in different ways. For example, it could be seen as a signal from the public that they distrust healthcare provision and that the state responds to such attitudes by introducing different accountability and surveillance mechanisms. This is likely to be the interpretation of government officials. However, as we argued earlier in the book, there are a number of different assumptions within this argument that could be problematic. For example, there is strong evidence that health professionals are the most trusted professionals while the NHS is among the most trusted institutions in the UK. This does not necessarily mean that health professionals and the NHS are trustworthy, and indeed it might be the case that we as users of services sometimes naïvely, and blindly, trust professionals (as demonstrated by many of Harold Shipmans' patients, see Chapter 6). Another irony at the time of writing is that whilst central governments may be keen to problematize the trustworthiness of local clinical staff, the latter are highly regarded by the general population, whereas politicians themselves are one of the least trusted social groups in current British society.

Further, if we assume that health professionals are untrustworthy, it cannot be taken for granted that introducing mechanisms of formal surveillance is the only possible remedy. For example we argued earlier in this chapter that there are different governance models that are logically and politically possible. Moreover, as we noted at the start of this chapter, the topic of trust is currently a reflection not so much of trust in itself but of *change* in healthcare systems. That change requires trusting the new and criticising the old (or its opposite in those challenging change).

Notwithstanding the above considerations, there appears to be a shift in the perceptions and expectations of the public and the government towards healthcare professionals. Professional groups are seen as more closely resembling interest groups rather than moral communities and thus there is a suspicion among other stakeholders that professionals have neither the willingness nor the capability to lead reform in the healthcare system that will make it more patient-centred. This suspicion led to the introduction of changes in the functioning and relationships between different governing bodies, so that the power of patients and policy makers in setting the priorities of the healthcare system was increased. This was both on the macro level (where new regulatory bodies were created and existing ones were reformed), and the micro level where the doctor–patient relationship is now expected to be 'patient-centred'. These changes require less professional paternalism and more patient power and responsibility.

With regard to the question about changing the mechanisms through which healthcare is regulated, this suggests a move from trust in people we encounter to trust in formal rules and regulations. Trust in persons can be associated with trust in the moral responsibility and professional ethics on the part of professionals in their varied, extensive and moment-to-moment clinical encounters. By contrast, trust in formal rules focuses more on mechanisms of surveillance, accountability to formally defined targets and threats of punishment in case of malpractice. In the latter case, users of the system put their trust in a set of procedural mechanisms developed to address a set of expected scenarios of possible failure.

This recent offer of quasi-legal organizational mechanisms to ensure *post hoc* justice and reparation if things go wrong can be compared with the older tradition of *a priori* confidence in practitioners encouraged in the public. The latter suggested that all professionals should be trusted by all patients in the present to act now and henceforth properly *because they are professionals*. The circularity of this assumption is reflected in the connotation of the word 'professional' to mean a unique blend of selfless service, technical competence and ethical probity. In this Durkheimian view, all that patients need to do is trust every practitioner because the latter will *always* embody the trustworthiness of a shared moral community

The two systems of regulation, trust in persons and trust in formal rules, operate through different assumptions about the way in which the relationship between the stakeholders is projected from the present into the future. These two ways of thinking about trust in clinical professionals can be thought of by using the distinction made by Luhmann (1979). He usefully distinguished between *present in the future* and *future in the present*. Thus, by trusting persons we allow for a substantial component of uncertainty and complexity of the future to be solved through a relationship of trust that we have with the professional. This relationship operates in the present but is oriented towards the future which is from the perspective of the present left open (*present in the future*). In this arrangement, trust is like confidence that the sun will rise in the morning in the east. Each *individual* practitioner is trusted in a similar manner to the reliability of the sunrise; it is about confident and taken-for-granted predictability.

By contrast, in the case where formal principles are used, the individual agency of the practitioner is reduced to a minimum. Instead, possible future scenarios that practitioners and patients could encounter, as well as probable failures in these relationships, are more clearly identified in the present. These possible futures are often regulated in the present through rules that specify what outcomes could and should be expected. Moreover, it also regulates what measures would be taken in case a set of specifically defined expectations are not met. Both cases are examples of a trust where the future is orientated in the present. In this arrangement trust is like a car insurance policy system.

This system stipulates what is expected of the individual policy holder (their bona fide driving licence, their past good driving and their motivation and competence to avoid accidents) but it is the *system* which is there to pay out if something occasionally goes wrong. At any such point of redress and recompense it is the metaphorical insurance company (the healthcare system) not the individual driver (the professional) that pays out. As with the errant driver, there *may* still be consequences at the practitioners level – but not inevitably.

To give an example of the routinization of this method of future in the present accountability, we can turn to the overlapping work of the NHS Litigation Authority (NHSLA), the National Patient Safety Agency (NPSA) and the Care Quality Commission. In 2000, the government's review of incidents, accidents and iatrogenic damage in the NHS (a report tellingly called 'Organization with a Memory') revealed that every year around 400 people die or are injured in incidents, 10,000 people have adverse reactions to drugs and about 10 per cent of hospital admissions involve adverse events (DoH, 2000). The NHSLA was set up in 1995 to improve patient safety, reduce the cost of clinical negligence and to pool the legal risk of the latter to sub-systems of the NHS (now called 'Trusts'). The legal cost incurred to the latter in 2007/08 was £456,301,303. The NPSA acts as the 'intelligence wing' of this administrative admixture by building up a data base of the type of incident and their causes. The Healthcare Commission monitors the organizational health of NHS sub-systems and provides public feedback to make the NHS more transparent and to raise its quality.

In addition to these mechanisms of looking back and learning, there are also formalised ones now to prospectively measure performance and set targets. Comparisons between different organizations or practitioners are only possible through some degree of such formalization demanded by the arrangement of monitoring and public reporting by the state. If we trust the present in order to address the unpredictability of the future, then we put our trust in persons and assume that healthcare professionals are trustworthy. If we decide to put our trust in a system of rules and procedures individual practitioners are either presumed to be untrustworthy or the question of their trustworthiness is deemed irrelevant. We are now predominantly in a healthcare culture in which this is the case and the old-fashioned discourse of 'present in the future' has been superseded by system accountability. This has required a discursive shift for both staff and patients.

Thus, discourses on relationships on the micro level that used to be dominated by the 'staff–patient' dyad have more recently been challenged and there are currently other alternatives, such as 'consultant–customer' for example. The latter is favoured at present by UK government. A mere change in language is not sufficient to create changes in practices, although it could contribute to such change by imposing a new cognitive framework within which problems are defined and solutions are developed.

Thus, changing the governance of the healthcare system towards a managerial model requires cultural, cognitive, and institutional readjustments, as well as the re-codification of practices in a way in which they can be made measurable and comparable. The latter is based on the belief that it is both desirable and possible to enhance the mechanisms that monitor, compare, and assess performance. The model also offers a readiness to respond to new policy demands or even to adopt very specific practices, when the evidence warrants it or the political requirement is irresistible.

However, the earlier discussion of the different aspects of quality and the interests of different stakeholders demonstrated that the codification and formalisation of different aspects of healthcare provision could be problematic and possibly unrealistic because of the open-ended challenges in the system. Which practices do we need to monitor? Which ones should take priority and be given more weight in assessment? What about the variations in baseline activity and standards in different parts of the country or within different specialities? What is to be done if despite all the monitoring and performance management investment, standards remain unaltered?

Therefore it could be argued that while monitoring and assessment *could* have a role to play in improving quality in healthcare provision this could only contribute in a rather limited way. It is certainly not a reliable formula to create trustworthy systems for the public. More specifically, formal assessment would be more useful in assessing the cost-effectiveness of the system and thus could be a useful tool of financial control for central governments. However, it is less persuasive as a method to ensure proper democracy and public trust in the healthcare system. More patients being seen or shorter waiting time can be demonstrated but can it alter the rate of iatrogenic damage or reassure each patient that their idiosyncratically expressed needs will be responded to in all cases with due respect? The evidence to date is that such reassurances have not been delivered by a government-led preoccupation with consumerism and accountability mechanisms.

The meaning of the collected performance data is not self-evident. It is open to different interpretations and these interpretations need to also be communicated to different stakeholders. As far as the government is concerned, the interpretation of assessment data is linked to the immediate pressures that governments could exercise through increasing or reducing funding (depending on how organizations and individual practitioners meet specific targets). However, as far as users are concerned the availability of performance data leads to a kind of a paradox: the interpretation of this data would still need to be done by the same professionals who are monitored.

Furthermore, there is a widespread distrust of official statistics across the population in general, as such data is often perceived to be 'doctored' for political purposes. Interpretations offered by government spokespersons and media experts are often seen as partial, selective, manipulative and so unreliable 'spin'. Indeed, as we noted above, politicians and government officials are consistently rated among the least trusted people in society. The latter could raise further doubts about the benefits for users from the availability of such information. All it may do is alter the political dynamics *between different groups of professionals* in healthcare, with no clear advantage experientially for patients. For example, one of the foreseeable outcomes of the availability of performance data could be in strengthening the role of GPs *vis-à-vis* hospitals. Thus, hospitals may need to convince GPs of their trustworthiness, as reflected in performance data, to maintain a needed flow of referrals from primary care.

Further contradictions within the management model could be related to the tension between meeting government expectations and offering independent advice. For example, there is a tension between the doctor offering best advice to an individual patient and the need to meet aggregate targets (say about immunization) which are financially rewarded. Other influences outside of oft-quoted but simplistically expressed 'clinical need' of patients (which is constructed in the service not self-evident in one party, the patient) are from the drug companies. They influence prescribing practices through marketing and research.

Debates within the medical profession about the undue influence of drug company activity once more demonstrate how patients are frequently excluded from, or are ignorant of, background influences on professional practice. When these do become apparent to patients, then their trust in the profession may be undermined. An example of this is the pressure from the drug companies to alter the diagnostic threshold for the prescription of statins and anti-hypertensive drugs. Clearly the more patients on these drugs the more profits accrue. Can the public have confidence that clinical practice is there, at their service, rather than at the behest of drug company manipulation?

The emphasis on management techniques in the governance of healthcare is also challenging the traditional conflation of 'professional authority' and 'moral authority'.

Professional, scientific and moral authority used to be very closely linked in the past. The Milgram experiment demonstrated the almost blind faith in science (see our discussion of this in Chapter 3). The much more recent Alder Hey scandal (discussed in Chapter 6) showed how such assumptions of overlapping professional and moral authority, which were normalized and routinized in professional practice (presumed consent), could also be challenged. The subsequent and consequent introduction of informed consent reflected and reinforced a changing cultural landscape about trust in professionals.

Thus, it could be argued that professional authority and moral authority have now become separated to some degree. Professional authority is at present most closely associated with competence and expertise in a specific field of knowledge and skill. By contrast, *moral authority* has now extended beyond professional boundaries and jurisdiction into a wider and more diffuse contested realm of civil society. Many are now actively involved in this, including patient groups and faith groups. Examples here include debates about abortion, euthanasia and stem-cell research. However, lay people and politicians still tend to look to professionals as a moral community to speak with authority about such matters. Thus whilst moral authority has now leaked into wider civil society, professional dominance remains evident to some extent.

Patient-centred services and the dominant models of healthcare governance

Here we can come back to the five models of healthcare governance suggested by Rowe and Calnan (2006) that we briefly discussed earlier in this chapter (see Figure 7.1). Actual healthcare governance can incorporate aspects of all five models, yet with different emphases.

The model that is currently dominant in the UK is located in the space between the market and the new public management models. The controlling role is partly occupied by the state that seeks to protect, and/or be seen as protecting, the interests of users as individuals. While a state withdrawal could lead to strengthening a market model, it could also support a model that incorporates aspects of market and stakeholder models. In such a model the individualized markets could be countered by the establishment of effective stakeholder groups, such as patient and professional organizations (possibly also including government), where a degree of negotiation could take place. Finally, the state could also adopt a steering role within a stakeholder model, where broad principles are defined by the state but are then interpreted and implemented on the local level through an active dialogue between different stakeholders.

Stakeholders and diversity of needs

The emphasis on 'stakeholders' is relatively recent in debates about healthcare. It is linked to the growth of consumerism in health and welfare policies. It emerged in the 1980s and has now developed an institutionalized status in the policy developments of political parties of all hues. Prior to that, the unfettered jurisdiction of clinical professions produced its own good and bad outcomes. Then, as now, professionals were at their best when dealing very publicly with acute trauma; when rescuing the injured and saving lives in A&E Departments.

This provides a model for an ideal type of healthcare. Paternalism is maximized heroically to save lives and mitigate trauma. Consequently it has becomes the stuff of TV representations of healthcare and it reinforces public trust in *both* persons *and* systems. From *Dr Kildare* in the 1960s to the unstoppable record of *ER* and *Casualty* today, an image of trustworthy optimal hospital-based healthcare has been brought into our sitting rooms at peak viewing times. The recovered patients we identify with on screen offer grateful devotion to their professional life savers. The latter are represented as devoted albeit fallible humans, always going the extra mile in the interest of their duty of care to the injured and dying. This is a moral community *par excellence* with professional interest work hardly evident. Though sometimes there is an implied criticism of residual medical dominance, unfettered power is criticized overwhelmingly in the actions of managers. These cultural images in the mass media suggest the optimality of professionally led action and the undesirable cold impersonal power play of managerialism.

However, most encounters in healthcare, past and present, have not been of this type. Most are mundane events about minor illnesses or referral decisions in primary care. Many others have been far more sinister. For example, in his book on 'scandal hospitals', Martin (1984) examined, what he called, the 'corruption of care' in large isolated institutions; these contained patients with learning disabilities or chronic mental health problems. They were unrewarding and socially rejected patients shut away in systems of multiple isolation. The hospitals were geographically isolated and the professionals in them often isolated from colleagues in other localities. Further isolation was compounded at the ward level, where a 'fiefdom' mentality developed among staff. The fate of patients might rely on the ward they were placed on or even on the particular shift and its leader at a moment in time. This picture of vulnerable unrewarding low-status patients combined with multiple forms of isolation was a recipe for disaster. Patients were neglected, abused and in some cases killed.

The healthcare regimes associated with the corruption of care disappeared, generally, when they were closed down. However, even today their residue remains. The large high-security psychiatric hospitals were preserved and, in line with Martin's analysis, continued to produce scandals (Pilgrim, 2007). Moreover, his point about low status and unrewarding patients remained important despite de-institutionalization. In the early 1990s a *cause célèbre* was Graham Pink, a nurse 'whistleblower', who drew attention to the poor care of elderly patients in the NHS.

In recent years, British TV viewers have endured appalling scenes of starvation and neglect in Bulgarian residential care homes populated by disabled children, many of them Roma. These victims of the corruption of care were in isolated systems and suffered multiple rejection on the basis of age, disability and often race. Nearer to home, a full-scale inquiry was initiated into the neglect of patients in the learning disability services of Cornwall. De-institutionalization has been replaced in part not by ordinary living arrangements but by re-institutionalization. This being the case, the corruption of care is likely to continue but now it will be on a smaller scale at dispersed sites of nursing and residential homes.

These current resonances suggest a limit to the democratic optimism of consumerism in healthcare. Its ethos has been driven by assumptions of patients as worthy, morally valued, reflective, assertive and articulate consumers. But many who use healthcare do not fit this pattern. Those who are profoundly disabled (those with learning disabilities or deteriorating neurological disease) are not typical 'consumers' and they invite support and advocacy to prevent the scenarios noted above. As we noted at the beginning of this chapter, they highlight our interdependency. Consumerism assumes our existential separation. Consumerism and even one-to-one, rather than collective, advocacy are individualistic responses to untrustworthy people and systems.

Where there is systemic isolation and secrecy then supra-personal solutions are required about openness, transparency and social inclusion. In recent years, the British government has recognized the particular vulnerability of older frail patients and younger patients with learning disabilities. Its guidance on vulnerable adults (DoH, 2001) was reviewed in 2008 as stories continued to come to light in the mass media of financial and other forms of exploitation in care homes and in ordinary living arrangements.

As with Martin's review of the corruption of care in scandal hospitals, these reflections have also highlighted that the human right to safety and care can only be protected if systemic features are also addressed. An *a priori* emphasis on consumer rights and the *post hoc* availability of mechanisms of accountability and punishment for errant practitioners, discussed earlier, between them will not make systems trustworthy, though they may have a moderately beneficial impact.

Throughout this book we have tried to offer different perspectives on trust (distinguishing between levels of analysis, empirical focus, assumptions about the nature of agency, historical changes, ideological and normative perspectives). Generally, we have tried to avoid making normative statements about those perspectives, in order to offer a clearer presentation of the complexities of the subject, yet our own position would sometimes, and unavoidably so, have been evident. Here, towards the end of the book, and more so in the concluding chapter, we would like to make our view on these debates much clearer.

From our perspective, the improvement of healthcare will only be maximized with the development of services based upon *collective* demands from user and advocacy groups, rather than a reliance on the aggregate impact of individual 'consumer' behaviour and the offer of advocacy for individuals. We do not oppose these efforts but in our view they are not *sufficient* to ensure the democratic control of healthcare and its improvement for the greatest number. Consumerism will start a process of democratic feedback but it will be limited to those with the education, technical competence, confidence and ability to contribute. Politicians and professionals between them, to date, have not produced systemic safety for unpopular and vulnerable patients. They have offered no coherent ideology of democratic interdependency to protect them. Instead consumerism is considered the norm and vulnerable patients are provided with a bolt-on policy, in response to scandals, of more monitoring and advocacy.

Returning to the potential logic of a stakeholder ethos, what the idealistic image of A&E and the horrors of the corruption of care both draw attention to is the possibility of synergies and conflicts of interest. Williamson (1998) when analysing these in healthcare pointed out that the interests of patients and professionals may be in conflict or in synergy. She also noted that the uneven power relationships between stakeholders lead to a variety of scenarios depending on these synergies and conflicts. Moreover, benign paternalism may lead to patient-centred care being enacted in the ignorance of patients. For example, professionals might make a number of decisions in the patients' interest that the latter are not informed of.

This complexity introduced by Williamson suggests a continuum. At one end would be professionals making decisions in their own interests and without reference to patients. At the other end the opposite might occur – patients might actually avoid professional influence or even campaign for its erosion or abolition. For example, some ex-psychiatric patients argue for the abolition of psychiatry. In the middle are a variety of scenarios which are negotiated between the interests of each group. These forms of negotiation and consensus lead to various degrees of transparency for patients and partnership arrangements with professionals.

Power differentials are a product of differences in knowledge and in vulnerability. In any clinical encounter, the patient is disempowered on both counts (this is why patients tend to under-report concerns and complain less often as true consumers might). The professional knows more than the patient and the patient is in a state of anxiety and regressed dependency because they are ill or disabled. It is so easy in these circumstances for professionally centred rather than patient-centred processes to develop. This is why direct appeals to professionals to be 'patient-centred' will be met easily with agreement. How will those who dissimulate be detected? It is easy for any of us to say that we care in a patient-centred way, when in practice we may or may not deliver this promise.

Stakeholders and patients in the context of models of governance

So let us place these observations in the context of the models of governance discussed earlier. In the bureaucratic and managerial versions, patient interests are mainly defined and mediated by the state. Similar to the professional model, the patient experiences, opinions and expressed needs only enter into the system through the direct patient–doctor encounters, which however are in this case mainly structured by the state. In a market model the involvement of the patient is again primarily in the doctor–patient encounter, but it is the patient (who can pay) that is much more important in defining the nature of exchanges.

While in the other two models the role of patient and professional groups could have some impact, it is in the market-based model where such an impact could be most significant. However, a market-based model favours different patient groups according to their visibility and financial power. This does not necessarily correspond evenly to the types of illness and disability which exist in society. The needs and rights of the latter could only be addressed by a robust stakeholder model. Some degree of government involvement in a steering role could be helpful in addressing such power differences. Government steering is also necessary for countering the financial power that commercial interests (pharmaceutical companies, for example) could have in a stakeholder model.

Coming back to the managerial model, by introducing principles of accountability and surveillance this model of governance is undermining professionals' traditional reliance on ethics. It is also weakening established interpersonal and organizational practices associated with the latter and the ethos of 'present in the future' noted earlier. Within such a context relationships on the micro level are now mediated by either systemic principles of accountability and surveillance (the new 'future in the present' ethos and culture). But systemic guarantees are rather distant for comfort to the patient in their immediate encounters with professionals (legal action is rarely what we have in mind when we need to consult a healthcare professional). Other specific contextual factors still co-exist with or even override in some circumstances general system reform. Establishing good interpersonal relations in specific clinical encounters to maximize the chances of humane treatment and empathy is open to highly contextual factors. These include familiarity, fondness, mood, day work-load, class, race, gender, and so on.

'Future in the present' forms of trust in systems cannot on either logical or practical grounds displace these subtle contextual influences to create standardized clinical performances. Generally, higher significance of contextual factors is introducing a higher level of uncertainty on the micro level but it is likely to favour people who have a higher social status and thus is likely to further marginalize groups that are already in a disadvantaged position. Where there is symmetry, of socio-economic background, between professionals and patients this lessens the power asymmetry inherent in the relationship. This is why better educated and more self-confident patients obtain greater access to services, such as the NHS, which are free at the point of need to all comers.

Furthermore, it could also be argued that different governance models also prioritise different types of doctor–patient relations. Thus, while in the traditional, professional model the doctor resembles a parent, in the managerial model, he or she would be more like a stranger. More involvement of patients within a stakeholder-led model would have a different outcome. By developing mechanisms that would both change professional culture while also strengthening the role of ethical conduct, that model is more likely to offer an alternative. Relationships with professionals would resemble more closely those of a friendly acquaintance. The latter means higher levels of equality as well as more guarantees for care and empathy with the suffering of the patient.

Thus, the changing governance structure in the healthcare system is at present primarily a two-way communication between state and the profession while the 'interests of the patient' are still represented in a relatively tokenistic way within these discourses. While undermining direct user participation is undemocratic it also has very significant consequences for the quality of healthcare provision (discussed in Chapter 4). More broadly, each of those models offers a different formula about democratic participation. Each also makes different assumptions about the relationship between state and citizens (see Turner, 1997; 2003; 2007), the nature of their mutual responsibilities, the degree of solidarity and the permeability of social boundaries.

Summary

'Trust in persons' and 'trust in systems' can be explored from a few different perspectives:

- from familiarity within traditional communities towards trust in highly functionally differentiated, complex modern societies;
- a way of exploring the interdependencies of relationships of trust on the micro (interpersonal) and macro (system–institutional) levels;
- as two alternative mechanisms of regulation of the relationships within specific healthcare systems;
- as a reflection of change that could be most closely associated with government and the professions.

Quality of healthcare can be discussed in relation to effectiveness, efficiency, optimality, acceptability, legitimacy, and equality, however:

- understanding of quality and priorities change with the change of positioning;
- there are irreconcilable contradictions between principles of quality and interests between groups; those could be balanced but cannot be permanently resolved.

We can distinguish between five, ideal-type, models of governance of the healthcare system. These are: market, management, bureaucratic, stakeholder and professional models.

- The dominant ones are the professional and more recently the managerial.
- Actual models of healthcare governance necessarily incorporate aspects of all five models, yet with different emphasis.
- Each model makes a number of assumptions and normalizes specific (usually in some respects unequal) distribution of power among stakeholders and social groups.
- There is a tendency to move towards a managerial model.
- Changes in the governance of the healthcare system towards a managerial model requires cultural, cognitive, and institutional readjustments as well as the re-codification of practices in a way in which they can be made measurable and comparable.
- All ideal type models could be 'patient-centred' to some extent. However, it is only in the stakeholder model, where patients would have an unmediated voice in the organization and day-to-day functioning of the healthcare system, as well as in personalised clinical encounters, that would minimize power discrepancies and maximize healthcare democracy.

CHAPTER 8

Conclusion

Below we offer an overview of our overall approach and what we consider that it adds to the debate on trust in healthcare. At the end, we lay out some analytical and political implications of the preceding chapters. There has been an unashamed complexity in our exploration of our topic throughout the book – because the topic is complicated. We hope that readers have been able to hold that complexity in mind when moving from chapter to chapter. At the outset we suggested a form of *triangulation* to ease the challenge of such a complicated picture. This approach has entailed three modes of analysis deployed with different nuances or emphases in each chapter:

- *Perspectives on trust* are the most obvious modes of analysis. We start with an ordinary language perspective on trust (Chapters 1 and 2), and then move on to chapter headings that headline academic frames of understanding that reflect some of our joint disciplinary expertise. The latter is generally divided into psychology, philosophy and sociology, although more specifically, subdivided into chapter headings that partly reflect sub-disciplines, for example psycho-social and psycho-ethical aspects of trust (Chapter 3); ethics and trust (Chapter 4); social aspects of trust (Chapter 5) and in systems that involves political sociology (Chapter 7). As well as giving these disciplinary perspectives, in Chapter 6, we examine case studies that strategically bring together other illustrated discussions elsewhere into one place.
- *Levels of trust* are also a clear mode of analysis. Again, we begin with the more ordinary and common level – the interpersonal perspective, which involves discussions about how trust between persons is maintained. Whilst we provide an ordinary language account in Chapter 2, we also theorize this from disciplinary perspectives, for example, ethics (Chapter 4). This said, we offer two other levels of trust: the sub-personal and supra-personal, which

involves trust in systems. The sub-personal is where we are concerned with discussions and debates on how trust originates in persons and how this motivates and shapes them to be trustworthy and trusted (Chapter 3 specifically, but also Chapters 4 and 5). We also examine trust in systems, where we are interested in notions of accountability, management, audit and public confidence (mainly Chapter 7 but also Chapter 5 and to a lesser extent Chapters 3 and 4)

- **Depth and relational proximity of trust** is the third and most undervalued mode of analysis. This involves less thought about levels of trust and more about its *character* in different proximal relationships – one's relationship with oneself ('self-trust' or 'basic trust'): one's relationship with others (for instance, 'encapsulated interests') and trusted systems (such as, 'super-accountability'). Whilst, at first, this seems to be another way of talking about levels of trust, it is actually more about the different 'characters' of trust and how they inter-relate in various contexts. For example, trust in the self or basic trust, as we saw in Chapter 3, is about a sense of security in ourselves and how this is formed in early childhood. While this is often overlooked, self-trust or basic trust in daily living is the cornerstone of being trusted and being able to trust others. Moreover, at the other end of the scale, trust in systems is about accountability and may, ironically, be a corrective, when trust in persons fails. In other words, we look to *impersonal* aspects of lives, when and if the personal, in and of itself, might fail us. What we bring into question though in this book is whether such an impersonal set of assurances might actually undermine the advantages of reliance on ordinary interpersonal trust. Most importantly, trust in terms of its relational character, is also about understanding the character of *intensity* in our trusting relationships with others – for example, whilst 'rational' accounts of trust may be appropriate amongst colleagues and strangers, its character is quite different in kith and kin relationships where it is affected by emotional intensity, which makes it more existentially risky. Finally, this 'character' is reflected in the disciplinary perspectives we talk about. For example, trust as virtue has a very different character from trust as a duty or obligation (see Chapter 4).

What we offer in this book, as an original contribution to debates on trust in healthcare, is an attempt to triangulate all three modes of analysis. To date there have been attempts to negotiate one or other of the levels described. For example, Harrison *et al.*, (2003) mobilise a 'levels' approach (following Sztompka, 1999) to illuminate different ways in which trust in healthcare fails as well as how it may be built up again. Whilst this is partially successful, it omits the complexity and depth of our triangulation approach. Neither do we rely on over rationally deterministic accounts of trust (such as those from Hardin). As we demonstrate, trust certainly *includes* rational calculation but it cannot be *reduced to it*; the non-rational aspects of our experience in ourselves and others must also be considered, a point we return to for emphasis in the next section.

Analytical considerations

Trust is complex even in terms of its ordinary usage. Moreover, not only is it semantically elastic, as we noted in Chapter 1, the ordinary experience of trust happens in specific contexts. For this reason, it is difficult to make generalisations about when trust is, or is not, easy to achieve and when it may be betrayed.

Staying with its semantic affinities, once we start to consider trust then a range of other close or overlapping words pour in, especially 'risk', 'confidence', 'predictability' and 'reliability' (the evidence of trust well invested) and even 'social capital', 'solidarity', 'social support' and 'friendship'. If trust is broadly conceived as the 'glue' in relationships then these sorts of interpersonal successes emerge for us in our lives. Moreover, sometimes these are best understood when trust is betrayed: we think more extensively when things go wrong and often take life for granted when everything is going well. Thus we should be wary to invest too much linguistic confidence in the word 'trust', as these other close affinities and reversals are all relevant to consider in relation to our topic.

Another analytical point to make is that 'trust' denotes and connotes many things for us. That is, it is a *polyvalent concept* and the experience of it does vary from person to person (from gullibility and naïvety to cynicism and paranoia) and across situations, even for the same person over time. The meaning of trust also varies across cultures and even within different social fields of the same culture. This might be called a 'polysemic' dimension to trust (as with many other forms of experience): that is, the same word ends up meaning different things to us in different contexts.

Moreover, trust will not be reduced to the rational and calculative aspects. We clearly cannot understand the nuances of trust without thinking analytically about the *non-rational* aspects of our experiences; our feelings, fantasies, hunches and intuitions all play their part in trust. This is why subjectivist accounts from human science in the traditions of psychoanalysis and existentialism are a rich seam to mine about trust.

Another analytical consideration is *historical*. The way we think about trust in healthcare has changed. The recent era of 'super-accountability' discussed in the previous chapter is just that: recent. Prior to that, we witnessed traditional medical paternalism, as the sole repository of the trust of patients and their relatives but this operated ostensibly in a sensitive framework of ethical duty, especially after scandals, linked to *modern* medicine were exposed during the twentieth century.

The next shift to undermine ethical medicine post-Second World War were the types of events discussed in Chapter 6. In the NHS this meant doctors who killed their patients or treated their remains with arrogant contempt. If we add to this picture the controversies of recent times (such as the concept of a good death, genetic screening and mental health) we find that the legitimacy of medical paternalism was becoming precarious by the 1980s. Thus another way of analysing trust in healthcare is in terms of *historical changes* about the way it is considered and reformed.

A different analytical point relates to the importance given over to *rebuilding trust in healthcare when it breaks down*. This has both an individual and a collective dimension. The case studies given in Chapter 6 indicate that patients or their relatives betrayed by healthcare professionals required personal acknowledgement and justice, but their experiences were also at the heart of a more general challenge for healthcare about its reputation. In other words, when individuals lose their trust in healthcare because of unexpected injury or even death at the hands of healthcare professionals, there is also a wider loss of confidence triggered in onlookers in the lay arena. The rebuilding of trust following untoward events has to be offered to direct victims and the wider population witnessing those events.

We are inside a period at the moment when different models of governance are being invoked, intended to minimize risk and re-build trust in healthcare. In this era of 'super-accountability' and recurrent 'checking', we are still not clear whether 'trust in whom' and 'trust in what' questions are being fully answered. Nor is it clear whose interests are being served by introducing these mechanisms: is 'super-accountability' truly increasing trust in the healthcare system? Is it about resting power from clinical professionals and shoring up the new powers of a managerial stratum in healthcare? Is it about governments devolving blame 'downwards' for problems in healthcare?

But, more importantly for most of us, will this managed systemic emphasis be effective at increasing trust in the routine experience of service users (patients and their relatives), and will it reduce or further increase the gap in access and quality of services? What if, despite all of the *post hoc* learning from public inquiries and local critical or untoward incidents, trust remains damaged? When 'lessons have been learned' and new polices, procedures and protocols have been 'put in place' by professionals and their managers, what of the aggrieved patients and relatives? What of their sense that systemic learning may have occurred and new checking procedures may have been introduced *but* their subjective experience of injustice, trauma or grief have still not been properly resolved – what then? At the time of writing, we pose these questions rhetorically because, having reviewed so much material relevant for the book, we have ended up lacking confidence in a 'managerial fix' to a very complex matter.

In particular, a reliance on accountability cannot substitute for a virtuous culture, shared by professionals and patients alike, in which care is encouraged, intended and received in both its practical and emotional sense (see Chapter 4). What can be done is done in good faith and the patient feels truly cared for. Accountability mechanisms, no matter how sophisticated or elaborate, are not sufficient for the building of that virtuous shared culture. Accountability can look good on paper, and in practice it might even be very evident, but in of itself it does not ensure such a culture. Indeed, there is the risk that preoccupation with accountability becomes a rhetorical and practical diversion from the achievement of that virtuous culture of trust (see Chapter 4). It might be damaging over time to the personal mutuality and good faith required for successful provider–user transactions in daily encounters in healthcare.

Having said all of the above, probably most of healthcare has always carried on, in a practical sense, in ways with which both staff and patients are satisfied, as human beings. Most of the time healthcare professionals are neither heroes nor villains: they simply do things which they are trained to do competently and respectfully. For their part, most of the time, patients engage with healthcare systems and feel that their care has been good or at least good enough. And when the latter is less than perfect the patient understands the immediate reasons for this, when observing the constraints on the staff looking after them. Much of what happens on a daily basis in healthcare entails unremarkable scenarios and is simply about people who are physically or psychologically vulnerable being looked after by others in a good enough way. This goes unnoticed because, as we noted earlier: we mainly tend to demand accounts and explanations when things go wrong in life (Scott and Lyman, 1966).

Finally in this section on analysis, we can note the need for *constant reflection about trust in healthcare*. All of the above points suggest that the literature on trust in general, and in healthcare in particular, including now this book, is in its infancy. It is a sketch of the map. This challenge of largely uncharted territory is foreclosed by the overblown promises of technocentric solutions from medical scientism, the simplistic bureaucratic formulae of politicians and bullish managers, compounded at times by the magical thinking of the voting public. Experts and politicians are prepared to tell us how trust will be fixed about healthcare and how we can avoid the unbearable messy contingencies of morbidity and death by believing that such fixes are possible. This book has been one effort at critically questioning quick and impulsive fixes. We now move from these analytical points about trust in healthcare to their political implications.

Political considerations about trust in healthcare

When writing this book we have often returned in our three-way preparatory discussions to a set of political questions about transparency and democracy, as well as about where the responsibility for maintaining our health resides. In the light of our discussions, we offer below a few points to consider about the politics of trust in healthcare.

Democracy is a central challenge

The scandals and controversies we described, and the doubts we expressed about the current political fixes designed to minimize risk in healthcare systems, point in one direction only. The building and maintenance of trust in healthcare is fundamentally a democratic challenge. We are of the view that old-fashioned professional paternalism and current managerialism in different ways are not democratic. This is because both situate power about healthcare in the hands of one or other group of technocrats, at the expense of citizens facing existential challenges about their health and those they care for.

Traditional criticism of the autonomous power of the clinical professions, especially medicine, is now well known. The scandals and controversies rehearsed in Chapter 6 made this clear, as did the limits of traditional professionalism set out in Chapters 2 and 7. However, we have also challenged the assumption of easy alternatives to the tradition. The shift to consumerism and managerialism has led to the rise of new political forces. In the final chapters we built up a picture of emergent communities of interest involved in the 'new public management' form of governance.

Currently, there are no grounds to consider that this, recently arrived, political elite governing healthcare should be trusted by ordinary people, simply because its task is to displace traditional clinical professional discretion and autonomy. The risk is that this task becomes an end in itself, without reference to the democratization of healthcare, especially in the UK, where the NHS is viewed by most as a virtuous and venerated public institution. While the strengths and weaknesses of clinical professionals, as autonomous moral communities, have been tested out over centuries, the new healthcare managers have yet to prove themselves in this regard. How can they be truly accountable to the general public, when most of their activity occurs in a myriad of closed meetings and private unexplained deliberations?

Here lies a paradox, which parallels governments demanding 'evidence-based practice' in state apparatchiks working in clinical contexts, even though *their own* policies are frequently not derived from evidence. Likewise, managers demand unending accountability from clinicians yet it is not clear how *their own routine actions* can be made transparent. What we are offered instead are glossy annual reports and some accounting mechanisms that do not necessarily offer a true reflection of a real improvement in healthcare and patient satisfaction. This is a very low level of accountability, which is easily ensured by the art of rhetoric honed by healthcare managers. And yet, is more accountability likely to produce better results? How much improvement can we realistically expect by following such a route? Although accountability is currently overly focused on clinicians, would additional accountability about managers still miss a fundamental point about the imaginative democratization of healthcare?

In Chapter 2 we introduced one version of the notion of 'health literacy', as part of the professional discourse on the limited competence of ordinary people to understand their health and the expectations health-care professionals have of them. However, from a political perspective we could also imagine a higher order of such literacy. The most power-less are those with least knowledge and confidence to pursue the inter-rogation of elite groups. Thus, a different form of health literacy may now be required to democratise healthcare. This would be about the *collective* awareness of those disempowered groups and their advocates, rather than the limited 'empowerment' of atomized individual consumers of healthcare.

Consumerism and the 'audit explosion' have contributed to a shared delusion

There is no one-size-fits-all policy solution to trust building in health-care (or any other public set of processes in civil society). The current fetish of consumerism may excite a few who are convinced by its perceived ability to solve all problems of trust. However, as we high-lighted in Chapter 7, whilst consumerism is predicated on the premise that individual choice in a market place leads to good outcomes, this assumption can be challenged forcefully in relation to healthcare.

The 'super-accountability', which has lived cheek by jowl with consumerism in recent times, and been expressed largely through vari-ations on the new public management style of governance, has entailed a massive economic investment. And yet, to date, its success is far from clear. Leaving aside the financial costs involved, whatever gains it has achieved in public confidence have been offset by spirals of distrust between politicians and practitioners, practitioners and managers and, some of the time and maybe counter-intuitively, the public and all of these groups.

The clinical professionals, who were previously presumptuous about their own integrity and competence as sources of personal reliability for patients, were at times undoubtedly found lacking. The scandals inside the NHS outlined in Chapter 6 were grounds enough to give confidence to those demanding greater external control over clinical activity. Now the prospect of errors and malpractice has become the focus of constant managerial surveillance. In turn this encourages 'back covering' and, with it, perennial low-grade anxiety and episodic demoralization.

Entreated and commanded to be 'patient-centred' all practitioners will assent but then find ways of personally complying with or resisting its demands. Their managers, who might be senior clinical colleagues, have accrued some autonomy in this devolved system of state-controlled surveillance, as quality controls have increasingly co-opted clinical managers to implement local mechanisms (what can be called 'soft governance'). They are responsible within professions and localities to set targets and audit activity. As we indicated in Chapter 7, professionals are not merely in competition with the state, they also, at times, share its power.

This new form of healthcare governance has triggered the paradox of the information gap widening, as more information is sought and found. This means we need to repeat some of our earlier questions for emphasis. What should we prioritize to measure? How do we measure it? When do we stop? Who audits the auditors? Is audit about public accountability or political surveillance? Is healthcare governance a basis for displacing blame and responsibility? What if the 'audit cycle' is broken by systemic and personal resistance – what then? All of the effort in generating and answering such questions requires a constant replenishment of time and money, triggering an unending demand for more of the same. At some point we all need to ask where it will all end and what benefits are accruing from endless auditing and 'performance management'.

Even more troubling, auditing the activity may take on a reified role and become more important than the activity itself. Procedures are followed at the expense of personal connection. Targets are achieved but the point is missed. A large number of 'boxes can be ticked' with not a patient in sight. The strategic drive to ensure the trustworthiness of systems can lead to trust as a desired and desirable *personal* experience being undermined in practice by impersonal targets and audit mechanisms. And, at the end of all the expensive efforts at 'super-accountability', there is no absolute guarantee that patients will not be abused and made sick or even that practitioners will no longer kill their patients.

Such expectations would be unrealistic under any model of governance. However, the managerial model, especially when combined with a discourse that tends to interpret all complexities through a language of 'risk', thrives on such unrealistic expectations and is prone to encouraging them. Thus, all actual and potential failures are interpreted as 'risks' and therefore mechanisms are 'put in place' that are intended to prevent and respond to such failures. The more 'risks' are identified the more scope there is for introducing mechanisms to manage them, and the more we all are encouraged to think about and express complexities as 'risks' that can and should be managed.

Despite the proliferation of standardization and review of policies, procedures and protocols about clinical activity and how it is recorded, there remains no single pathway to resolve the complexities of trust in healthcare given the vast array of people who use it or at times might even be in its coercive receipt. A cosmetic surgeon and a forensic psychiatrist have as much in common as a primary-care podiatrist and an occupational therapist working with people with profound learning disabilities – that is, very little. They all work in healthcare but the recipients of the latter are massively diverse, with different needs and vulnerabilities to iatrogenic risk. Accordingly, trust building in healthcare will necessarily vary from one specific situation to another: in sum, context is all important.

Trust needs to be understood in context

Healthcare is multilevelled and complex, when viewed as a wide-ranging system with many types of client group. From the questions of trust we discussed in relation to clinical encounters, through to the strategic intent of governments with their healthcare policies, we have illuminated what the concept means at many intermediate levels. Because of this complexity, trust means a variety of things to different people within different contexts of experience.

Clinicians are easy targets for testing and evaluating trust because this is where the 'face work' in clinical encounters happens. At this point failures in trust are most visible. But what of the powerful forces outside of those encounters? The democratic measures that would need to be put in place to increase trust in healthcare commissioners or the pharmaceutical companies are less easy to fathom than the constant emphasis on practitioner performance and how to get it right. Thus, although we drew proper attention to the interest work of professionals, they are disproportionately scrutinized and criticized in respect to those who continually politicize, shape and manage the process. These groups are less visible and accountable to ordinary people; indeed many citizens are oblivious to their influence.

Open systems, though not completely random, are fairly unpredictable. The complexities of healthcare mean that the building of trust will necessarily be messy and uncertain, not least because trust is most tangible through our interpersonal relationships with others. Ironically, trust in systems, which demands super accountability, highlights the erosion and failure of personal trust. Trust in systems is curiously tricky. On the one hand, it involves shoring up an intangible public confidence that has already been eroded. On the other hand, it involves building up an objectivity and transparency in trying to objectify and limit risk. This makes it a much more complex form of trust than interpersonal trust not least because restoring public confidence is difficult to measure once the achievement of interpersonal trust – which is to an extent blind and implicit – fails. Furthermore, the objectification and transparency of risk only allays our insecurity up to a point. This is because objective and transparent risk factors do not necessarily or easily translate into any tangible existential uncertainties. Paradoxically the latter are brought to our attention through the rhetoric of 'risk', its management and expectation elicited about its elimination.

Health institutions can, in various ways, increase their luck and learn from experience to improve matters but, ultimately, personal trust in healthcare is always an uncertain business and so we are wise, some of the time, to distrust it. But as we often are reliant on it, out of habit or necessity, we can only hope for the best (the kindly cure, speedy recovery, support in times of need and lives prolonged or even saved) and prepare for the worst (the hospital acquired infection, the loss of liberty, the honest mistake).

Those like Illich, McKeown and Dubos may have been prematurely nihilistic about medical nemesis and the limits to techno-centric medicine – writing as it was before the evidence of the effectiveness of healthcare to impact on health. Nonetheless, an honest appraisal of this proven impact of services on health leaves the social causes of ill-health and its personal consequences largely in place. As we noted earlier, the sources of ill-health still lie largely outside of healthcare influence. Poor people get sick more and die significantly earlier than rich people, even when they have access to healthcare.

The political costs and benefits of late modernity can be weighed up

Technological changes may furnish much of the content of healthcare systems. However, the personal and interpersonal expectations of comfort and recovery when ill, or constant support if disabled, which have existed since antiquity, remain. They are now embedded in the elaborate conditions of 'distanciation' emphasized by Giddens. Kith and kin now vary in their availability to care for us and large impersonal systems complement, and may even completely substitute for, that traditional response to illness and dying.

While our need to trust others when sick, injured, disabled and vulnerable remains, we still all have to contend with systems of health-care, which are frequently unfamiliar and not geared up to respond to our idiosyncratic requirements. If our understanding of, and response to, morbidity has been increasingly technicalized and depersonalized, the existential challenges are the same as ever. If many of us, much of the time, are still tired of living and scared of dying, healthcare is there to respond. However, it does not have all of the answers, and will throw up some new challenges, especially in relation to reconciling levels of trust.

There are no simple solutions to this reconciliation. However, we have proposed some critical dimensions to the consideration of trust in the context of healthcare for the reader's reflection. One of these relates to the imperfection and imperfectability of human relationships and humanly created social forms, such as healthcare systems. Despite this ubiquitous imperfection, the risk of trusting others most of the time works for us. Risk cannot be *eliminated* and the more we believe it can then the less we might enjoy the benefits of trust for that majority of time. Our enjoyment of trust in healthcare might be spoiled, in good part, for the very reason that we are encouraged to think about the risks it undoubtedly contains. However, we should also not be naïve and trust it too much; healthcare deserves to be distrusted some of the time with good reason. Maybe we would be wise to proceed, in some version of a middle way, with a combination of sceptical caution and faith in others.

Glossary

Accountability/super accountability is about trust in systems. That is to say, it involves making people accountable to procedures and systems. Ironically, it often becomes an issue when trust in people fails. It is useful because trust in others is a risky business and since accountability makes people accountable to outcomes, it is maybe a useful strategy to supplement trust between people. Super or hyper accountability is a form of accountability that is so totally orientated to external checks and balances within systems that people are continually held to account by proper procedures and its demands. This undermines personal trust.

Affect is a verb that usually means 'to influence'. However, in the human sciences it is also used as a noun to mean emotions or feelings. 'Affective' or 'affectional' are then adjectives derived from this sense. Affect is typically then distinguished from rational thought or rationality.

Ascribed bonds refer to relationships that are given by birth (for example, parents, children, relatives) rather than developed through one's choices, interests, and coincidences of life. It is often argued that in modern societies, in contrast to traditional societies, ascribed bonds, but also ascribed status, or position in society, have become less significant.

Attachment theory was developed by the British psychoanalyst John Bowlby, who incorporated the implications of studies of early infant–parent attachments in animal studies. This led him to study attachment and loss in young children. He traced feelings of depression and anxiety to these early developmental difficulties. According to this theory we all develop a particular attachment style when encountering new situations and people, which is based on our pattern and quality of attachments to caregivers in early childhood.

Authenticity/inauthenticity – see existentialism.

Autonomy/principled autonomy – we distinguish between individual autonomy and principled autonomy. Whereas the former is associated with the notion of independence, the latter is expressed in actions whose principle could be adopted by all others. Principled autonomy is an important safeguard in universalizing trust in relation to consent.

Basic trust – see self-trust.

Biological sciences are the academic disciplines, which understand plant and animal life at different levels. They predominate in the training of most clinical professions but the latter also learn about the human sciences. The biological sciences particularly relevant for clinical education are cytology, histology, anatomy, physiology, neurology and pharmacology.

Case studies – as well as framing trust from different academic perspectives (Chapters 3–5), we also frame trust in terms of case studies distinguishing between medical scandals (that involve high profile or catastrophic failures of public trust in healthcare), medical controversies (that involve uncertainty and therefore trust in healthcare) and routine breakdowns of trust (that involve everyday failures in trust in healthcare).

Clinical professions are those which focus on the assessment and treatment of patients. They also conduct research on patients ('clinical research') and on healthcare ('health services research'). The most numerous clinical professions working in healthcare settings are medical practitioners and nurses but a range of other smaller professions are also found (such as paramedics, physiotherapists, occupational therapists, speech therapists, health and clinical psychologists) which assess and treat sickness and injury or support those with disabilities. In health services research, clinical professions work closely with others, such as sociologists and economists.

Commodification refers to treating relationships and things as commodities, that is, things that are primarily produced for the market and acquired via markets. This also implies that relationships mediated by money, rules of supply and demand are dominant, and the primary motivations of sellers and producers are ones of profit and individual interest.

Community refers to a specific type of a group that is unified through a shared set of cultural symbols and practices (that could be related to, for example, language, religion, locality), and where its members have a sense of belonging to, and identify with, the group. There are different types of communities but the two main types that are usually discussed are: (a) face-to-face communities, and (b) 'imagined communities' (such as, nations, religious communities).

Communitarianism is an ideology or a belief that affirms the interests of the group over those of its individual members.

Discourse is a term that is mostly associated with the French philosopher Michael Foucault and refers to the way in which the use of language could be based on a set of usually invisible common assumptions. This suggests that the way in which we talk and think about things already carries a set of believes about how things are as well as assessments about how things could and/or should be. Competing discourses co-exist at any moment in time but they are often unequal and some of them tend to establish themselves as dominant ones. The term 'discursive practices' is also common and it indicates that ideas and practices are often intertwined in everyday life.

Duty ethics involves questions about 'What should I do?' Goodness is defined in terms of moral rightness. That is, we are obligated or duty bound to do the right thing. Duty ethics is based on principles that are subject to the founding and universal reasons. In this way there are impartial reasons to do the right thing. Duty ethics takes into account the autonomy of the patient and is a means to found patient rights.

Embeddedness refers to relationships and organizations being an integral part of their immediate environment. This emphasizes the presence of close interdependences between what we are interested in and its local context. Where there is a lack of interdependence we speak of 'disembeddedness'.

Empiricism is a form of philosophy which builds up knowledge (both everyday and scientific) via the senses. Put simply, it is what scientists agree about what they hear, see, smell, taste or touch. Unlike phenomenology or existentialism, which emphasise unique experience, empiricism is about a stable or repeatable consensus about observations across a number of observers. These observations are then recorded as objective facts. The method is then extended to experimentation, where scientists test hypotheses. By holding all conditions constant and then introducing a new condition they observe the impact of the latter. In this way they test hypotheses and deduce knowledge from experimentation. Thus empiricism includes systematic observation and experimentalism. The use of methods of audit and checking in modern healthcare systems follow in this tradition to quantify evidence and make objective claims.

Existentialism is a form of philosophy that focuses on the close expe-riential study of human existence – what it means to be human. Its ancient roots can be found in Buddhism and its modern expressions can be found in forms of both Christianity and atheism. Existentialists emphasise that we are self-conscious and thoughtful beings, who are constantly faced with choices about how to live our finite lives. With this common condition comes anxiety and guilt – the products of the struggle to confront or evade the authentic nature of our limited exis-tence. Existentialism emphasizes the contingent or context-specific aspect of being alive – this particular person in this particular time and place seeing their lives in a unique manner.

Faith: good and bad – faith has both an ordinary and technical mean-ing. In ordinary language, faith is a special kind of trust, a trust that is 'blind' to the extent that it is based on some un-testable belief. While this may be 'examined' it cannot be 'proved' – in this sense it is 'blind'. In existentialism 'bad faith' has taken on a particular meaning. Bad faith is not *just* self-deception; it also has an element of *faith*. That is to say, while self-deception is 'bad', it involves a wrong belief in what one has deceived oneself about. According to Sartre at least, we are all in bad faith to some degree or other, leaving us with the option to resist and try and be honest with ourselves, no matter how difficult this turns out to be. Being in relatively good faith, we are being as authentic as we can be. Resisting bad faith and living authentically we shore up the capac-ity to trust ourselves (self-trust).

Four principles – these are autonomy, non-maleficence, beneficence and justice. They are principles that are used on a conditional basis to make certain clinical judgements. While each clinical situation demands a skilful use of one principle or another, there are often clashes of priority. While the arbitration of what principle, when there is a clash, is situation dependent, certain principles clearly take priority. For example, non-malificence must trump beneficence, that is to say, first do no harm, takes priority over doing good for others.

General systems theory was developed by the biologists Paul Weiss and Ludwig von Bertalanffy. They argued that human activity can only be properly understood as part of an open system. Open systems are constantly affected by their environment or context, whereas closed systems are isolated from these influences. For example, a physics labo-ratory experiment involves examining a closed system, whereas the human sciences study people in their social context (an open system). Systems involve activities of varying levels of organization, with new characteristics emerging with each level. Cells, tissues, organs, organ systems, bodies, dyads, families, large groups, cultures, societies – entail more and more complex forms of organization, with new qualities emerging at each level. One level is necessary for the other to exist but one level cannot be explained by another (the error of reductionism).

Hermeneutic circle of understanding – our experiences accrue to what we already have tacit knowledge of, contributing to a deeper understanding. Take healthcare work: it cannot be taught successfully in a direct way in 'one shot' of basic training. Professional competence is accrued through a hermeneutic circle of understanding acquired by problem-based learning, clinical practice, learning from 'role' models and having mentors that develop one's professional competence and trustworthiness over time.

Human sciences refer to the range of academic disciplines that are interested in human conduct and experience. The main ones are sociology, anthropology and psychology (which also studies animals) but several other disciplines are in large part interested in human action or provide insights about human life and its context (especially branches of philosophy, theology, geography, economics and political science). Because clinical professionals are involved in the care of others, their education draws upon the human sciences (as well as the biological sciences). All of these sciences are disciplines and so largely focused on rules of academic inquiry or research. By contrast the clinical professions are mainly concerned with the practical application of knowledge distilled from all of those disciplines for the benefit of patient care. The latter benefits from the former but sometimes they are in tension.

Iatrogenesis refers to the adverse impact on patients of contact with healthcare. Its original meaning referred to 'doctor-made-illness' but is now used in this general way to signal negative impacts of entering the patient role. We can think of clinical iatrogenesis (such as adverse reactions to medication, hospital acquired infections); social iatrogenesis; and cultural iatrogenesis.

Ideology is a set of ideas, values and beliefs that tend to be developed on the basis of widely ranging assumptions about, for example, what human beings are like and what they should be like; what should be the relationship between individuals and society; what are the causes of inequality and whose responsibility these should be, and so on. While ideologies are primarily about beliefs and values they tend to be closely associated with individual and group interests and class position. The notion of ideology has been increasingly displaced recently in social science by the closely associated one of 'discourse'.

Individualism is an ideology or a belief that affirms the centrality of individuals and their interests, priorities, and freedoms *vis-à-vis* those of the group (such as, community, society, the state). It may reflect assumptions about the centrality of causes in our relationships to one another and the world ('psychological reductionism') or a moral or spiritual emphasis on individuals. In the latter regard discourses about personal freedom and human rights or civil liberties are common.

Informed consent involves a number of components: competence; disclosure; understanding; voluntariness and consent. One gives informed consent to a procedure or treatment: if one is competent to act, receives a thorough disclosure and comprehends what this entails, acts voluntarily and consents.

Institution can be used to refer to an organization (such as the NHS, for example), but is more broadly used as a reference to patterned social practices and relationships, as well as to the ways in which they are stabilised through both formal (for example, law) and informal mechanisms (for example, shared norms and values). In human systems, institutions are one example of stable arrangements or 'structures'.

Instrumental refers to something that is used or thought of as a means to an end, rather than as something that is important in itself. It indicates goal directedness and may also imply manipulative selfishness and amorality, when used in relation to human action.

Intersubjectivity refers to a wide set of understandings and emotions that are developed through interaction and constitute a sphere that cannot be fully understood by reference to any of the parties involved, but is instead better understood as an attribute of the relationship and its history.

Intrapsychic refers to inner life or the contents of our mind. It is usually associated with the work of psychoanalysis but is sometimes used to refer generally to inner experience (which we may or may not be consciously aware of). In this broad sense it refers to any internal experience in or out of our immediate consciousness.

Legitimacy refers to the ability of modern social systems, for example political systems such as nation states and their governments, to make an effective claim on representing the views and interests of their members. such as, the citizens. Questions of legitimacy could be raised in relation to whole social systems, such as the political system, for example, or to some of their constitutive elements, such as the current government or even specific government decisions. This could lead to different types of legitimation deficit or problem most of which are a normal part of the democratic process and can be dealt with through existing procedures such as withdrawing and revising policies, changing members in government, and changing political parties in office through democratic elections. However, if broader concerns are raised by citizens about the capability of the current political system, based on the nation state, and its dominant mode of political representation, based on democratic elections, this could lead to a broader crisis of the political system as such.

Medical scandals, controversies and routine breakdowns – see case studies and trust.

Medicine for our purposes refers to the broad field of the assessment and treatment of sickness and disability. Its narrower allusion can be to pharmacological treatments (medication) or to one of the clinical professions (medical practitioners). When used to refer to 'medical training' it is important to note that the latter draws on a range of biological and human sciences and so it is not strictly a single academic discipline (see other entries).

Modern society is usually defined in contrast to traditional, or pre-modern, society and in terms of key changes that gathered speed around the beginning of the nineteenth century. These changes are mostly associated with the process of industrialization, the establishment of capitalist relations of production, the rise of the nation state, the declining power of the church and religion, and the growing faith in the power of reason. Traditional societies are usually described as being dominated by face-to-face relationships in small and tightly knit rural communities, where one's place in society was largely defined by birth, and where most of the things needed for one's life were made within one's family or by someone else living in close proximity. In contrast, modern societies are predominantly urban, with agriculture accounting for only a very small proportion of economic activity, a high level of division of labour across space, and with relationships between people to a large extent mediated by impersonal systems.

Nation state is a notion that is used in order to describe most contemporary states and refers to a particular type of state in which the physical boundaries of the state, as a political community, overlap with the boundaries of a nation, as an affective, imagined, community. The citizens of nation states tend to have a strong sense of belonging to the state, identify with its territory and symbols, and feel a sense of solidarity with other members of the national community. Such a sense of mass solidarity is made possible by a combination of highly centralized power, efficient bureaucracy, and effective state–national ideology that characterize nation states. Nation states are widely recognized as a modern phenomenon and their emergence is usually associated with the processes of industrialization, the development of new communication technologies, and especially the printing press, and the transition from feudal to capitalist societies. It should be noted that the process of nation-state building has been uneven across Europe and the world, and that the extent of overlap between nation and state varies, while nations as imagined communities can be defined to a larger or lesser extent in ethnic, cultural, or civic terms.

NHS is the abbreviation used in the UK to refer to its National Health Service, which has been in existence since 1948 and continues to be financed centrally by the British government from general taxation.

Normalized refers to relationships, attitudes, believes, and so on, that are taken for granted and have come to be treated as unproblematic and 'normal'. Referring to such relationships as 'normalized' rather than as 'normal' is in order to question their underlying assumptions and the power relationships that they hide. The latter could be about, for example, class, gender, ethnicity, race.

Normativity refers to making value judgements about what is right and how things should be.

Ontological insecurity/security is about how secure or insecure we feel in ourselves. It has implications for how secure/insecure we feel in what we do, where we are and how we self and other. It is fundamental to the idea of self-trust.

Paternalism refers to specific type of unequal relationships where, similar to the relationship between father and child, there is a tension between inequality and care. Medical paternalism in particular refers to the belief that medical professionals would (and should) know what is best for their patients and would (and should) take decisions on their behalf, and in their best interest. The latter makes an assumption that patients are not capable of making the right decisions, and while it gives much power into the hands of health professionals, medical paternalism is also associated with an expectation that this power will not be abused.

Patient rights nests in an older tradition of human rights and are justified, ethically, by a duty-based approach.

Patients are people who are assessed and treated by clinical professionals. The term is used to cover those who are currently sick, injured or disabled *and* those who might become so in the future (hence general practitioners have 'patient lists' for all people when and if they present for a consultation). With this wide potential status in mind, arguably we are all patients from cradle to grave. In healthcare in recent times other terms have been applied to patients, including 'service users', 'service recipients', 'consumers' and 'clients'.

Phenomenology is the study of how people subjectively perceive the world. Its subjective emphasis places it near to existentialism. Occasionally in the literature we find the terms linked, as in an 'existential-phenomenological approach'. However, strictly speaking, phenomenology is a *method of investigation* derived from philosophy (Hegel and Husserl), whereas existentialism is a philosophical orientation towards life and its challenges. Also, it can be distinguished from traditional scientific methods, which seek to identify essential aspects of the world – attempts at the objective description of reality. Phenomenology is interested instead in the way that reality appears to people, not reality in and of itself.

Philosophy is an academic discipline which reflects on ways of thinking about ourselves and the world. Its longstanding interest in the human mind and its workings mean that it was in large part the forerunner of modern academic psychology. Philosophy focuses on the understanding of rationality (logic), knowledge (epistemology) and moral systems (ethics). In doing so it offers general advice about investigations in the human sciences. In relation to the topic of this book, moral philosophy and the ethics of healthcare (including 'medical ethics') are particular fields of interest.

Political aspects of a question refer, in the narrow sense, to the existing political process, parties, elections, voting rights, and so on. In the broader sense, the political aspects of a question are about understanding, voicing, debating the often incompatible interests and wishes of different individuals or groups implicated in the issue at hand.

Psychoanalysis is a term used now to describe a range of approaches to understanding unconscious life following its founder, Sigmund Freud.

The idea of an inner cauldron of irrational life, which can be distinguished from rationally and consensually agreed facts (see empiricism), is traceable to work of the Ancient Greek philosopher Heraclitus. One version of psychoanalysis is discussed in this book of particular relevance to its topic. 'Object–relations theorists' were psychoanalysts who developed the idea that the internalization of early personal relationships was central to understanding our personal lives as we grow and relate to others. The wider term 'psychodynamic' can be found referring to any notion arising from psychoanalysis and its developments.

Psychology is an academic discipline that studies experience and behaviour (in humans and other species). It became differentiated from academic philosophy at the turn of the twentieth century. Its main focus is the individual but its interest also extends at times to small and large groups, where it shares some common ground with sociology. In the context of healthcare, some psychologists with postgraduate training are employed to work with patients or conduct research (health psychologists and clinical psychologists).

Rational refers to a thought process or a decision where one is fully aware of the different options and plays an active part in taking the decision or in developing a plan for action. Rational is often discussed in relation with 'calculation', where decisions and actions are based on the careful weighing up of different arguments. However, the latter should not necessarily be the case.

Self-trust (or basic trust) has an internal (intra-personal) as well as an external (interpersonal) dimension. It involves trusting ourselves, our thoughts, emotions and actions in the situations we find ourselves in. It establishes how secure we feel in ourselves and the world we inhabit (ontological security). It is the cornerstone for our capacity to trust others. Self-trust is important for professional confidence, competence, interpersonal skills and mental health – whether it be patient or professional.

Social class is primarily associated with one's position within the economic field and access to material resources. In empirical research social class is often defined in relation to occupational status and wealth.

Social roles refer to the different positions that we occupy in society, such as for example, nurse and patient, woman and man, ill and healthy, parent and child, employer and employee, student and teacher, and so on.

Sociology is an academic discipline which studies social groups and their relationships in their wider social context. The range of interest of the discipline is from the study of people's experience in everyday settings (where it overlaps with social psychology) to the investigation of larger social structures and processes (where it overlaps with political science and economics). Some sociologists are employed in healthcare settings to study aspects of patient care and the activities of the clinical professions ('health' or 'medical' sociology).

Stakeholders are people, institutions, organizations that have an interest, a 'stake', in the issue, or problem at hand. The notion of 'interest group' is one version of stakeholder but usually implies one which is in regular internal deliberation and which develops strategic aims to advance its own position in society. For example, patients are stakeholders (because of a common social role in relation to healthcare) but typically they do not regularly reflect together on their collective interests. This can be contrasted with the clinical professions which are interest groups; these do regularly reflect on their own roles and ambitions.

Status refers to one's position in society. This is usually less about one's material wealth, than it is about how one is perceived by others and to what extent he/she is seen as deserving respect for what they do and who they are.

Supranational institutions are institutions beyond the nation state, such as, for example, IMF, OECD, EU, UN, World Bank, and so on.

Trust (an overview) – our discussion of trust in this book can be understood from a number of constituencies of debate – see conclusion – that triangulate three ways of thinking about the subject. *Perspectives on trust* involve ordinary language uses of the word as multidisciplinary academic frames of understanding. In our academic treatment of trust we make deliberate connections to a number of other concepts in a multidisciplinary literature, namely: attachment, dependency, recognition (psychology and philosophy), existentialism, authenticity, ontological security, good and bad faith (philosophy) risk (sociology), power, identity, solidarity, belonging (sociology/philosophy) and governance (political sociology). While the glossary is not an exhaustive treatment of terms related to trust in the academic literature, it does reflect the more technically difficult terms used from the academic literature. We also take a case study perspective that frames trust in terms of catastrophic failure (medical scandals), everyday failure (routine breakdowns) and uncertainties (medical controversies). *Levels of trust* involve a view of trust at different social levels of analysis, namely: the intrapersonal (self-trust), interpersonal (trust between persons) and systems of trust (accountability). *Depth and relational proximity* involves the 'character' of trust within different levels understanding.

Unilateral refers to something that is one-sided, and/or something that is taking into account only the wishes, interests, perspective of only one of the sides in a relationship where it could be individuals or groups that are implicated.

Virtue is a good quality or excellence of character predisposing the virtuous agent to want to do what morality requires. The virtuous medical professional possesses both intellectual virtues, such as prudence, and virtuous character, such as compassion and caring.

Virtue ethics is about questions of moral character: what should I be? Or, how should I live? Goodness is defined in terms of human excellence and perfectibility. They are internally motivated. That is, we are virtuous for the sake of wanting to be virtuous. Virtue ethics is responsive to particular situations and cultural norms and involves a partial perspective on what it is to be a virtuous agent within a community. Unlike duty ethics there is no universal or God's eye view of what is morally right and what is not. Virtues for medical professionals include: fidelity to trust; benevolence; effacement of self-interest; compassion and caring; intellectual honesty; justice and prudence.

Welfare state refers to the services and support provided to citizens by the state in relation to healthcare, social care, unemployment, disability, old age, education, child care. The specific form of support offered by governments would vary across countries, but the underlying assumption is that it is a responsibility of the state to offer such support to its citizens. The size of the welfare state and the distribution of funds between different forms of support vary between countries and different political parties and interest groups would have different position on that.

Bibliography

Adorno, T.W., Frenkel-Brunswick, E., Levison, D.F. and Sandford, R.N. (1950) *The Authoritarian Personality* (New York: Harper & Bros).

Alaszewski, A. (2002) 'The Impact of the Bristol Royal Infirmary Disaster and inquiry on public services in the UK' *Journal of Interprofessional Care*, 16: 4, pp. 371–8.

Allsop, J. (2003) 'Regulation and the medical Profession' in J. Allsop and M. Saks (eds) *Regulating the Health Professions* (London: Sage).

Allsop, J. and Saks, M. (2003) 'Introduction: the Regulation of Health Professions' in J. Allsop and M. Saks (eds) *Regulating the Health Professions* (London: Sage).

Anderson, B. (1983) *Imagined Communities: Reflections on the Origin and Spread of Nationalism* (London: Verso).

Anderson, J. (1996) 'Translator's introduction' in A. Honneth *The Struggle for Recognition: The Moral Grammar of Social Conflict* (Cambridge: Polity).

Anderson, R.M. and May, R.M. (1990) 'Vaccination and herd immunity to infectious diseases' *Nature*, 318, pp. 323–9.

Arendt, H. (1963) *Eichmann in Jerusalem: a report on the banality of evil* (Harmondsworth: Penguin).

Aristotle, (1999) (trans. Irwin, T.) *Nicomachean Ethics* (Indianapolis/Cambridge: Hackett Publishing Co).

Aurelius, M. (2004) (trans. G. Hays) *Meditations, Living, Dying and the Good life* (St Ives, UK: Phoenix).

Baier, A. (1994) *Moral Prejudices: Essays on Ethics* (Cambridge: Harvard University Press).

Baird, P.A., Anderson, T.W., Newcombe, H.B. and Lowry, R.B. (1988) 'Genetic disorders in children and young adults: a population study' *American Journal of Human Genetics*, 42, 1, pp. 677–93.

Baker, D.W., Parker, R. M., William, M. V. and Clark, W. S. (1998) 'Health Literacy and the Risk of Hospital Admission' *Journal of General Internal Medicine*, 13, 12, pp. 791–8.

Balint, M. (1952) *Primary Love and Psychoanalytical Technique* (London: Hogarth).

Barber, B.R. (2007) *Consumed: How Markets Corrupt Children, Infantilize Adults and Swallow Citizens Whole* (New York: Norton).

Bauman, Z. (2004) *Europe: An Unfinished Adventure* (Cambridge: Polity).

Baumrind, D. (1985) 'Research using intentional deception: ethical issues revisited' *American Psychologist*, 40, 2, pp. 165–74.

Beauchamp, T. and Childress, J. (2001) *Principles of Biomedical Ethics*, 5th edn (Oxford: Oxford University Press).

Beauchamp, T. and Walters, L. (eds) (2008) *Contemporary Issues in Bioethics* (New York: Thomson Wadsworth).

Beck, A. (1960) 'Issues in the anti-vaccination movement in England' *Medical History*, 4, 1, pp. 144–58.

Beck, U. (1992) *Risk Society: Towards a New Modernity* (London: Sage).

Beck, U. and Beck-Gernsheim, E. (1995) *The Normal Chaos of Love* (Cambridge: Polity).

Bendelow, G. (2006) 'Pain, suffering and risk' *Health, Risk and Society* 8, 1, pp. 59–70.

Blackburn, S. (2001) *Ethics: A Very Short Introduction* (Oxford: Oxford University Press).

Block, P. (2002) *Essays on Trust and Government, Part I and II* (New York: Peter Block Inc).

Borkovec, T.D. and Newman, M.G. (1998) 'Worry and Generalised Anxiety Disorder' in A.S. Bellack and M. Hersen (eds) *Comprehensive Clinical Psychology*, Volume 6 (London: Pergamon).

Bostock, D. (2000) *Aristotle's Ethics* (Oxford: Oxford University Press).

Bourdieu, P. *et al.* (2002) *The Weight of the World: Social Suffering in Contemporary Society* (Cambridge: Polity).

Bowlby, J. (1953) 'Some Pathological Processes Set in Train by Early Mother–Child Separation' *Journal of Mental Science*, 99, pp. 265–72.

Bowlby, J. (1969) *Attachment* (London: Hogarth Press).

Brendan, N. (2010) 'Why the "Death Panel" Myth Wouldn't Die: Misinformation in the Health Care Reform Debate', *The Forum*, 8, 1, article 5.

Briere, J. and Runtz, M. (1987) 'Post-Sexual Abuse Trauma: Data Implications for Clinical Practice' *Journal of Interpersonal Violence*, 2, 4, pp. 367–79.

Brown, P. (2008a) 'Legitimacy Chasing its Own Tail: Theorising Clinical Governance Through a Critique of Instrumental Reasoning' *Social Theory and Health*, 6, 2, pp. 184–99.

Brown, P. (2008b) 'Trusting in the new NHS: Instrumental *versus* Communicative Action' *Sociology of Health and Illness*, 30, 3, pp. 349–63.

Browne, K., Davies, C. and Stratton, P. (eds) (1988) *Early Prediction and Prevention of Child Abuse* (London: Wiley).

Bunker, J.P. (2001) *Medicine Matters After All* (London: Nuffield Trust for Research and Policy Studies in Health Services).

Burleigh, M. (1994) *Death and Deliverance: "Euthanasia" in Germany 1900–1945.* (Cambridge: Cambridge University Press).

Calnan, M. and Rowe, R. (2008) 'Trust, accountability and choice' *Health, Risk and Society*, 10, 3, pp. 201–6.

Cerbonne, C. (2006) *Understanding Phenomenology* (Chesham: Acumen).

Chadwick, R., Levitt, M. and Shickle, D. (eds) (1997) *The Right to Know and The Right not to Know* (Avebury: Aldershot).

Chadwick, R., Schickle, D., ten Have, H. and Wiesing, U. (1999) *The Ethics of Genetic Screening* (The Netherlands: Kluwer).

Chattoo, S. and Ahmad, W. (2008) 'Moral economy of selfhood and caring: negotiating boundaries of personal care as embodied moral practice' *Sociology of Health and Illness*, 30, 4, pp. 550–64.

Cichetti, D., Toch, S.L and Lynch, M. (1995) 'Bowlby's dream comes full circle: the application of attachment theory to role and psychopathology' *Advances in Child Clinical Psychology*, 17, pp. 1–75.

Clarke, A. (1991) 'Is non-directive genetic counselling possible?' *Lancet* 338, pp. 998–1001.

Cochrane, A. and Holland, W. (1971) 'Validation of screening procedures' *British Medical Bulletin*, 27, 1, pp. 3–8.

Commission for Healthcare Audit and Inspection (2009) *Investigation into Mid Staffordshire NHS Foundation Trust* (Concordat gateway number: 167 March).

Council on Scientific Affairs for the American Medical Association (1999) 'Health literacy: report for the AMA Council on Scientific Affairs' *Journal of the American Medical Association*, 281, pp. 552–7.

Cuckle, H. and Wald, N. (1984) 'Principles of Screening' in N. Wald (ed.) *Antenatal and Neonatal Screening* (Oxford: Oxford University Press).

Davies, H. and Mannion, R. (1999) 'Clinical Governance: Striking a Balance Between Checking and Trusting' *REPEC*, University of Connecticut, Working paper, http://www.york.ac.uk/inst/che/pdf/DP165.pdf Accessed 14 December 2008.

Delanty, G. and Jones, P.R. (2002) 'European identity architecture' *European Journal of Social Theory*, 5, 4 pp. 453–66.

Department of Health (2000) *An organisation with a memory: Report of an expert group on learning from adverse events in the NHS, London* (Gateway Reference: Crown).

Department of Health (2001) *The care standards tribunal: regulations comprising procedural rules of the Tribunal (The protection of children and vulnerable adults and care standards Tribunal regulations)* (Gateway Reference: Crown).

Department of Health (2003) *Building on the Best: Choice, Responsiveness and Equity in the NHS* (Gateway Reference: Crown).

Department of Health (2006) *Our Health, Our Care, Our Say: Making it Happen* (Gateway Reference: Crown).

Dimsdale, J. (1980) *Survivors, Victims and Perpetrators: Essays on the Nazi Holocaust* (Hemisphere PB Corp).

Donabedian, A. (2003) *An Introduction to Quality Assurance in Health Care* (Oxford: Oxford University Press).

Douglas, M. (1992) *Risk and Blame: Essays in Cultural Theory* (London: Routledge).

Douglas, M. And Wildavsky, A. (1982) *Risk and Culture: An Essay on Selection of Technological and Environmental Dangers* (Berkeley: University of California Press).

Dubos, R. (1987) *Mirage of Health: Utopias, Progress and Biological Change* (New Brunswick, NJ: Rutgers University Press).

Durbach, N. (2000) '"They might as well brand us". Working class resistance to compulsory vaccination in Victorian England' *Social History of Medicine*, 13, 1, pp. 45–62.

Durkheim, E. (1992) *Professional Ethics and Civic Morals* (London: Routledge).

Dunn, C., Crowley, P., Bush, J. Pless-Mulloli, T. and Mckinney, P.A. (2008) 'Expertise and scientific uncertainty: understanding trust amongst professional stakeholders in environment and health' *Environment and Planning,* 40, 3, pp. 696–714.

Erikson, E. (1965) *Childhood and Society* (Harmondsworth: Penguin).

General Medical Council (1992) *Professional Conduct and Discipline: Fitness to Practice* (London: General Medical Council).

Evetts, J. (2006) 'Trust of professionalism: challenges and occupational changes' *Current Sociology*, 54, 1, pp. 515–31.

Eysenck, H.J. (1949) 'Training in clinical psychology: an English point of view' *American Psychologist* 4, 2, pp. 173–6.

Fairbairn, W.R.D. (1952) *An Object-Relations Theory of the Personality* (New York: Basic Books).

Feinman, J. (2006) 'How to Have a Good Death' published to accompany BBC television programme first broadcast on BBC 2 television in March 2006.

Fenwick, E. and Fenwick, P. (2008) *The Art of Dying* (London: Continuum).

Fisher, C.B. and Fryberg, D. (1995) 'Participant Partners: College Students Weigh the Costs and Benefits of Deceptive Research' in D.N. Bersoff (ed.) *Ethical Conflicts in Psychology* (Washington DC: American Psychological Association).

Foucault, M. (1973) *Discipline and Punish: the birth of the prison* (New York: Vintage).

Foucault, M. (1990) *The History of Sexuality* (New York: Random House).

Freidson, E. (1970) *Profession of Medicine: A Study in the Sociology of Applied Knowledge* (New York: Dodd Mead).

Freud, S. (1926) *Standard Edition of the Complete Works of Sigmund Freud (Standard Edition 20)* (London: Hogarth Press).

Fromm, E. (1941) *Escape from Freedom* (New York: Holt, Rinehart & Winston).

Fromm, E. (1955) *The Sane Society* (New York: Holt, Rinehart & Winston).

Fromm, E. (1973) *The Anatomy of Human Destructiveness* (Harmondsworth: Penguin).

Furedi, F. (2005) *Culture of Fear: Risk-taking and the Morality of Low Expectation* (London: Continuum).

Gambetta, D. (ed.) (1988) *Trust: Making and Breaking Co-operative Relations* (Oxford: Blackwell).

Giddens, A. (1990) *The Consequences of Modernity* (Stanford: Stanford University Press).

Giddens, A. (1992) *Transformation of Intimacy: Sexuality, Love and Eroticism in Modern Societies* (Cambridge: Polity Press).

Giddens, A. (1998) *The Third Way* (Cambridge: Polity).

Gillon, A. (1986) *Philosophical Medical Ethics* (London: Wiley).

Gilson, L. (2006) 'Trust in health care: theoretical perspective and research needs' *Journal of Organizational Change Management*, 20, 5, pp. 359–74.

Glover, J. (2002) *Humanity: A Moral History of the Twentieth Century* (London: Jonathan Cape).

Goffman, E. (1961) *Asylums: Essays on the Social Situation of Mental Patients and Other Inmates* (New York: Anchor Books).

Goodrich, J. and Cornwell, J. (2008) *Seeing the Person in the Patient* (London: King's Fund).

Guntrip, H. (1977) *Schizoid Phenomena, Object Relations and the Self* (London: Hogarth).

Guyer. P. (2006) *Kant* (Abingdon: Routlege).

Habermas, J. (1987) *The Theory of Communicative Action* (Cambridge: Polity).

Halligan, P.W., Bass, C. and Oakley, D.A. (eds) (2003) *Malingering and Illness Deception* (Oxford: Oxford University Press).

Hardin, R. (2006) *Trust* (Cambridge: Polity Press).

Harlow, H.F. (1961) 'The Development of Affectional Patterns in Infant Monkeys' in B.M. Foss (ed.) *Determinants of Infant Behaviour* (New York: Wiley).

Harlow, H.F. and Zimmerman, R.R. (1959) 'Affectional responses in the infant monkey' *Science*, 130, 3373, pp. 421–32.

Harrison, J., Innes, R. and van Zwanenberg, T. (eds) (2003) *Rebuilding Trust in Healthcare* (Oxford: Radcliffe Medical Press).

Harrison, S. and Ahmad, W. (2000) 'Medical autonomy and the UK state 1975 to 2025' *Sociology*, 34: 1, pp. 129–46.

Harrison, S. and Smith, C. (2004) 'Trust and moral motivation: redundant resources in health and social care?' *Policy and Politics*, 32, 3, pp. 371–86.

Hart, J.T. (1971) 'The Inverse Care Law' *The Lancet*, 1, 7696, pp. 405–503.

Halligan, P.W., Bass, C. and Oakley, D.A. (eds) (2003) *Malingering and Illness Deception* (Oxford: Oxford University Press).

Hegel, G.W.F. (1977) *Phenomenology of Spirit* (Oxford: Clarendon Press).

Higgs, P. and Scambler, G. (1998) 'Explaining Health Inequalities: How Useful are Concepts of Social Class?' in G. Scambler and P. Higgs (eds) *Modernity, Medicine and Health* (London: Routledge).

Honkasalo, M. (2006) 'Fragilities in life and death: engaging in uncertainty in modern Society' *Health, Risk and Society*, 8: 1, 27–41.

Honneth, A. (1996) *The Struggle for Recognition: The Moral Grammar of Social Conflicts* (Cambridge: Polity).

Hope, C. (2003) *Brothers Under the Skin: Travels in Tyranny* (London: Macmillan).

Horne, G., Seymour, J. and Shepherd, K. (2006) 'Advance Care Planning for Patients with Inoperable Lung Cancer' *International Journal for Palliative Nursing*, 12, 4, pp. 172–8.

Illich, I. (1976) *Limits to Medicine: Medical Nemesis: The Exploitation of Health* (London: Marion Boyars).

Ipsos-MORI (2009) *Trust in Professions* http://www.ipsos-mori.com/research publications/researcharchive/poll.aspx?oItemId=15&view=wide

Jarman, B. (1983) 'The identification of underprivileged areas' *British Medical Journal*, 286: 6379, pp. 1705–9.

Jessop, B. (2008) *State Power: A Strategic-Relational Approach* (Cambridge: Polity).

Jodelet, D. (1991) *Madness and Social Representations* (London: Harvester Wheatsheaf).

Johnson, T. (1972) *Professions and Power* (London: Macmillan).

Jonsen, A. and Toulmin, S. (1988) *The Abuse of Casuistry* (Berkeley: University of California Press).

Kennedy, I. (2001) *Learning from Bristol: the Report of the Public Inquiry into Children's Heart Surgery at the Bristol Royal Infirmary 1984–1995* (London: Crown).

Kershaw, I. (1998) *Hitler: 1889–1936, Hubris* (London: Penguin).

Klein, R. (1989) *The Politics of the National Health Services* (Harlow: Longman).

Kleinman, A. (1988) *The Illness Narratives: Suffering, Healing and the Human Condition* (New York: Basic Books).

Kleinman, A. (2008) 'Catastrophe and caregiving: the failure of medicine as an art' *Lancet*, 371, pp. 22–3.

Knoppers, B. M. and Chadwick, R. (2006) 'Human genetics research: emerging trends in ethics' *Focus* 4, pp. 416–22.

Kojève, A. (1969) (trans. James H. Nichols) *Introduction to the Reading of Hegel: Lectures on the Phenomenology of Spirit* (Ithaca: Cornell University Press).

Kolthoff, E., Huberts, L. and Van Den Heuvel, H. (2007) 'The ethics of New Public Management: is integrity at stake?' *Public Administration Quarterly* (Winter 2006/2007) pp. 399–439.

Laing, R. D. ([1959], 1990) *The Divided Self* (Harmondsworth: Penguin).

Laing, R. D. (1961) *Self and Others* (Harmondsworth: Penguin).

Lambert, M.J. (2007) Presidential address: a program of research aimed at improving psychotherapy outcome in routine care: what we have learned from a decade of research. *Psychotherapy Research* 17, 1, pp. 1–14.

La Rochefoucauld, de (2003) (trans. Prime, I.) *Moral Maxims*, (New Jersey: Associated University Press).

Larson, M.S. (1977) *The Rise of Professionalism* (Berkeley: University of California Press).

Latour, B. (1987) *Science in Action* (Cambridge, Massachusetts: Harvard University Press).

Lawton, J. (2000) *The Dying Process: Patients' Experience of Palliative Care* (London: Routledge).

Lifton, R.J. (1986) *The Nazi Doctors – Medical Killing and the Psychology of Genocide* (New York: Basic Books).

Lindholm, C. (1990) *Charisma* (Cambridge: Basil Blackwell).

Luhmann, N. (1979) *Trust and Power* (New York: John Wiley).

Luhmann, N. (1988) 'Familiarity, confidence, trust: problems and alternatives' in D. Gambetta (ed.) *Trust: Making and Breaking Cooperative Relations* (Oxford: Basil Blackwell).

McCollough, B. and McGuire, A. *et al.* (2007) 'Consent: informed, simple, implied and presumed'. *American Journal of Bioethics*, 7, p.12.

Mackenzie, C. and Stoljar, N. (2000) 'Autonomy Refigured' in C. Mackenzie and N. Stoljar (eds) *Relational Autonomy: Feminist Perspectives on Autonomy, Agency, and the Social Self* (Oxford: Oxford University Press).

Martin, D., Thiel, E., and Singer, P. (1999) 'A new model of advance care planning: observations from people with HIV' *Archives of Internal Medicine*, 159: 1, pp. 86–92.

Martin, J.P. (1984) *Hospitals in Trouble* (Oxford: Basil Blackwell).

Mauss, M. (1970) *The Gift: Forms and Functions of Exchange in Archaic Societies* (London: Cohen and West).

McKeown, T. (1976) *The Role of Medicine: Dream, Mirage, or Nemesis?* (London: Nuffield Provincial Hospitals Trust).

Milgram, S. (1963) 'Behavioral study of obedience' *Journal of Abnormal and Social Psychology*, 67, pp. 371–8.

Misztal, B. (1996) *Trust in Modern Societies* (Cambridge: Polity).

Moncrieff, J. (2008) *The Myth of the Chemical Cure: A Critique of Psychiatric Drug Treatment* (Basingstoke: Palgrave Macmillan).

Nolte, F. and McKee, M. (2004) *Does Healthcare Save Lives? Avoidable Mortality Revisited* (London: The Nuffield Trust).

Nuernberg, October 1946–April 1949 (1949) *Trials of War Criminals before the Nuernberg Military Tribunals under Control Council Law No. 10* (Washington, DC: U.S. Government Printing Office).

Nuffield Council on Bioethics (1993) *Genetic Screening Ethical Issues* (London: Nuffield Council on Bioethics).

O'Neill, O. (2002) *Autonomy and Trust in Bioethics* (Cambridge: Cambridge University Press).

Parsons, T. (1951) *The Social System* (London: Routledge).

Pence, G. (1995) *Classic Cases in Medical Ethics*, 2nd edn (New York: McGraw-Hill).

Pencheon, D. (1998) 'Managing demand: matching demand and supply fairly and efficiently' *British Medical Journal*, 316, 7145, pp. 1665–7.

Personal Communication Prof, Sheila Payne, Help the Hospice Chair in Hospice Studies, International Observatory on End of Life Care, Lancaster University, (2008).

Pilgrim, D. (ed.) (2007) *Inside Ashworth: Personal Accounts of Institutional Life* (London: Radcliffe Medical Press).

Pilgrim, D. and Guinan, P. (1999) 'From mitigation to culpability: rethinking the evidence on therapist sexual abuse' *European Journal of Psychotherapy, Counselling and Health* 2, 2, pp. 155–70.

Pilgrim, D. and Vassilev, I. (2007) 'Risk, trust and mental health services' *Journal of Mental Health*, 16, 3, pp. 347–57.

Pilgrim, D. and Rogers, A. (1997) 'Two Types of Risk in Mental Health' in T. Heller *et al.* (eds) *Mental Health Matters: A Reader* (London: Macmillan).

Pilgrim, D. and Rogers, A. (2003) 'Mental disorder and violence: an empirical picture in context' *Journal of Mental Health*, 12, 1, pp. 7–18.

Pilgrim, D., Rogers, A. and Bentall, R.P. (2009) 'The centrality of personal relationships in the creation and amelioration of mental health problems: the current interdisciplinary case' *Health*, 13, 235–54.

Pirmohamed, M., Brown, C., Owens, L., Luke, C., Gilmore, I.T., Breckenridge, A.M. and Park, B.K. (2000) 'The burden of alcohol misuse on an inner-city general hospital' *Quarterly Journal of Medicine*, 93, pp. 291–5.

Porter, D. and Porter, R. (1998) 'The politics of prevention: anti-vaccinationism and public health in nineteenth-century England' *Medical History*, 32, pp. 231–52.

Post, S.G., Botkin, J.R. and Whitehouse, P. (1992) 'Selective abortion for familial Alzheimer's Disease?' *Obstetrics and Gynaecology* 79, pp. 794–8.

Power, M. (1997) *The Audit Society: Rituals of Verification* (Oxford: Oxford University Press).

Putnam, R.D. (1993) *Making Democracy Work: Civic Traditions in Modern Italy* (Princeton: Princeton University Press).

Putnam, R. (2000) *Bowling alone: the collapse and revival of American community* (New York: Simon & Schuster).

Rabinow, P. and Rose, N. (2006) 'Biopower today' *BioSocieties*, 1, 2, pp. 195–217.

Rank, O. (1929) *The Trauma of Birth* (London: Paul, Trench & Trubner).

Read, J., Agar, K., Argyle, N. and Aderhold, V. (2003) 'Sexual and physical abuse during childhood and adulthood as predictors of hallucinations, delusions and thought disorder' *Psychology and Psychotherapy: Research, Theory and Practice*, 76: 1, 11–22.

Redfern, M. (2001) *The Report of the Royal Liverpool Children's Inquiry* (UK: Crown).

Riceour, P. (1994) (trans. K. Blamey) *Oneself as Another* (Chicago: University of Chicago Press).

Rogers, A. and Pilgrim, D. (1995) 'The risk of resistance-perspectives on mass childhood immunisation' *Medicine, Health and Risk (Sociology of Health and Illness Monograph)* pp. 35–50.

Rogers, A., Hassell, K. and Nicolaas, G. (1998) *Demanding Patients? Analysing the Use of Primary Care* (Buckingham: Open University Press).

Rogers, R. (ed.) (2008) *Clinical Assessment of Malingering and Deception* (London: Routledge).

Rose, N. (2008) 'The value of life: somatic ethics and the spirit of biocapital' *Daedalus*, 137: 1, pp. 36–48.

Rose, N. and Novas, C. (2003) 'Biological citizenship' in A. Ong and S. Collier (eds) *Global Anthropology* (London: Blackwell).

Rowe, R. and Calnan, M. (2006) 'Trust relations in health care: developing a theoretical framework for the "New" NHS' *Journal of Organizational Change Management*, 20, 5, pp. 376–96.

Salter, B. (2003) 'Patients and doctors: reformulating the UK health policy community?' *Social Science and Medicine*, 57: 5, 927–36.

Sartre, J.-P. (2006) (trans. Hazel E. Barnes) *Being and Nothingness* (London: Routledge).

Sartre, J.-P. (1973) (trans. Philip Mairet) *Existentialism and Humanism* (London: Methuen).

Sayer, A. (2005a) *The Moral Significance of Class* (Cambridge: Cambridge University Press).

Sayer, A. (2005b) 'Reductionism in social science' *Department of Sociology, Lancaster University*, www.lancs.ac.uk/fass/sociology/papers/sayer-paris1.pdf, accessed on 14 December 2008.

Schneidman, E. (2007) 'Criteria for a good life' *Suicide and Life Threatening Behaviour*, 37: 3, pp. 245–7.

Scott, M.B. and Lyman, S. (1968) 'Accounts' *American Sociological Review*, 33, 1 pp. 46–62.

Seligman, A. (1997) *The Problem of Trust* (Princeton: Princeton University Press).

Shaw, M., Davey Smith, G. and Dorling, D. (2005) 'Health inequalities and New Labour: how the promises compare with real progress' *British Medical Journal*, 330, 7498, 1016–21.

Sheaff, R. (2002) *Responsive Healthcare: Marketing for a Public Service* (Buckingham: Open University Press).

Sheaff, R. and Pilgrim, D. (2006) Can learning organizations survive in the newer NHS?' *Implementation Science*, 1, p. 27.

Shieff, E.M. (2003) 'Media frames of mental illness: the potential impact of negative frames' *Journal of Mental Health*, 12, 3, pp. 259–70.

Simpson, K. (1980) *Forty Years of Murder* (London: Grafton Books).

Simpson, N., Lenton, S. and Randall, R. (2001) 'Parental refusal to have children immunised: extent and reasons.' *British Medical Journal*, 310, pp. 225–7.

Smith, A. (2002) *The Theory of Moral Sentiments* (Cambridge: Cambridge University Press).

Smith, C. (2001) 'Trust and confidence: possibilities for social work in "high modernity"' *British Journal of Social Work*, 31: 2, 287–305.

Smith, J. (2002) *The Shipman Inquiry: First Report – Death Disguised* (UK: Crown).

Smith, J. (2003a) *The Shipman Inquiry: Second Report – The Police Investigation of March 1998* (UK: Crown).

Smith, J. (2003b) *The Shipman Inquiry: Third Report – Death Certification and the Investigation of Deaths by Coroners* (UK: Crown).

Smith, J. (2004a) *The Shipman Inquiry: Fourth Report – The Regulation of Controlled Drugs in the Community* (UK: Crown).

Smith, J. (2004b) *The Shipman Inquiry: Fifth Report – Safeguarding Patients: Lessons from the past – proposals for the future* (UK: Crown).

Spier, R.E. (2001) 'Perception of risk of vaccine adverse events: a historical perspective.' *Vaccine* 20, pp.78–84.

Stakettee, G.S. and Frost, R.O. (1998) 'Obsessive compulsive disorder' in A.S. Bellack and M. Hersen (eds) *Comprehensive Clinical Psychology*, Volume 6 (London: Pergamon).

Stewart, M., Brown, J.B., Weston, W.W., McWhinney, I.R., McWilliam, C.L. and Freeman, T.R. (1995) *Patient-centred medicine transforming the clinical method* (Thousand Oaks: Sage Publications).

Stone, J. (2003) 'Evaluating the ethical and legal content of professional codes of ethics' in J. Allsop and M. Saks (eds) *Regulating the Health Professions* (London: Sage).

Storr, A. (1968) *Human Aggression* (London: Allen Lane).

Strathern, M. (ed.) (2000) *Audit Cultures: Anthropological Studies in Accountability, Ethics, and the Academy* (London: Routledge).

Streefland, P. (1999) 'Patterns of vaccination acceptance' *Social Science and Medicine*, 49, pp. 1705–16.

Suttie, I.D. (1935) *The Origins of Love and Hate* (London: Kegan Paul).

Sztompka, P. (1999) *Trust: A Sociological Theory* (Cambridge: Cambridge University Press).

Taylor, C. (1992) *The Ethics of Authenticity* (Harvard: Harvard University Press).

Taylor-Gooby, P. (2002) 'Varieties of risk. Editorial' *Health, Risk and Society*, 4, 2, pp. 109–11.

Thomas, C. (2008) 'Dying, places and preferences' in S. Payne, J. Seymour, and C. Ingleton (eds) *Palliative Care Nursing, principles and evidence for practice* (London: Open University Press).

Thomas, R. and Davies, A. (2005) 'Theorizing the micropolitics of resistance: New Public Management and managerial identities in the UK public services' *Organisation Studies*, 26, pp. 683–706.

Thompson, M. (1982) 'A three-dimensional model' in M. Douglas (ed.) *Essays in the Sociology of Perception* (London: Routledge & Kegan Paul).

Thorne, B. (1996) 'Person-Centred Therapy' in W. Dryden (ed.) *Handbook of Individual Therapy* (London: Sage).

Trials of War Criminals before the Nurenberg Military Tribunals under Control Council Law No. 10 (1949) (Washington DC: US Government Printing Office).

Turner, B.S. (1995) *Medical Power and Social Knowledge* (London: Sage).

Turner, B.S. (1997) 'Citizenship studies: a general theory' *Citizenship Studies*, 1, 1, pp. 5–18.

Turner, B.S. (2001) 'Risks, rights and regulation: an overview' *Health, Risk and Society*, 3: 1, pp. 9–18.

Turner, B.S. (2003) 'Social capital, inequality and health: the Durkheimian revival' *Social Theory and Health*, 1, 1, pp. 4–20.

Turner, B.S. (2006) *Vulnerability and Human Rights* (University Park, PA: Penn State University).

Turner, B.S. (2007) 'The enclave society: towards a sociology of immobility' *European Journal of Social Theory*, 10, 2, pp. 287–303.

van Hooft, S. (2006) *Understanding Virtue Ethics* (Chesham: Acumen).

Veatch, R. (1991) *Medical Ethics*, 2nd edn (Sudbury Massachusetts: Jones & Bartlett).

Wahl, O.F. (1995) *Media Madness: Public Images of Mental Illness* (New Brunswick NJ: Rutgers University Press).

Waller, S., Thom, B., Harris, S. and Kelly, M. (1998) 'Perceptions of alcohol-related attendances in accident and emergency departments in England: a national survey' *Alcohol and Alcoholism*, 33, pp. 354–61.

Wark, P. (2006) 'How to Have a Good Death' published in the Times Online http://www.timesonline.co.uk_and_style/health/features/article695832.ece? pri...

Watt, J. (1980) 'Conscience and responsibility.' *British Medical Journal* Dec 20; 281(6256), pp.1687–8.

Westermeyer, J. and Kroll, J. (1978) 'Violence and Mental Illness in Peasant Society: Characteristics of Violent Behaviours and "Folk Use" of Restraints' *British Journal of Psychiatry*, 133, 6, pp. 529–41.

Whitfield, C., Dube, S., Felitti, V. and Anda, R. (2005) 'Adverse Childhood Experiences and Hallucinations' *Child Abuse and Neglect*, 29, 7, pp. 797–810.

Whitney, S., McGuire, A. and McCullogh, L. (2004) 'A typology of shared decision making, informed consent and simple consent' *Annals of Internal Medicine*, 140, 1, pp. 54–9.

Widiger, T.A. and Trull, J.T. (1994) 'Personality disorders and violence' in J. Monahan and H.J. Steadman (eds) *Violence and Mental Disorder* (Chicago: Chicago University Press).

Wilkinson, I. (2006) 'Health, Risk and 'Social Suffering' *Health, Risk and Society*, 8, 1, pp. 1–8.

Wilkinson, R.G. (1996) *Unhealthy Societies: The Afflictions of Inequality* (London: Routledge).

Williamson, C. (1998) *Whose Standards? Consumer and Professional Standards in Healthcare* (Buckingham: Open University Press).

Wilson, J.M. and Jungner, Y.G. (1968) *Principles and Practice of Screening for Disease. Public Health Paper 34* (Geneva: World Health Organization).

Winnicott, D.W. (1967) 'The Location of Cultural Experience' *International Journal of Psychoanalysis*, 48, pp. 368–78.

World Health Organization (2004) *Immunization in Practice: A Guide for Health Workers* (Geneva: World Health Organization).

World Medical Association (1964) *Declaration of Helsinki: Ethical Principles for Medical Research Involving Human Subjects* (Helsinki: WMA).

World Health Organization/Council for International Organisations of Medical Sciences (CIOMS) (2002) *Ethical Guidelines for Biomedical Research Involving Human Subjects* (Geneva: World Health Organization).

Web sites used

http://www.angelfire.com/fl5/ikill4attention/

Council for Healthcare Regulatory Excellence: http://www.chre.org.uk/

Local Involvement Networks: http://www.dh.gov.uk/en/Managingyour organisation/PatientAndPublicinvolvement/dh_076366

Parliamentary and Health Service Ombudsman: http://www.ombudsman.org.uk/

The Audit Commission: http://www.audit-commission.gov.uk/

The Care Quality Commission: http://www.cqc.org.uk

The General Medical Council: http://www.gmc-uk.org/
The Health Professions Council: http://www.hpc-uk.org/
The Health Protection Agency: http://www.hpa.org.uk/
The National Clinical Assessment Service: http://www.ncas.npsa.nhs.uk/
The NHS Litigation Authority: http://www.nhsla.com/
The National Institute for Clinical Excellence: http://www.nice.org.uk/

Index